The Discourse of Disability

This book explores the concept of disability through a social, political, cultural, religious, and economics lens. It challenges the categorization of "physically disabled" produced by way of legal, medical, political, cultural, and literary narratives that comprise an exclusionary discourse.

The volume discusses themes like disability and identity politics; disability and the Western epistemology; disability in India; disability and Indian English fiction and Hindi cinema to question the embodied hegemony of "norms" and their effects on the construction and history of societies. It analyses select literary and cinematic texts like *Trying to Grow*, *Fireproof*, and *Animal's People*, as well as the movies *Black* and *Lafangey Parindey* to critically examine the representation of disabled people as freak, monstrous, and animal. The book also makes policy recommendations for inclusive education and work norms for disabled people.

This book will be beneficial for scholars and researchers of disability studies, cultural studies, film studies, and English literature.

Vivek Singh is Assistant Professor of English at Banaras Hindu University, India. He pursued his PhD from the University of English and Foreign Languages, India. To pursue his research, he went to Potsdam University, Berlin, and received DAAD fellowship. He has delivered more than 15 lectures in various reputed institutions and has published more than ten papers in international journals. His edited works include *The Crisis in Humanity* (2022). Currently, he works as a language instructor and cultural ambassador at Mississippi Valley State University, USA.

The Discourse of Disability

Indian Perspectives

Vivek Singh

Routledge
Taylor & Francis Group

LONDON AND NEW YORK

First published 2024
by Routledge
4 Park Square, Milton Park, Abingdon, Oxon OX14 4RN

and by Routledge
605 Third Avenue, New York, NY 10158

Routledge is an imprint of the Taylor & Francis Group, an informa business

British Library Cataloguing-in-Publication Data
A catalogue record for this book is available from the British Library

ISBN: 978-1-032-53619-4 (hbk)
ISBN: 978-1-032-72206-1 (pbk)
ISBN: 978-1-032-72205-4 (ebk)

DOI: 10.4324/9781032722054

Typeset in Sabon
by Taylor & Francis Books

For my parents

Contents

Foreword

I write this Foreword not as a scholar, for I have little academic expertise in the field of disability studies, but essentially as a person born (or "afflicted" early on) with partial deafness. I consciously avoid using the politer term "hearing impairment," as I want to call it what I heard it being called when I was growing up. Except that it was not applied to me.

I was born into a privileged, successful, educated, small-town family. My mother suffered from a hearing impairment (but did not wear hearing aids), and yet, when a visiting aunt suggested that maybe I should get my hearing checked, the suggestion was roundly dismissed by everyone in the family. It was only when I moved to Denmark and started learning Danish, at the age of 30, that my Danish teacher told me to get my hearing checked: "You cannot hear some consonants and vowels," she told me. Subsequent tests showed that I suffered from significant deafness in both ears, and, because it had been part of my life for years, I subconsciously lip-read.

Why did it take so long for this condition to be diagnosed? There are many reasons. Small-town India is not a place where older people really have discussions with children on an equal basis. Even teachers, in schools and elsewhere, issue orders, and seldom engage in conversation. But some of it was also subterranean social prejudice that even an educated family like mine had internalized: deafness (or any impairment) is a subject of subtle or obvious ridicule in most circles. No wonder my elders unconsciously refused to see the signs. It was their deep love for me that made them blind to my condition.

Looking back, I realize that there were obvious signs. I was a weak student in primary and secondary school, and often did not do my homework. I improved only in high school, when homework and other assignments were given to us in writing, and were not issued verbally by the teacher – "Read pages 40 to 78 of this book for tomorrow!" – on the way out of class. I was considered absent-minded, a dreamy boy who wrote poems. I was also a voracious reader, often so deeply lost in my reading that I did not hear my name being called at home. All these signs started making sense once I was diagnosed, not with deafness, but with a "hearing impairment" in Denmark.

Early on in this necessary study, Vivek Singh notes that

[M]ost people assume that functional impairments cause disadvantages. They presume that the life of the non-impaired individual is better than that of the impaired individual. People with disabilities are disadvantaged because they have a functional limitation which is wrong; functional limitations do not always guarantee that the individual possessing them will be disadvantaged.

I can relate to this and many parts of the book, despite suffering from a "minor" impairment. The fact that I am a writer today might well have a lot to do with my deafness: I was not just lost in the books I read as a child; I really did not hear my name being called. Books gave me voices and sounds that I could hear in my head, even as, unknowingly, I failed to hear all the varied voices and sounds around me in the real world. Perhaps my family was not wrong: had I been diagnosed with "deafness" early on, I might have experienced the condescension, pity, or ridicule which meet many of those who are functionally impaired. I saw this happen to my mother, whose increasing deafness was sometimes constructed by outsiders as "slowness of understanding," which of course it wasn't.

Of course, there are many people whose impairments are far greater than mine was or is. Neither I nor this book advocate that impairment should be ignored or wished away. But what this book insists on, correctly in my view and experience, is the realization that most of the negative aspects of physical impairment are socially constructed. It remains an urgent perspective, especially in India, and the book is written solidly for Indian readers. But these readers are not just the physically impaired or scholars like Vivek Singh and me; they should also be those who do not experience any obvious impairment. It is they who are the bigger part of the problem. That is why this book engages with religio-political discourses, literature, culture, legal matters, etc.: as the author puts it, "disability is not merely a subject of medical science but also a subject of humanities through which we can actively engage with the bio-ethical issues." This book is absolutely right in arguing that prejudices and ignorance about "disability identity" is just as serious a problem as that about "the categories of race, caste, gender, class and sexuality," and that urgent work needs to be done across the board, including at the governmental level, to begin to remedy this matter in India.

I hope that this book finds many readers, especially those without any impairment, and that it helps to change the dominant perception of "disability" in India.

Tabish Khair, PhD, DPhil
Associate Professor, Aarhus University, Denmark

Preface

Disability studies (DS), disability activism, and disability legislation have become well known in the Western world, particularly in the United States, the United Kingdom, and Europe. As someone who has been part of this development, I have found it heartening to see that this field is now expanding to parts of Asia, South Asia, the Middle East, Africa, and post-Soviet countries in Eastern Europe. Concomitant to this expansion is of course a curation and redefinition of DS. It could be said that the origins of this scholarship created a kind of founder template of certain ideas and approaches which have had both a generative and a deleterious effect on other iterations of DS. In fact, it is not unreasonable to consider the deployment of DS as a kind of colonialism or imperialism of ideas. It is therefore reasonable and necessary for the decolonizing of DS that local cultures create new visions and voices that will change the assumptions of the field.

Vivek Singh's book *The Discourse of Disability: Indian Perspectives* provides an excellent example of the way that national perspectives can alter our way of thinking about disability. Starting with an overview of the global disability studies approach, Singh then goes on to provide readers with a uniquely Indian perspective. I say "Indian," but Singh signals early on that because India contains a multiverse of perspectives and religions, it would be a false start to assume a unified historical and current view of disability in a nation that is composed of diverse populations.

Notably, one of the differences between India and the West is that disability awareness and activism is still somewhat nascent. Historically, according to Singh, India, like almost all the countries in the world, paid little attention to people with disabilities. Singh notes that, for example, ten years after independence, the majority of children with disabilities were not even in school. Despite some activism, currently the situation is improving but it is still inadequate, particularly as concerns the educational system. In sum, Singh emphasizes that "the life of people with disabilities remains miserable and economically challenging." Particularly worthy of note is that gender discrimination against women in India is ramped up when it comes to disability. Women and girls with disabilities are intersectionally discriminated against in ways that are painful to read about. Obviously, caste and social status figure in this algorithm of discrimination as well.

The situation with the social construction of disability is also somewhat perilous. Indian English fiction and Hindi cinema present us with disabled characters who are not fully developed, and who serve in minor roles that are largely metaphorical and particularly stereotypical. Given the political fractures in India between Hindu and Muslim demographics, the depiction of disabled people as "abject" or even "unclean" signals the gap between a disability-centered approach and an ableist one. The way that racialized and religious politics filters into the algorithm of discrimination is a striking insight of Singh's book. And the way, for example, that fiction might use a calamity like the Bhopal chemical disaster to discuss physical difference against the context of biopolitics in India is crucial to a nuanced and non-Western understanding of disability. In addition, the depiction of females with disabilities, particularly in Hindi films, seems to follow along patriarchal lines with agency and hegemony ascribed to masculine and masculinized subjects, while disabled people and women in particular serve a subordinate, de-eroticized, and negatively feminized role.

This book is invaluable in promoting a disability studies approach in India. While drawing on the work of postmodern theorists as well as that of disability studies scholars, Singh manages to strike a balance between theory and practice. The book's conclusion touches on the author's own difficulties within academia and makes recommendations concerning the government's policies of including disabled people in the workforce and in the field of education. Overall, the reader of this book will profit from the varied approach that includes the social, political, and artistic aspects of the complexity of disability.

Prof. Lennard J. Davis

Acknowledgements

This book began as a dissertation at the University of English and Foreign Languages (EFL), Hyderabad, and I hope that my mentors, Prof. Maya Pandit Narkar and Prof. Dilip K. Das can still see their influence on it and on me. I continue to feel the benefit of their guidance. Thanks to Dr. Shilpaa Anand and Prof. Anita Singh for pushing me to think critically. I am grateful to Prof. Anita Singh and Dr. Rahul Chaturvedi for helping me to imagine an academic career for myself.

I am immensely grateful to Dr. Tabish Khair for writing the Foreword and Prof. Lennard J. Davis for writing the Preface to this book. I have grown intellectually through reading their work, and there is no one better than they when it comes to examining the disability discourse.

It is no exaggeration to say that I could not have written this book without the books and peace I had in accessing the Ramesh Mohan Library at the EFL, and the University Library of Humboldt-Universität zu Berlin.

Deep thanks to Antara Ray Chaudhary, Anvitaa Bajaj, and Shashank Shekhar Sinha for their steady and enthusiastic support and for this project. Anvitaa Bajaj made every step of this process easy and pleasant.

I am lucky to have my brother, Ravi, without whom this project would have been much more difficult and far less enjoyable. Finally, and happily, to my beloved wife, Pragya, with whom I share my life.

Vivek Singh

Chapter 1

Introduction

The structure of society predominately privileges normal bodies and excludes the body marked with differences. Society prefers everyone to be normal and attempts to avoid those who are not. To normalize a body marked with differences, modern society puts them under the jurisdiction, control, and surveillance of biomedicine. The knowledge produced by modern society constitutes such bodies as the epitome of dependency. People with disabilities are categorized as dependent. Modern society views the disabled body as a corporeal problem and perpetrates systematic discrimination against it.

Disability is understood as a medical problem and our social responses to it focus on medical intervention, rehabilitation, and charity. People fighting for disability rights argue that such a view stigmatizes people with disabilities; they become the objects of pity and are regarded as undesirable. Disability studies activists challenge the traditional understanding of disability. They question the medical model of disability that conceptualizes disability as an individual defect that is lodged in the individual. Unlike the medical approach, disability rights movements define disability not as an individual defect but as the product of social injustice (Priestley 2011: 34). They claim that people with disabilities require significant changes in the built environment. Disability studies activists do not want the body to be cured; rather, they study the social meaning embedded within the body, symbols, and stigma attached to people with disabilities and ask how they relate to enforced systems of exclusion and oppression, "attacking the widespread belief that having an able body and mind determines whether one is a quality human being" (Siebers 2008: 4). Furthermore, they argue that disability is a social construction, and that no causal relationship exists between impairment and disability. In his 1996 book *Understanding Disability: From Theory to Practice* Michael Oliver says that disability is wholly and exclusively social. Due to the prejudices and stigma that are attached to people with disabilities, society excludes them from the physical and social world.

Historically, people with disabilities have suffered from disadvantages; they have been segregated from the social, political, and economic worlds. Disabled people frequently live in deplorable conditions, owing to the presence of

DOI: 10.4324/9781032722054-1

physical and social barriers which prevent their full integration and participation in the community. As a result, millions of disabled people throughout the world are deprived of virtually all their rights and lead a wretched, marginal life (Shakespeare and Watson 2001: 547). This is because most people assume that functional impairments cause disadvantages. They presume that the life of a non-impaired individual is better than that of an impaired individual. People with disabilities are viewed as being at a disadvantage because they have functional limitations; however, this is wrong. Functional limitations do not always guarantee that the individual possessing them will be disadvantaged. Wheelchair users are faced with the problem of inaccessible architecture, such as buildings that lack access ramps. People with disabilities are disadvantaged not because of their functional limitations but because of architectural choices that do not meet their needs and expectations.

The social model of disability critiques the medical model of disability and ensures empowerment, choice, and citizenship for people with disabilities. It claims that disability is the result of society's failure to provide adequate and appropriate services. The social model of disability perceives disability in attitudinal terms; it questions the understanding of disability as a biological construct. Harlan Hahn states that disability stems from "the failure of a structured social environment to adjust to the needs and aspirations of citizens with disabilities rather than from the inability of the disabled individual to adapt to the demands of society" (1986: 128). They are subjected to oppression and negative social attitudes that inevitably undermine their personhood and their status as full citizens. Therefore, it is not illogical to say that society is characterized by conflict between two competing groups: the dominant and the subordinate. In the same context James Charlton argues that

> Oppression is a phenomenon of power in which relations between people and between groups are experienced in terms of domination and subordination, superiority, and control. Those with power control; those without power lack control. Power presupposes political, economic, and social hierarchies, structured relations of groups of people, and a system or regime of power. This system, the existing power structure, encompasses the thousands of ways some groups and individuals impose control over others.
>
> (1998: 30)

He believes that society's psychological oppression of disabled people has made them feel that their disability is natural. We can apply the Marxian notion of "false consciousnesses" to people with disabilities who have come to believe that they are less capable than others. Consciousness is a process of awareness that is influenced by social conditions and chance. False consciousness originates from self-pity, self-hate, and shame in people's minds. False consciousness is a state of awareness that, according to Charlton, can prevent people with disabilities from knowing their real selves, their real needs, and their real capabilities and from recognizing the options they have. False consciousness and alienation also obscure the real source of oppression. They cannot recognize their self-perceived pitiful lives are simply a mirroring of the pitiful world order. In this regard, people with disabilities have much in common with others who have internalized their oppression.

(1998: 27)

Other minority groups are also the victims of social oppression; however, we cannot equate the oppression of people with disabilities with the oppression of other minority groups. Social oppression is specific in the manner in which it operates in terms of form, content, and location, so an analysis of the oppression of disabled people partly involves pointing out the essential differences between their lives and those of other sections of society, including those who are, in other ways, oppressed (Abberley 1977: 163). Social oppression leads to institutional discrimination. Barton (1993) says in the same context that research findings have demonstrated the extent of the institutional discrimination that disabled people experience in our society. This involves access and opportunities to work, housing, education, transport, leisure, and support services. Thus, the issues go far beyond the notion that the problem is one of individual attitudes. These are not free-floating but are set within and structured by specific historical and material conditions and social relations. "Goodwill, charity, and social services are insufficient to address the profundity and stubbornness of the factors involved" (242). People with disabilities are subjected to horror, distrust, pity, anxiety, fear, hostility, and patronizing behaviors. Such pejorative attitudes, coupled with an inhospitable physical environment such as inaccessible buildings and unusable transport systems, are considered by disabled people to be of real concern. Therefore, it can be concluded that we live in a disabling world.

The social model of disability negates the importance of the body; indeed, it makes a dualistic Cartesian distinction between disability and impairment. Disability scholars such as Michael Oliver argue that disablement has to do with the body and that "impairment is, in fact, nothing less than a description of the physical body" (1996: 5). A person who lives with an impaired body does experience disablement. There is a possibility that the discussion of the personal experience of people with disabilities may hinder the achievement of disability movements' main objectives. It may divert scholars to question the oppressive structure of society. Vic Finklestein has stated that "attitudes and emotions [come] from experiencing discrimination" (1981: 465). Writers such as Jenny Morris have elevated the importance of the personal and the psychological in understanding disability. Such arguments have encouraged a shift away from thinking about changing the real world. However, other disability theorists such as Bill Hughes and Kevin Paterson, who are influenced by postmodern ideas, argue that engaging with debates concerning the body strengthens the potency of the explanatory power of the social model. The social model of disability critiques the medical model, but discourses regarding the body and impairment fall into the domain of biomedicine. They purport that impairment and the body can also be examined from a sociological perspective. The social model offers a pertinent critique of capitalism but does not touch on the paradigm of modernity that maintains the rigid distinction between impairment and disability. According to Hughes, "it restricts the analytical power and 'reach' of disability studies: in particular, it confounds the possibility of developing a social theory of impairment which is largely dependent upon escape from Cartesian categories" (1999: 156). In the social model, the body is rendered synonymous with its impairment and physical dysfunction. However, impairment is more than a medical issue; it is an experience and at the same time a discursive construction. Feminist disability theorists such as Liz Crow and Jenny Morris call for the social model of disability to be reconceptualized and suggest incorporating the sociology of impairment. They claim that we can deny the fact that the physical and emotional pain that people with disabilities experience due to their impairment affects their everyday life. The sharp distinction drawn between disability and impairment has compartmentalized bodily experience from social experience—pain from politics. The existence of impairment is an objective reality as well as one that is subjectively experienced. Liz Crow states that

> an impairment such as pain or chronic illness may curtail an individual's activities so much that the restriction of the outside world becomes irrelevant ... for many disabled people personal struggles relating to impairment will remain even when disabling barriers no longer exist.
>
> (1996: 9 and 209)

Such contrasting perspectives of disability are accommodated by disability studies.

This book seeks to analyze how certain bodies have been considered disabled and looks at the tools which have facilitated their construction as disabled subjects. It will question the production of the abled body through ideological apparatuses such as literature and cinema and will critique the biased language which interpellates the human subject and stigmatizes the body of difference. The body has been redefined by the claim that physical form is not a natural reality, but a cultural concept: a means of encoding a society's values through its shape, size, and ornamental attributes. The body comes to exist through linguistic representation. Language is not an object of representation as humanistic thought; rather, language functions as an agent of ideologies and values. In this book I will investigate the following key questions: why is it important to form certain bodies as disabled? What are the concepts of disability and how are they perpetuated in society? When do these concepts change? How has language perpetuated the notions of ability and disability and naturalized their normalization in terms of inclusive and exclusive practices? The book will explain how both disabled and able bodies are represented. It will examine a selection of Indian literary texts and cinematic works which seem to construct disability in diverse ways. I will compare and contrast the literature and output of Hindi cinemas in the decades that followed independence and from a contemporary ethos. Finally, I will look at works containing narratives that show how bodies of difference have been produced.

This book argues that through radical changes in narratives and representation the bodies of difference can be included in mainstream society, and that marginalized bodies can carry a strong sense of identity. In order to unravel the politics led by the oppressive structure of the society that produces violence against people with disabilities, this book asks the following questions: what counts as violence against disabled people? And when we think of violence, what do we have in mind? While is it morally and politically necessary to recognize and challenge physical acts of violence—epitomized by hate crime—do other subtler forms of violence exist that are equally damaging to disabled people?

1.1 Chapter plan

The book has been divided into seven chapters. Chapter 1, the introduction to this book, weaves an eclectic conceptual framework of disability theory borrowing theoretical insights from structuralism and psychoanalysis.

Chapter 2, "Disability Studies and Identity Politics," engages with issues of identity and their intersection with gender and sexuality. It challenges the dichotomy of ability and disability. In order to explore disability identity, I examine narratives in literary works to discover whether they employ an adaptive approach or offer a productive possibility for people with disabilities.

Chapter 3, "Disability in the Western Epistemology," examines the question of the development of norms throughout the ages and the conceptualization of the disabled body as an undesirable subject. In order to understand the disabled body, one needs to look at the conceptualization of the norm, i.e., the normal body. The chapter looks at the Western sociological history through which normalcy has been constructed. It shows how people with disabilities were participating in various sociocultural performances but were later segregated because of their differences. It also examines how certain practices created discourses, such as that on sanitation, that believed in social division. Furthermore, it delves into the discourse of industrialization that constructed hospitals and asylums for people with disabilities and distanced them from mainstream society. The industrial revolution created the social process of disabling a set of practices and discourses that are linked to the late 18th- and 19th-century notions of nationality, criminality, gender, and race, etc. This chapter explores the politics of medical institutes that empowered able-bodied and devalued bodies marked with differences. Moving ahead, it explores the notion of fingerprinting through which medical scientists brought up the question of corporeal identity. Such experiments did not only affect the sociopolitical lives of people with disabilities but also influenced the policy that affected their economic lives. This chapter aims to question the normative mechanism that tends to capitalize on the lives of individuals and contradicts the ideologies that superimpose the dominant normal order.

Chapter 4, "Disability in India," contextualizes the lives of people with disabilities. It explores the significance of disability as it has been understood in the Indian context. It will seek how the Western notion of disability differs from the Indian notion of disability. People with disabilities in India do not only encounter discrimination based on their physical differences but are also discriminated against based on caste. India is a caste-based country; therefore, any study is incomplete if it ignores the issues of caste and religion. This chapter examines how religion and caste have influenced society in general and the lives of people with disabilities in particular. Needless to say, colonialism transformed the socio-political and economic lives of people living in India. Policies were also influenced by the colonial powers and tagged people with disabilities as useless individuals. One of the main aims of this chapter is to position disability within the colonial era, the real and the imagined, through which to explore a range of inter-sectionalities as disability is theorized, constructed, and lived as a post/neocolonial condition. Education is one of the important factors in the lives of individuals. In the context of people with disabilities, this chapter engages with the issues of education and its relationship to government policy. It draws attention to the fact that the government promised to improve the lives of people with disabilities but lacked the conviction to do so. Innumerable policies have been drafted by the government in the name of inclusive education which have not been implemented properly. The way policies were being implemented reflected the prejudiced attitude of the government towards people with disabilities. A brief study of the drafted policy by the Indian government will show how education was not inclusive in either form or content.

In Chapter 5, "Disability and Indian English Novels," I analyze selected literary works from a disability perspective. I argue that to be disabled is not something that one *is* but something that one *becomes*; furthermore, disability is ordered and enacted in situated and quite specific ways. Moreover, it can be added that disability studies attempt to denaturalize disability. The chapter explores how the disabilities of disabled characters in literary texts are the result of social discrimination, disabling barriers, and disablist politics, and are not an inevitable outcome of individual bodily conditions. The chapter seeks to respond to the following questions: how is normativity enacted? What does one seek to achieve? What specific configurations of subjectivity, embodiment, and disability can we see emerging in the literature? Moving ahead with the questioning of stereotypes of disability, this chapter engages with questions about what is made of disability and ability, and what is made of the disabled subject and body? It delves into the unexplored question of pain in terms of disability. It weaves together characters' experiences of pain with a critical reading of cultural discourses to make several key interventions into knowledge produced about and through pain. It lays out a corporeally infused cultural analysis of pain and excavates the felt experiences of cultural discourses. It situates those experiences within a broader cultural politics of ableism. By applying the methodology of animal studies, the oppression of disabled people and devaluation of their differences will be sought which will be an attempt to bring animal studies and disability studies together to question the exclusionary structure against these differences and to open up a new paradigm of ethics. This chapter will criticize the Americanism and consumerism that has confined the spaces for the body marked with differences.

Chapter 6, "Disability and the Hindi Cinema," analyses the contemporary situation in which people with disabilities live and feel discriminated against. Films are another form of popular culture that reflect the attitudes of society while at the same time ridiculing them. It investigates how people with disabilities are living with their family members, what their responses are, and how they are excluded from society. The discussion highlights the fact that women with disabilities encounter more problems compared to men with disabilities because of their gender construction. Narratives included in this chapter not only tell us a great deal about contemporary situation of women with disabilities and their sexualities but help to question these categories as well.

The chapter explores how the sexualities and gender identities of women with disabilities are regulated. It engages with the narratives that highlight how social control is routinely enforced through definitions of what is natural and normal. Aspects of gender identity and sexuality are controlled through notions of normality. This chapter questions the way categories of disability are made to appear natural and coherent in our lives.

The concluding chapter of the book, "New Directions for Future Work," offers a summary of the research findings. It suggests new areas to be explored for the transformation of the normative structure of society. It suggests new ways of thinking and analyzing the discourse of disability.

This book is an outcome of my immense interest and careful and intensive reading in the area of disability studies. My findings originally appeared in a PhD thesis on which I had worked extensively for a few years when I finally decided to rework, revise, and publish it in form of a book. I started my research knowing that little work had been done that directly relates to my topic and this further piqued my interest in the field. Later, working in the field in which the present book is largely grounded helped me to find areas that had yet to be explored, which I have incorporated in the last chapter of the book. This book seeks to encourage and assist all those who wish to critically engage with this field of study, especially in the context of India.

Disability Studies and Identity Politics

Representation is never neutral; in fact, it tends to establish binaries. The representation of people with disabilities establishes the notion that the disabled body is dependent upon the abled body. In its broadest sense, it is interesting to investigate how representation attaches meaning to bodies. Although recent scholarship has explored the way in which difference and identity operate in politicized constructions such as gender, race, and sexuality, cultural and literary criticism, conventional scholarship has generally overlooked the related perceptions of corporeal otherness that we term variously as "monstrosity," "mutilation," "deformation," "crippledness," or "physical disability."

The book seeks to challenge the entrenched assumptions that able-bodiedness and its conceptual opposite "disability" are self-evident physical conditions. The aim is to defamiliarize these identity categories by disclosing how the physically disabled are produced by way of legal, medical, political, cultural, and literary narratives that comprise an exclusionary discourse. Disability functions as a multivalent trope, which I will examine in this chapter, although it remains a mark of otherness. By examining disability as a reading of the body that is marked by race, ethnicity, and gender, I hope to reveal possibilities for signification that go beyond a monologic interpretation of corporeal difference as deviance. Thus, by first theorizing disability and then examining several sites that construct it, I intend to uncover the complex ways in which disability intersects with other social identities to produce the extraordinary yet ordinary figure that haunts us all.

2.1 Representation and reality

Representation means using language to say something meaningful about world, or to represent it meaningfully to other people. Representation is an essential part of the process by which meaning is produced and exchanged between members of a culture. But it is important to notice how representation fails to imbibe the complexity of the experience of disability. The experience of the encounter between an able body and a disabled body is more complex than representation usually suggests. In this respect, Rosemarie Garland-Thomson,

DOI: 10.4324/9781032722054-2

in her book *Extraordinary Bodies* (1997), talks about the initial or casual exchanges between normates. According to Garland-Thomson, the term normate usefully designates the social figure through which people can represent themselves as definitive human beings. Normate, then, is the constructed identity of those who, by way of the bodily configurations and cultural capital they assume, can step into a position of authority and wield the power it grants them and disabled people which differs markedly from the usual relations between readers and disabled characters. She goes further by saying that when a person has a visible disability it almost always dominates and skews the normate's process of sorting out their perceptions and forming a reaction. The interaction is usually strained because the non-disabled person may feel fear, pity, fascination, repulsion, or merely surprise—but none of these feelings can be expressed owing to social protocol. The discomforting dissonance between experienced and expressed reaction notwithstanding, a non-disabled person often does not know how to act toward a disabled person: how or whether to offer assistance; whether to acknowledge that person's disability; what words or gestures to use or avoid; and what expectations they should have. This is not to suggest that all forms of disability are interchangeable or that all disabled people experience their bodies or negotiate their identities in the same way. Indeed, it is precisely the variation among individuals that cultural categories trivialize and that representation often distorts. Garland-Thomson adds that disability is an overarching and in some ways artificial category that encompasses congenital acquired physical differences, mental illness and retardation, chronic and acute illness, fatal and progressive disease, temporary and permanent injuries, and a wide range of bodily characteristics considered disfiguring, such as scars, birthmarks, unusual proportions, or obesity. Representation frequently obscures these complexities in favor of the rhetorical or symbolical potential of the prototypical disabled figure, which often functions as a lightning rod for the pity, fear, discomfort, guilt, or sense of normalcy of the reader or a more significant character. I intend here to shift from this usual interpretive framework of aesthetics and metaphor to the critical arena of cultural studies to denaturalize such representations. We find that bodies of difference are seldom represented in literature and cinema. In an essay entitled "Subjectivity in Language" Emile Benveniste (1971) explains that language shapes our attitudes and subjugates us. Meanwhile, Tobin Siebers says that "the body figures as a language effect rather than as a causal agent; excluding embodiment from the representational process almost entirely" (2010: 2). So, careless use of language and political representations of impaired bodies may result in their subjugation. It is often done to privilege certain identities and to marginalize others. Garland-Thomson (1997) studies different literary and cultural representations of physical disability in which privileged identities are under-recognized. The majority of literary and cinematic works produced thus far have made a deliberate attempt to marginalize the body of difference; it should be noted that such works are also intended to support commercialism. The emergence of a somatic society is a better context through which to understand the sociology of impairment. This is a society in which major political and personal problems are both problematized within the body and expressed through it. This suggests that, in the contemporary world, the body has come to be recognized as the key domain in which struggles for power and control are contested. Biopolitics has come to dominate contemporary politics to the extent that we have witnessed a somatic turn whereby the focus is on the social regulation of individual and collective bodies to promote social stability. The body, here, is a central metaphor for social, political, and cultural activities and anxieties. From a Foucauldian position, the impaired body is inseparable from the power that is visited upon it. As a discursive construction, impairment is culturally complex. It is a product of the intense disciplinary practices that produce it. Bill Hughes (1999) states that there is a struggle in contemporary culture between an agenda that celebrates physical difference and one that valorizes impossibly rigid regimes of bodily maintenance and consumer asceticism. Discrimination is built into the everyday world in such a way that impaired bodies disappear. This describes the process whereby the impaired body-as-subject—in the process of everyday social encounters—is objectified and thus experiences itself as an awkward presence. As we know, liberal modernity cuts across differences in the body and suggests a homogenous aesthetic of the built environment that will exclude disabled people. Architectural practice is informed by a normalizing discourse that serves to alienate impaired bodies and to prioritize what one might term the mobile body. So, the third model which refuses the medical model and the social model arises out of the erosion of the legitimacy of a world conceived in dualistic terms. The post-Cartesian age is one of the body politics in which society is somatic, disability is embodied, and impairment social. Mitchell and Snyder (1997) say that regardless of whether the focus is on the body itself or on the sociopolitical context, there is broad agreement among analysts that far from being a bioscientific fact, disability is a category that is constituted, given meaning, and expressed through an endless set of cultural, historical, political, and mythological parameters that ambiguously define disabled people as excessive, contaminators, or both malign and helpless.

2.2 The production of the normal body

Throughout history, any society affected by capitalism has excluded the abnormal/diseased/disabled body or disrespected the body of difference. By extension, modern society has reconfigured the boundaries of the body and reconceptualized the notion of the normal body which is valuable and respected. This does not mean that in the past another form of body was neglected or excluded from society; rather, in the words of Roberto Esposito (2011), it was "immunized," which denotes the inclusive exclusion of the disabled body and in this respect the body of difference has a desire for sameness. The polarity between the abled body and the disabled body was marked at the point of labor power. Ability becomes the ideological baseline by which humanness is determined—the lesser the ability, the lesser the human being. In these terms only the normal body is valuable, and we already know that the ideology of ability simultaneously banishes disability and turns it into a principle of exclusion. The notion of aberrancy was attached to the body of difference to exclude them and to determine the criteria of the normal body. The criteria for being a normal body were founded upon what is considered an abnormal body. But there were no unchanging criteria for deciding what is aberrant. Perceptions of madness, sickness, disability, and criminality alter radically over time. What needs to be taken into consideration is we do not define the abnormal through the normal but vice versa. In other words, we do not decide that a certain kind of body is valuable and legitimate and then go on to decide what kinds of bodies are aberrant or unacceptable. Instead, we first figure out what abnormality is in order to frame the concept of normality. At the sociocultural level the abnormal/disabled body is regarded as a threat to the integrity of the normal/abled body. To maintain the order of the sociocultural paradigm, abnormality of the body has to be eliminated. Disabled bodies emerge as discordant social elements and their elimination of them is a logical extension of a capitalist ideology that esteems national and individual progress toward self-reliance, self-management, and self-sufficiency. In *Purity and Danger*, Mary Douglas (2004) explains how culture does not tolerate the anomalies that are produced by the communal narratives of order. That which emerges from a given cultural context as an irremediable anomaly is translated not as a neutral difference but as pollution, taboo, contagion. That irremediable anomaly, moreover, is seen historically as a matter of medical intervention. Such anomalies have been a medical matter for as long as human beings have sought to escape the stigma of death, disease, and injury, which is why the elimination of the body of difference seems to be necessary. But here it is pertinent to examine the following: is the boundary of bodies fixed and stable? Can we have a pure social order by exterminating the anomalies? Do anomalies lie outside the sociocultural order? Here I am trying to conceptualize the normal body as fluid and incomplete and that functions in the same way that the so-called abnormal body functions. The constitution of the normal body is always in progress and is never completed. The intervention of postmodern discourse about the body sweeps away the Enlightenment's way of thinking of the body as perfect, fixed, and as being rather than becoming.

Let us return to the social model of disability in which we find that it is the environment that disables those bodies which do not fit into the structure. It opposes the labeling of disability as "a physical or mental defect but defines it as a cultural and minority identity" (Siebers 2008: 4). The concept of identity has been broadly debated in the field of disability studies and remains a contested and prolific issue in recent years. Siebers' argument that disability is a cultural and minority identity rejects identity as essential, fixed, and stable. As we know, identity is not a universal entity but is produced by sociocultural discourses, and it attacks the notion of essentialism whereby we find that language reflects reality but does not construct reality. Language is a structure not of representation but signification. It does not represent a reality that is outside of it or before it. Language is a structure of signs; it constitutes the reality that is to be represented. It is not denied here that there is no reality outside language, but the knowledge of reality that we have is constituted in language. Language, Austin (1962) argues, constitutes the "I" through the process of signification and utterances. Saussure argues that the sign constitutes both the signifier and the signified because the relationship between the signifier and the signified is arbitrary, while both the word and the concept are constructed through the differences. Thus, we cannot think about reality without language. Benveniste (1971) argues that the subject is the effect of the structure whose self is represented in language. Therefore, "I" does not represent the self but constitutes it through the process of signification. Even Austin (1962) proposes that if a person makes an utterance, it signifies that they are not simply saying something but is performing that action intended in utterance. The anti-essentialist claims that identity is a process of becoming and is always produced by similarity and difference. As Jacques Derrida (1967) argues, the meaning of identity categories—Britishness, Blackness, Masculinity, etc.— are deemed to be subject to continual deferral through the never-ending process of supplementarity or difference. So, it may be concluded that there is no such identity that is essential and natural. Disability as an identity is a social category rather than a biological and natural property.

The medical model identifies certain bodies as disabled/diseased and exerts power over them that results in the marginalization of those bodies. It empowers the dominant model of ability by differentiating it from the disabled/diseased body. As I have argued above, language generates meaning through relational differences. The abled body comes to acquire meaning in its difference from the disabled body. However, it is also regulated within the discourses by producing knowledge. "Norms" are constituted by the population and are constitutive of the population. Norms constitute the essence of the sense of the self. Norms emerge through community experiences. The question arises as to how norms that regulate discriminatory practices come into existence. Norms prescribe certain "performances" which are perpetuated by the subject. The individual becomes the subject by putting themselves into the process of performance. They perpetuate the structure of normality by reiterating that performing process. Norms come into existence by restraining certain behaviors or practices, and by attaching negative meaning to certain performances and stigmatizing them. Judith Butler (1990) argues that the subject is produced through the performativity of norms (normative representations, normative practices). It is very clear that certain practices are abhorred or considered deviant if they do not fit into the norm. We have seen in our society that if a person behaves abnormally they are treated as a mad/diseased person and become subject to medical treatment.

Undoubtedly, the central purpose of disability studies is to reverse the negative connotations of disability, but this pursuit tends to involve disability as an identity formation rather than as a physical or mental characteristic (Siebers 2008: 4). Thus, it appears that negative connotations have been attached to those bodies that do not properly fit into the norm. For example, if a body cannot run, it is deemed not fit for purpose and can be considered a problematic body for the coherence of norms or society.

2.3 The genealogy of ability

During the time of globalization, disability was medicalized and institutionalized. A new form of power was generated by instituting hospitals and a new form of medicine was produced to be practiced on healthy and sick/mad bodies. Hospitals were constructed to create a new power relationship between the state and the citizenry through which a new kind of discourse was shaped. Discourse as a total system of knowledge makes true or false statements possible. The disabled believe unreal things to be true because the discourse that structures their belief dictates it. Disability discourse does not originate in the mind or body. Disability is part of a historically constructed discourse, or as Lennard Davis (1995) puts it, it is an ideology of thinking about the body under certain historical circumstances. Disability is not an object but a social process that works on everyone who has a body and who lives in the world of senses. The disabled body adapts to the phenomenon of disability discourse which has the motive to regulate that body, and through this process the normal structure is empowered. I am not going to discuss here the various apparatuses of ideology such as art, religion, and institutions that control human behavior and reshape it. Instead, I want to trace the genealogy of disability to question the constructed identity of disabled people as well as to look at how it has been perpetuated.

Let me first question the idea of adequation that the norm always looks for. We have already seen in Saussure (1916) that each signifier has a signified and that each signifier differs from another signifier. The difference between one signifier and another signifier is negative. The word "signifier" constitutes meaning through relational differences too. But in Derrida we find that there is no fixed meaning, and that each signifier refers to another signifier rather than to a fixed signified. The effect of difference generates the "unfinalizability" of the meaning, the perpetual postponement of the closure of meaning in the sign, and the postponement of the sought-for adequation of signifier to signified. So, there is no such body that can properly fulfill the expectations of the norm. In the case of the disabled body, it poses a continual threat to the coherence of the norm because it does not emerge as adequate to the norm. Needless to say, the disabled subject is also the effect of that same structure that has produced the able/normal subject. But to escape from incoherence and the threat of that structure it excludes the disabled subject and exercises discriminatory practices by attaching negative connotations to it.

Many disability theorists argue that disability as an identity is never negative. In India there is a heterosexual normative culture in which sexual relations among people of the same sex are prohibited. It produces the practices of homosexuality as abhorrent and deviant. The body which desires the same sex is labeled as a disabled/deviant body and is kept under medical supervision. But we also live in a democratic society in which each person has equal rights and to disparage a person because of their disability should not be normalized and legitimatized. There are groups of people who celebrate the difference in their bodies. For instance, in the postcolonial discourse, white people discriminated against third world people based on the color of their skin and considered them as some sort of surrogate people, and even conceptualized them as the underground self. The negritudists propagated to celebrate their difference rather than feeling bad about the color of their skin and applauded with a new aphorism, "black is beautiful." The feminist movement which ran parallel to the postcolonial movement celebrated women's biology and sexuality, which were major causes in the subjugation of women in the patriarchal society, in narratives rather than suppressing their inherent biological traits. According to Anthony Giddens, "self-identity is not a distinctive trait or even a collection of traits, possessed by the individual ... it is the self as reflexively understood by the person in terms of his or her biography" (1991: 53). Identity is how an individual interprets the sense of his self. According to Giddens, we are free to choose our identity and can reject identities imposed on us as a result of ascribed characteristics. A disabled person may not carry a disability identity because they have never felt discriminated against in the environment and have never regarded their body as being incapable of performing certain acts. A so-called able person may fit into the ascribed characteristics of disability because they have always found their sense of self weak and disabled. Here the words "able" and "disabled" are used as they have been understood in "normal" society. We reject fostered identities by the creation of narratives about the self and "provided [that] we can sustain these narratives, we are able to maintain our sense of self" (Giddens 1991: 54). This understanding of self and identity questions the ascription of the single identity which was supported by essentialists. Our sense of self is continuously evolving and every day we emerge with a new sense of self. We interact with new situations every day which make us feel abled, sometimes disabled, sometimes possessing masculinity, sometimes femininity, etc. However, these all categories are culturally constituted. Disability identity is a possibility of being which is carried by everyone.

In our society, discriminatory practices also emerge through the idea of difference. The idea of celebrating difference is one way of ignoring discriminatory practices. Therefore, in the case of disability studies it is necessary to question the idea of difference as it is manifested in the "cyborg."

The cyborg embodies the idea that there are no clear divisions between the nonhuman and the human, the technological and the biological, the artificial and the natural. The innovation in the field of technologies and medical science reshaped the human body. Prostheses, i.e., devices that replace a missing part of the body, are used to make the body stronger and are frequently used by disabled people. At present, virtually every part of the body can be replaced except the brain and the nervous system. By using the idea of the cyborg, disability scholars argue that the notion of ability can be incorporated by a disabled body and an able body also uses prostheses to feel strong and capable. The cyborg presents pure, clean, hard, and tight bodies that are associated with the notion of ability, namely that "the able body has a great capacity for self-transformation. It can be trained to do almost anything; it adjusts to new situations" (Siebers 2008: 10). Therefore, the notion of cyborg questions the notion of ability and challenges the notion of disability. "The disabled body is limited in what it can do and what it can be trained to do. It experiences new situations as obstacles" (Siebers 2008: 10). On the other hand, the cyborg has been heavily criticized by disability scholars who maintained that it has reproduced and empowered the notion of ability. Here it is important to problematize the distinction between ability and disability as well as the fixing of the identities of the disabled.

Certain signs and symbols are attached to impaired people. For instance, a wheelchair user is deemed to be a disabled person who cannot walk or run as an able body does. A normal person may discriminate against impaired people because they use wheelchairs. However, the impaired person uses a wheelchair simply to empower their physical capabilities and to make their work viable; by the same token, a normal person might use a car or a bike for the same purpose. It is an inherent problem in our society that prejudiced ideas have been attached to certain symbols and signs. People with disabilities do not want to be Othered on the basis of their impairments; they are normal and able in other ways.

The sense of self is a sense of knowledge about the self that questions any sort of knowledge that is imposed on one's self. It goes without saying that one's sense of self often derives from a normative knowledge of the human. Constituting one's identity is very much a political act that can be questioned by personal narratives which may challenge the stereotypical image of the disabled subject. On the other hand, it can be said that the able or the disabled may be biased in the production of their self-image and self-narratives. People whose bodies are not used as a signifier of difference claim that biographical narratives are one of the tools that can be used by those whose bodies are not universally accepted to construct a self and are a way of reconstructing bodily image and self-identity. But in contrast to this charge, it can be proved that a person who has never come across those obstructions which have impeded the functioning of their work or frustrated their wishes should not be identified as having a disability. Nick Watson concludes that

> [s]elf-identity and subsequently agency is achieved through a practical demonstration of his skill and abilities and it is through this agency that he is able to reaffirm his own sense of biography and challenge identities ascribed to him on the basis of his impairment"
>
> (2002: 256)

Earlier in this chapter I proposed that disability is not a property of individual bodies but the effect of social structure that privileges ability. Furthermore, with the help of prostheses and positive thinking an impaired person can overcome their condition which is disabling in this normative culture. My argument here is that aided by these mechanisms a disabled person produced in normative culture can challenge the privileged notions of ability. Such mechanisms create a space where both able and disabled bodies come together without having the sense of each other's bodily differences.

2.4 The idea of becoming

As the notion of becoming uncovers the inherent fluidity and lack of completion by reclaiming the body, it unsettles the notion that the body is complete and fixed; it is the process that shifts and flows just as the body itself undergoes modifications and changes. The general notion which lies behind the disabled body is that inability to meet normative expectations positions the disabled body as untrustworthy and less unique but that any mode of corporeality is merely porous and provisional. Moreover, as Maurice Merleau-Ponty's (1962) approach indicates, the phenomenological understanding is that biological, social, and discursive bodies are equally unfixed and mutually constitutive. No body is complete in itself, nor does it operate independently of the other. An individual's experience of anxiety while facing abnormal corporeality is not because such corporeal disorders are foreign or unknown to them, but precisely because it is already inside their repressed psyche, or it is their repressed experience of embodiment. In early infancy, everyone experiences the *corps morcelé* (fragmented body) as Jacques Lacan (1997) calls it, and it is only in the process of becoming a subject in the symbolic order that the image is dis-avowed. In other words, bodies that evoke anxiety and fear touch—those who are old, sick, and disabled—are not so much strange as all too familiar. Lacan tellingly names aggressivity as a correlative tension of the narcissistic structure of the coming-into-being of the subject. In the hostility, evasion, and para-doxically in the fascination that greets disability there is a moment of self-recognition or intuition of the Lacanian model of misrecognition that otherwise sustains the self in the symbolic. It is as though each one knows, but cannot acknowledge, that the disabled other is a difference within rather than external to the self. Proximity and touch are not without risk but the move to deny them is bound to fail. What phenomenology tells us is that we are always already exposed, already immersed in one another, and that in acknowledging our intrinsic openness to the other—all the others—lies the best hope of over-coming the insistent hierarchies that strip some bodies of meaning and value. As Merleau-Ponty notes, the blind man using a stick to guide his way is not made to do it in a utilitarian sense. Through the stick he enters into a new relationship with his world: "the stick is no longer an object perceived by a blind man, but an instrument with which he perceives. It is a bodily auxiliary, an extension of bodily synthesis" (1962: 176). The prosthetic aid evokes a very different body image to that of a sighted person, but both the blind and the sighted partake in what Merleau-Ponty calls a "total awareness of my posture in the world" (1962: 203). Having either a mental or physical disability does not break one's immersion in the flesh of the world, so rather than seeing it as negative, it might signal the opening up of new horizons. A person who has a spinal cord injury should see his becoming-in-the-world with others. It does not mean that his loss, pain, and despair are going unnoticed; rather, as the new phenomenology of embodiment becomes familiar, different forms of perceptual awareness and interrelationship may become a site of unexpected possibility (Shildrick 2009). The issue at hand is that we often fail to acknowledge the vulnerability of modern subjects. Rather than resisting this notion, we consistently question it within the context of intercorporeality and our shared existence in the world with others.

Miho Iwakuma's (2002) speculation on the extension of embodied subjectivity in the arena of sexuality—when a lover of a person in a wheelchair touches the chair, he or she shivers as if the flesh of the person were being caressed. In a sense, the person was touched but it is usually dismissed as fetishistic. Yet we are embodied in the flesh of the world where experiencing and being experienced by others is not a formal encounter between the self and the other but is a matter of intercorporeality. There is no transactional hierarchy. In the same reference, as Katherine Ott (2002) points out, the term prosthesis has acquired rich abstract meaning in both psychoanalysis and cultural studies as a metaphor signaling some kind of mediation between an artificial device and the supposedly natural body; however, it also has a complex material history mapping the literal interface between flesh and machine. Prosthetic devices are intended to replace or enhance normative function and appearance; in other words, there is a Foucauldian sense of the technological disciplining and regulation of the body. But their use may be radically subverted. The intercorporeality of the organic and the inorganic, the assembly and disassembly of surprising connections, the capacity to innovate, and the productive troubling of intentionality are all experienced by disabled people, particularly insofar as they are prepared to explore the uncharted potential of prostheses. As with other minoritarian thought and practices, such as the feminine, the breaking through of the expressed limits and constraints of the resource to hand intensifies the decomposition of binaries—body/machine, active/passive, biology/technology, interior/exterior and multiple non-repressive forms of passionate vitality.

2.5 Disability and sexuality

One major area in the field of disability studies is the discourse of sexuality. The sexuality of disabled people has been silenced, and any reference to sexuality in terms of disabled people is often constructed as asexual or hypersexual.

One reason may be that, as Foucault suggests, bodies and pleasure might subvert the normative stability. When considering the sexuality of disabled people, facilitated sex is a plausible way which is in opposition to the normative image of sexuality as heterosexual, private, ideally productive, and above all autonomous as sociocultural mores and law support. So, here I pose the question, are we trying to win access for disabled people to the mainstream of sexuality, or are we trying to challenge how sex and sexuality are conceived, expressed, and limited in modern society? I will seek to address the question of what is at stake in the cultural imaginary that requires such a closing down of possibilities, such as the possibility of being a sexual subject. Through the psychoanalytic approach, I will analyze the cultural imaginary that structures every sexual subject. Deleuzian notions such as desiring machines, assemblage, and body-without-organs are terms that have the potential to disrupt the devaluation of the disabled body. By turning to minoritarian thinking/practices, as recommended by Gilles Deleuze and Felix Guattari (1987), which seem highly appropriate to address the problem of disability, I want to explore not the shutting down or the governance of sexuality, but the potentialities of effectively queering the terms of reference. In the Butlerian sense, the embodied disabled subject is not a pre-existing agent, but one that comes into being and is materialized and sedimented as a result of a series of acts and expressions. Deleuzian embodiment persists only through the capacity to make connections, both organic and inorganic, and to enter into new assemblages which in turn are disassembled. His concept of body-without-organs is not intended as a denial of corporeality as such but is a rather way of rewriting it that avoids the Lacanian narrative of moving from fragmentation to a temporally and spatially stable unity that grounds the subject. It is a normative organization of the body that closes down and fixes its possibilities rather than operating as "a body populated by multiplicities" (Deleuze and Guattari 1987: 30). What Deleuze and Guattari want to promote is not a return to the staging of the pre-subjective infant body, but a deconstruction, a queering of all bodies that entails both taking apart egos and their presuppositions and liberating the pre-personal singularities that enclose and repress. We need to reimagine disability in terms of what Gibson (2006) calls transgressive connectivity. For example, a disabled man who uses a wheelchair, breathes with the aid of a ventilator, is nourished via a gastronomy tube, and speaks through a voice synthesizer might seem the epitome of conventional dependency but Gibson sees it very differently. In his multiple connections and the exchange of energy that facilitates his capacities, the man is freed of the burden of individual identity in a wider becoming: he is a fluid body, not a subject, but a conglomeration of energies. He has replaceable parts, "his organs are here, there and everywhere, he is an excitation, appoint of contact, a relay on a power grid, a plot point on the plane of consistency" (Gibson 2006: 187–196). Such descriptions connote both an individual moment of becoming through connection and modality of existence for all of us. So, the postmodernist analysis makes a point that all bodies—normative or non-normative—are in a constant process of construction and transformation.

A critical study of the disabled body cannot just change the lives of a significant minority of people who are categorized as disabled but has the capacity to disrupt the whole nature of the relationship between differently embodied subjects.

What is clear is that the notion of disability demands a reconfiguration of all our sociocultural, political, and ethical considerations and holds out the promise of culturally disrupting the existing imaginary. The deeply transgressive nature of the Deleuzian approach will perhaps appear too dangerous to many, but it is difficult to deny that the shift must be toward transformation, not accommodation.

It is also important to look at the way disability has been conceptualized and analyzed by the disabled person. One of the goals of disability studies is to provide a center stage for the voices of disabled persons, namely their feelings, thoughts, and experiences as members of an oppressed minority group and of an oppressive culture. In our normative society, disability is considered a negative identity; however, this is not always true as, it also has a positive valence. For example, many disabled persons do not consider their disability as a defect or flaw. Let me quote Nick Watson's interview with Joyce:

> Well, I know this is going to sound very strange to you, but I don't see myself as a disabled person. I see me as an ordinary person, sort of being a housewife, being an auntie, just doing ordinary things that ordinary people do.
>
> (2011: 234)

In Joyce's case, she puts herself in the category of a normal woman who performs social relationships properly. She is quite comfortable with her family and with her colleagues. She faces no problems in playing social roles. Her impairment never obstructs her from performing social relationships. These relationships construct her self-identity. I found it very true when I interacted with Harshini, a ninth grade student at the Durgabai Deshmukh Vocational Training and Rehabilitation Centre for the Handicapped, in Andhra Mahila Sabha, Vidyanagar, who has a profound hearing impairment. After talking to her, I concluded that she has never felt that she is different from other people. Meanwhile, Watson concludes that

> if this is accepted then it has to be acknowledged that identity formation for disabled people is not a unique experience contingent on the presence of an impairment ... but is part of the experience of identity formation common to people as much research has shown.
>
> (2011: 76)

Both Joyce and Harshini have impairments and feel as a normal person feels. Watson also references Jane, who was born and brought up in an environment in which being disabled was normal and her impaired body did not cause any problems for her: "I am a wheelchair user, big deal. The chair is my legs, I save a hell of a lot of money on shoe leather—I just don't see myself as disabled" (2011: 78).

Self and identity are always embodied. Giddens (1991) argues that most people are absorbed in their bodies, and feel themselves to be a unified body and self. But if it fails to meet the necessary standards, one's sense of self may be called into question. This may result in the dislocation of the self and may create an unembodied self, in which case, Giddens argues, the body appears as an object or instrument manipulated by the self from behind the scenes. What is an individual subjected to? Debate on this question will help to unravel the enigma of the "process of becoming a disabled subject." The subject is an effect of the structure in which she or he is produced. Butler (1993) and Lacan (1997) extend this argument which shifts from the structure that produces the "empty forms" as Benveniste suggests. According to Benveniste (1971), linguistic structure constitutes the empty forms that we come to occupy as speaking subjects. Butler and Lacan extend the arguments of structuralists by saying that the process of occupying these forms generates effects that the structure does not fully control.

According to Althusser (1971), we do not have pure, distinct ideas in our minds; it is the ideological structure that produces these ideas. Both ideology and language locate their structure in the unconscious. Althusser says that an individual is subjected to social order not only through the structure of ideology but also through the "process." Knowledge, as Foucault states, is produced about the disabled subject through the various apparatuses which are incorporated into the minds of the disabled subject, and the structure that is produced is normalized and perpetuated via the processes of the disabled subject. The very politics behind this is to insert social meaning into the social experience, through which power is linked to subjectivity. The subject looks at the social meaning as personal attributes such as self-esteem and empowerment. Individuals view this as a matter of personal growth and choice rather than an artifact of power. Constituting identity is a tool of government that is imposed on the subjects by governing their beliefs and behaviors. Government is in Foucault's words "conduct of conduct" which he discusses in his essay "The Subject and Power." Foucault goes further by saying that institutions help the government to regulate the behaviors of individuals and through which they exert power over the individuals; one such is the technology of the self that is deployed by the "pastoral power" in which one acts on their body/conduct. In that way, one transforms her/himself into the form of a subject and understands it as her/his freedom and her/his own choice. If we look back through history, we see that a new kind of knowledge emerged in the 18th and 19th centuries. Industries and technologies were progressing rapidly. During this era the administrative state, capitalism, positivist science, and liberal philosophy came into being.

Before industrialization, people with disabilities were associated with mainstream society. Their differences were accommodated and their skills were utilized. They were considered to be productive for their environments. For example, Aspasia from Athens, Greece, who died in 400 BCE never felt excluded; people learned rhetorical speeches from her. These allowed them to live in their communities and to have fruitful and happy relationships. In other words, they did not constitute a separate, socially discriminated group.

> With the onset of large-scale factory production came the requirement for workers to fit the mold stamped out by mechanization and the timetable, and this put people who lacked the qualities necessary for this kind of labor at a distinct disadvantage.
>
> (Galvin 2006: 98)

As Marx (1990) argues, mechanized production required a uniform workforce, and work was not organized to cater to the range of intellectual and bodily differences experienced by people. People were understood as people with disabilities who were unable to produce proper labor. It is the modernized labor force that is quite distinct from the ancient times that define people's lives and ensures their survival. Foucault argues that, while work has always had a productive function, in the modern era it has taken on two additional functions, namely the symbolic function and the function of dressage or discipline. Those who could not participate in this modern structured social sphere were considered as being unable to adapt to the new conditions and as not having symbolic qualities. They were defined as aberrant. Through this, two separate categories, abled and disabled, were established. The able person was understood as someone who possessed the disciplinary attributes necessary to be part of mainstream society because they could fit into the structured modern social spheres and could support the capitalist mode of production through the use of their body. The disabled person, however, was seen as posing a threat to the social order. But the medicalization of people with disabilities is an attempt to integrate them into mainstream society. They are being rehabilitated and normalized, so that they can be productive for modern society. Quoting Foucault, Galvin states that "as disabled people emerged from the close fortresses in which they functioned and [began] to circulate in a free state, the methods of control over their subjectification became more flexible and more diffuse" (2006: 98). Identity is very much unstable and unfixed compared to other minority identities. For example, a black man will never be a white woman but may turn up the very next day crippled. Disability as an identity can be occupied by anyone, at any time. Disability theorists consider disability as an anchor for other minority identities. Quoting David Mitchell and Sharon Snyder, Siebers argues that "stigmatized social positions founded upon gender, class, nationality, and race have often relied upon disability to visually underscore the devaluation of marginal communities" (2008: 6). Their discrimination is justified by considering them disabled. When minority identities are pathologized by association with disability, Siebers argues, the effect is never merely metaphorical; instead, it also becomes referential. Disability is the reality of the human condition. So, the association with the disability of other minority identities rationalizes the prejudiced attitudes of people toward them. In the case of minority identities, framing identity is considered politics. The individual needs an identity when they are in a crisis due to their helpless and hapless position. The identity is framed such that it seems to other people that they are in need and that they are demanding extra help because they cannot live independently. Siebers says that the word "identity" is seen as a crutch for them. It is perceived that they "lack" something. Psychoanalysts explain that lack lies at the heart of identity. And those who are unable to overcome this lack fall into patterns of dependence and aggression. Recent theorists reject identities associated with lack, dependence, and pathology. But identity is always thought of negatively in the case of minorities. It is seen that they possess unhealthy identities. But this can be justified because it is born due to pain, suffering, resentment, and bitterness. They have been repressed in the dominant culture by majority groups. Similarly to other contemporary theorists, Nancy Fraser (2010) argues that identity politics is a political action to homogenize the various marginalized groups. Identity politics is an attempt to recognize the suffering of other marginalized people. It is a political action through which people's genuine needs will be ignored. In defense of identity politics, Siebers says that it can be justified because it is linked to pain and suffering. This is very true in the sense that disability is not a pathological condition but disability identity is embodied via various apparatuses. Alcoff (2006) says that "identity is not merely that which is given to an individual or group, but is also a way of inhabiting, interpreting and working through, both collectively and individually, an objective social location and group history" (2006: 42). A person's identity is not always recognized by their individuality but the structure through which "that person identifies and becomes identified with a set of social narratives, ideas, myths, values and types of knowledge of varying reliability, usefulness and verifiability" (Siebers 2008: 15).

The constructed notion of disability defines the politics of imposing social codes and norms on bodies. Viewing disability as the mismatch between society and bodies is the strategy of imposing norms. We have already discussed how disability deconstructs the notion of norms and interrogates the politics layered behind their social construction. Social constructionism fails to see the physical realities of people with disabilities. We come to the conclusion that in this "normal" society the body hardly matters. It privileges performativity over corporeality. In addition to this Siebers favors pleasure over pain and illustrates social success in terms of intellectual achievement, bodily adaptability, and active political participation. It is power relations that bring us into a social relationship. As Foucault says, power is productive and it only functions on "free subjects." Social success can only be defined in terms of our relationship with ourselves which will change if the power structure is revealed. In order to transform the relationship of social exclusionary/discriminatory practices maintained by power, we need to know that subjectification is a socially mediated process. Galvin says in relation to this argument that "it is possible to build new identities within the fractures and fault lines out of which power erupts and along the border of the norm where new meaning and new identities can be created" (2006: 187). As Foucault says, we have to know the virtual fractures, because they open up a new space for freedom.

Unlike other identity categories such as race, sexuality, and gender, disability is not yet widely recognized. Michael Berube (1998), an eminent disability theorist, has admitted that he found disability too specialized a category to apply to general education. He says,

> I was kind to people who used wheelchairs ... and respectful of all persons regardless of their mental abilities, but when it came to whether disability should be a major academic subject, I just could not see the point of another additive studies programme in the curriculum.
>
> (1998: ix)

On the other hand, gender studies and race studies, for example, discuss the identity formation of women and black people, respectively. Like other identities, gender, sexuality, ethnicity, and race, disability is not a theoretical abstraction; rather it is a lived experience that is performed unconsciously. People with disabilities become adept at turning disability stereotypes and narratives to their own ends. They transform a potentially stigmatizing experience into an act of empowerment. However, there is always the possibility that some disabled people may choose not to perform or attempt to perform in the same way as able-bodied people. The goal of both the self-conscious performer and those who do not perform becomes an active maker of meaning, rather than a passive specimen on display. Choosing to perform disability is the starting point of people's lives as activists. Therefore, disability performers reject assumptions and prejudices that challenge narrative conventions and aesthetic practices. Petra Kuppers (2003) argues that physically impaired people have to negotiate two areas of cultural meaning: invisibility as an active member of the public sphere, and hyper visibility and instant categorization. We need to reflect on both the range of performances to which a disability perspective may be applied and the wide variety of approaches and methods that contribute to disability perspectives themselves.

Chapter 3

Disability and the Western Epistemology

3.1 Religion and discourse of disability

The political and social movements started by disability activists in the West acknowledged that people with disabilities are an oppressed and repressed group. Disability scholars' examination of people with disabilities rejected the need for the medical language of symptoms and diagnostic categories. They began to look for different kinds of signifiers and the identification of different kinds of syndromes for their material. In other words, their engagement with the issue of disability questioned the linguistic conventions that are used to institutionalize, control, regulate, incarcerate, isolate, indocrinate, and instruct the disabled. The structure of ableism reinforced the dominant culture's views on disability. Religious ideology plays an important role in structuring societal norms. Social practices have fluctuated among different cultures; for example, views on disability differ in Jewish culture from those in Christian culture.

The fact cannot be ignored that disability is an everyday reality. In bygone times, disabled people were not authorized to perform sacrifices in the same manner as priests, for example. People with disabilities were deemed to be legally unclean. They held the same lowly social positions as prostitutes or women who were menstruating. People with disabilities were faced with cultic impurity. "One had to be without defect in order to approach God's place of residence" (Stiker 1999: 24). In an article entitled "Blemish" the *Encyclopedia Judaica* enumerates the impairments borne by disabled people and develops the concept of cultic impurity thus:

> People with disabilities preclude the offering of sacrifices: blindness and certain eye diseases, injuries to the thigh, a deformed nose (flattened between the eyes), lameness, the loss of a limb, skeletal deformation, muscle degeneration, a humped back, skin diseases even if not precisely identified, the loss of a testicle.

> (Stiker 1999: 24)

DOI: 10.4324/9781032722054-3

Stiker (1999) makes the distinction between deformity and illness. A certain form of disability was categorized as being superior to another form of disability. For instance, Jewish law categorized the deaf and mute as subnormal beings, while the blind were deemed normal and able to enjoy their full rights. However, these distinctions do not suggest that disabled people used to take part in social functions. Owing to their disabilities they were judged to be impure, and they were disqualified from actively participating in society.

According to the Koran, disabled people's engagement in combat was avoided, because "no man, lame, blind, or crippled or having an incurable defect of the flesh, or afflicted by an impurity of the flesh, none of these shall accompany them to battle" (Stiker 1999: 24). They were not even allowed to participate in church congregations. The community of the Qumrān did not privilege any form of disability. In the name of the sanctity of the congregation or of the community, the exclusion of people with disabilities was proclaimed. The ritual nature of exclusion was also confirmed by the Koran, but it excluded bodies marked with differences from specific rituals. People with disabilities were exempted from battle due to their incapacity not because of their polluted bodies. By stating that "no reproach to the blind, no reproach to the lame, no reproach to the sick" (Stiker 1999: 25), the Prophet wiped out the pollution of the disabled.

Several passages in the Bible reveal that people with disabilities were excluded from society. Lepers were proclaimed unclean. Priests used their authority to determine whether or not a person was impure. As a result, those deemed "unclean" were secluded from the social group. They had to maintain their distance from the "clean" body. These trends promulgated the discourse of hygiene. The measure of cleanliness found in the biblical tradition protected the healthy body. It was required to do so because doctors, at that time, were ineffectual and were limited in their abilities. Therefore, such practices of prohibition started the discourse of sanitation that exacerbated such social divisions. It is also noted that disability represented the presence of God. Jews believe that God is omnipresent; i.e., he is everywhere at all times, and he is always present in the guise of Shekinah which is "very precise and very contingent: in the Ark of the Covenant, between the wings of the Seraphim, in the Temple and the Holy of Holies, and not elsewhere in the same capacity" (Stiker 1999: 26). In biblical times, the presence of people with disabilities was symbolized as the connection between God and the people. People with disabilities were conceptualized as being closer to God.

According to the Bible, physical defects are linked to sin, and as such they signify that an affliction is associated with man, not with God. The Bible states that

> man is the source of evil. It is not an inevitable destiny, nor is it an act of God. It is relatively simple to understand that this signification entails the pollution in disability; what derives from human sin has no part in God. But it is up to man to cure himself.
>
> (Stiker 1999: 27)

Thus, the Bible conceptualizes social morality as being applied to disability and the concept of charity that started from there because the Jewish people had the idea of reparation. This had far-reaching consequences, as shown in Exodus 21:28:

> When an ox gores a man or woman to death, the ox shall be stoned, and its flesh shall not be eaten; but the owner of the ox shall not be liable. If the ox has been accustomed to gore, and its owner has been warned but has not restrained it, and it kills a man or a woman, the ox shall be stoned and its owner also shall be put to death. If a ransom is imposed on the owner, then the owner shall pay whatever is imposed for the redemption of the victim's life. If it gores a boy or a girl, the owner shall be put to death according to the same rule. If the ox gores a man or female slave, the owner shall pay to the slave owner thirty shekels of silver, and the ox shall be stoned.
>
> (Stiker 1999: 27)

Here, it is pointed out that personal liability and social liability were legislated indirectly to others. The link between sin and defect was conceptualized so as to exclude people with disabilities and to deny them the right to perform religious roles, and was introduced as an ethical and social imperative. "The person who is so tried is not condemned, even if the religious signification that he bears dooms him to a very precise and circumscribed form of exclusion" (Stiker 1999: 27).

These examples from the Bible show that attitudes to disability were mixed. It was assumed that disability was punishment for a sin or that people with disabilities had been born under the hostile influence of the planet Saturn. Some believed that people with disabilities were closer to God and that they were born on Earth to repent and to be purged from sin. In medieval times, people with disabilities were highly visible in everyday life. They were treated as normal people by society. They were supported by their communities, families, and friends. The state did not have to provide for them. However, various historical sources report that some disabled people travelled to holy sites as pilgrims and had to resort to begging for their sustenance. The care of the sick and the disabled was based on the Church's teachings: "The monks and nuns would follow the seven 'comfortable works' which involved feeding, clothing, and housing the poor, visiting them when in prison or sick, offering a drink to thirsty, and burial" (Historic England n.d.). Therefore, such acts were not only confined to religious matters; the care of people with disabilities was conceptualized as a civic duty. In England, during the reign of Henry VIII hospitals that had been demolished were rebuilt and dilapidated buildings intended for disabled people were refounded to enhance the reputation of their rich benefactors. It was not saving the souls of the disabled that was previously the concern of religion. At the end of the 16th century, with the help of taxes and donations, new almshouses and hospitals sprang up.

New explanations started to emerge with respect to people with disabilities. People began to believe that madness and disability had nothing to do with God. They presumed that their disabilities were the result of their misfortunes, so therefore they deserved charity. Supporting disabled people was the responsibility of an individual, not of the State: "The parish might give you poor relief, but only if you were destitute as well as disabled. As a disabled person in the society, your life was often harsh and brutal, like everyone else's" (Stienstra 2002: 46). In the 17th century, people migrated from one place to another in search of a livelihood. Social and cultural values were rapidly changing. Every country wanted to show off its wealth and power. Rich traders and merchants started to establish hospitals after the Great Fire of London in 1666. Disabled soldiers and sailors used to shelter in these hospitals. To make them "normal" and healthy, institutes were built. The care of people with disabilities shifted from society to hospitals. To maintain civic order and progress, special schools were institutionalized for the mentally retarded and the disabled.

3.2 Industrialization and disability

At the beginning of the 18th century people with disabilities were sent to live in small charitable asylums or hospitals. In the United Kingdom, of a population of around nine million at the end of the 18th century, it is estimated that fewer than 10,000 individuals lived in an institution, which shows that such people were still being supported by the community and at home (Oliver 1996 :78). But there was an idea growing that hospitals and asylums were the right places for people with disabilities. The early decades of the 19th century ushered in many changes in the structure of society as well as in the architecture of the environment. The industrial revolution had a dramatic impact on the life of people with disabilities by showing them asylums and hospitals as the only spaces to live in. The asylum was defined thus:

> from any of the great main lines of railway which run through the shire ... a traveler will be sure to spy, in some comparatively secluded position, a great group of buildings, which by their modern air ... their tall chimney stacks ... their bulky water tower, seem to belong rather too busy towns than country seclusion.
>
> (Historic England n.d.)

People with disabilities were unwilling to stay there but they were left with no other options.

After the 1834 Poor Law Amendment Act was passed, new workhouses were built. Previously workhouses were built for destitute disabled people and were designed more humanely.

The new workhouses were designed to root out shirkers and scroungers. They were intended as miserable places to live, with Spartan conditions and harsh work regimes. The able-bodied poor avoided them if they could, so disabled and mentally ill people were moved into them.

(Historic England n.d.)

A historian of disability historian explains, "At the beginning of the 19th century, a few hundred people were living in nine small charitable asylums. By 1900, more than 10,000 idiots and lunatics were in 120 county pauper asylums. A further 10,000 were in workhouses" (Historic England n.d.).

The data shows that society considered the disabled as a burden and people thought that giving them financial relief would encourage laziness. "The truly destitute would be helped, but only in the workhouses, where no one could want to stay for long" (Historic England n.d.). Society failed to understand the impact that such policies and thinking would have on the disabled and mentally ill people.

By this time medical institutes had started to take shape. Medical professionals known as alienists, the forerunners of psychiatrists, believed that asylums were the best places for disabled and mentally ill people as here they could be treated and restored to moral good health. However, by the end of the century, they believed that they were incurable. By the end of the Victorian age, people with disabilities still lived with their family members and were supported by their communities, but by this time special schools and charitable institutes had been established.

Though some people begged on the streets, others prospered. The Blind Henry Fawcett (1833–1884) became Postmaster General in 1880. Young disabled people formed a self-help group called the Guild of the Brave Poor Things. Their coat of arms was sword crossed with a crutch.

(Historic England n.d.)

It also shows that mobilization for disability rights had started.

At the beginning of the 20th century, tensions between different attitudes had emerged. The return home of soldiers disabled in the First and Second World Wars challenged the widespread notion that people with disabilities were a burden to society. On the other hand, the development of science saw attempts to improve the human race. In 1930, Julian Huxley, secretary of the London Zoological Society and chairman of the Eugenics Society wrote, "What are we going to do? Every defective man, woman, and child is a burden. Every defective is an extra body for the nation to feed and clothe, but produce little or nothing in return" (Historic England n.d.). Westeners strongly agreed with the idea of eugenics and conceptualized people with disabilities as a threat to the health of the nation. The politics behind this idea of eugenics was to eliminate people with disabilities from society to build a stronger society. People with

disabilities were segregated in the name of perfecting the human race. However, the return of the disabled soldiers from the wars brought some changes
in the attitudes of the people. Disabled soldiers were heroes who had sacrificed their lives for the nation. The nation was responsible for treating them
with a positive attitude. Plastic surgery and prosthetics were major advance-
ments for society that aimed to "normalize" the life of disabled soldiers.
"Employers were urged to take on disabled workers and at the same time
sheltered employment workplaces sprang up, including the British Legion
poppy factory in south London" (Historic England n.d.). Following the
Second World War (1939–1945), many horrors emerged that included the
mass killing of people with disabilities in Germany. But at the same time, an
initiative by the state to take care of people with disabilities was started; the
1944 Disability Employment Act promised sheltered employment, reserved
occupations, and employment quotas for people with disabilities. Disabled
people also campaigned to increase awareness about disability among the
population.

> In the 1960s and 70s, the civil rights movement in America inspired dis-
> abled groups to take direct action against discrimination, poor access, and
> inequality. A "social" rather than a medical model of disability emerged
> and eventually, in 1995 the Disability Discrimination Act was passed.
>
> (Higgins 1992: 167)

The social model was concerned with the rights of people with disabilities.
There were tensions between industries fostered by globalization that had no
space for bodies marked with differences and disability activism that was
spreading the consciousness among citizens for the rights of people with disabilities. Undoubtedly, people with disabilities were discriminated against based
on their differences and the decision went in favor of the industrialists.

Disability came into existence with the conceptualization of ability.
Exploring the ideology of ability is also relevant to understanding the way the
notion of disability was formed. Disability is not a substance that existed
before ability; rather, the meaning of ability is founded upon the difference of
disability. The emergence of the ideology of ability and the discourse of normality originated in the form of disability because both ability and disability
complement each other. The institutionalization of medical science reflected
the urgent need to perfect the body:

> [W]hether the medical scientists are working on a cure for the common
> cold or the elimination of all disease, a cure for cancer or the banishment
> of death, a cure for HIV/AIDS or control of the genetic code, their pre-
> posterous, and yet rarely questioned goal is to give everyone a perfect body.
>
> (Siebers 2001: 7)

Western society led by medical scientists conceptualized a body that seemed to be inconsequential and as well as perfectible, and this can be considered an unreasonable understanding.

The incomprehensible proposition was to understand that medical scientists wanted to question the fragility of the body that consists of the reality of sickness, injury, disfigurement, enfeeblement, old age, and death. The proposition of the discourse of ability that believes in the principle of the medicalization of society constructed a world of norms in which we live—in other words the lesser the ability, the lesser the worth of the human being. Each of us attempts to be normal or at least deliberately attempts to avoid that state. One does think about the masses and reflect on their thinking. One cannot ignore the fact that they are evaluated according to the yardstick that is structured by the discourse of norms. Human beings' weight, height, sex drive, and bodily dimensions are measured from the line of above-average. Children are tested at school to determine whether they fit into the normal curve of learning. Therefore, it will not be a generalization to say that every area of contemporary life is calculated by some idea of the norm, and to understand the form of disability, there is a need to unravel the conceptualization of the norm. Disability is not a problem as such, but the construction of normalcy has constricted it.

3.3 Norm(s) and disability

Some concepts of norms already existed during the pre-medieval period when the notion of disability was different from today's notion of disability. The definition of a norm is not related to the condition of human nature; rather, it is a feature of a certain kind of society. The social process of disabling was not a feature of the medieval period, but seems to have appeared with industrialization and is related to sets of practices and discourses that emerged in the late 18th and 19th centuries with the notions of race, gender, sexual orientation, etc. Disability scholars have argued that words such as normal, normalcy, average, abnormal, and normality only entered European languages rather late in human history. "The word normal as constituting, conforming to, not deviating or different form, the common type of standard, regular usual only enters the English language around 1840 ... the word norm in the modern sense has only been in use since around 1855, and normality and normalcy appeared in 1849 and 1857, respectively" (Davis 2013: 3–4).

The concept of the ideal body that originated in the 17th century and was exemplified in the tradition of the nude Venus presents a mythopoetic body linked to the gods. This body of God is not attainable by human beings. The ideal body is imagined by human beings but can never be found in this world. Pliny tells us that the Greek artist Zeuxis tried to paint Aphrodite, the goddess of love, by using as his models all the beautiful women of Crotona in order to select each of her ideal features or body parts and to combine these into the ideal figure of the goddess. So, the point is that no one can conform to the ideal body—everyone is less than ideal.

It is important ask what caused the conceptualization of norms or averages in the 19th century. The concept of norms enters European culture to marginalize all the deviations. Norms or averages were debated in the branch of knowledge called statistics and were popularized by the Belgian mathematician, astronomer, and statistician Adolphe Quetelet. Quetelet made a huge contribution to a generalized notion of what it is to be a "normal" person. He was more impressed by the law of error which was used by astronomers to locate a star by plotting all the sightings and then averaging the errors. He applied this to the distribution of human features such as height and weight. Based on his calculations, he formulated the concept of the body of an average person. This abstract human was the average of all the human attributes in a given country.

Such constructions of an average person contributed paradoxically to creating a kind of ideal person. "An individual who epitomized in himself, at a given time, all the qualities of the average man, would represent at once all the greatness, beauty and goodness of the being" (Davis 2013: 2). Such a constitution of the average person not only hegemonized the moral qualities but hegemonized the body as well. Porter argues that "deviations more or less great from the mean have constituted (for artists) ugliness in the body as well as a vice in morals and a state of sickness with regard to the constitution" (Porter 1986: 103).

The concept of a norm was popularized in such a way that it became a moral obligation of the people to comply with it:

> The norm pins down that majority of the population that falls under the arch of the standard bell-shaped curve. This curve, the graph of an exponential function, that was known variously as the astronomer's "error law," the "normal distribution," the "Gaussian density function," or simply the "bell curve," became in its own way a symbol of the tyranny of the norm.
>
> (Davis 2013: 3)

Needless to say, any bell curve will have at its extremities those characteristics that deviate from the norm. Consequently, the concept of deviations or extremes was introduced with the concept of the norm. Therefore, in societies in which the concept of the norm began to be operative, people with disabilities came to be understood as deviants.

In the 19th century, statisticians such as Sir Francis Galton, Karl Pearson, and R. A. Fisher were working as eugenicists and the central insight of statistics was to measure human beings and improve them so that deviations from the norm could be diminished. In addition, eugenicists attempted to set the norm for populations and individuals as well. Therefore, the whole population was divided into two parts: the standard population and the substandard population. The standard population consisted of those who complied with the norms, while those who failed to comply with the norms were labelled substandard. In theorizing the tyranny of the norm, Davis says that "such an activity is profoundly paradoxical since the inviolable rule of statistics is that all phenomena will always conform to bell-curve norming the non-normal is an activity as problematic as untying the Gordian Knot" (1995: 25). In the same context, MacKenzie (1981) states that "Galton's statistics made possible eugenics but rather that the needs of eugenics in large part determined the content of Galton's statistical theory" (1981: 52). The relationship between statistical sciences and eugenicist concerns gave birth to the concept of the norm that substantiated the concept of the disabled body.

The rise of eugenics can be traced back to the notion of the evolutionary advantage of the fittest that was popularized by Charles Darwin. The belief that only the fittest survive in the process of evolution laid down the foundations for eugenics and for the idea of the perfectible body undergoing progressive improvement. Farrall says, "eugenics was in reality applied biology based on the central biological theory of the day, namely the Darwinian theory of evolution" (1985: 55). In addition, Davis says that "Darwin's theory served to place disabled people along the wayside as evolutionary defectives to be surpassed by natural selection" (2013: 5). Thus, eugenics became obsessed with the elimination of defectives, a category that included the feeble-minded, the deaf, the blind, the physically impaired, and so on.

Galton, the cousin of Darwin, introduced the technique of fingerprinting that is used for personal identification purposes. His interest in fingerprinting showed that certain physical traits could be inherited. According to MacKenzie,

> one of the inducements to making these inquiries into personal identification has been to discover independent features suitable for hereditary investigation ... it is not improbable, and worth taking pains to inquire whether each person may not carry visibly about his body undeniable evidence of his parentage and near kinships.
>
> (1981: 65)

Fingerprinting also tells us about people's parentage: a fingerprint is a kind of serial number that is marked on the body. According to the notion of fingerprinting, this serial number belongs to a person's parents and is transferred to their child. Through that serial number, the human body is standardized and the identity of the body cannot be altered by human will. The belief is that serial numbers identified by fingerprints are embedded in people's corporeality. "This indelibility of corporeal identity only furthers the mark placed on the body by other physical qualities—intelligence, height, reaction time" (Davis 1995: 32). If one accepts this logic, it can be argued that a person enters into an identical relationship with the body and thus the body forms a person's identity. It is believed that identity is not changeable. So, it can be argued that the politics behind the fingerprinting of the body is to differentiate bodies from one another and to identify them with their unique serial number, and this results in identifying the person with their marks of physical difference.

Eugenicists did not distinguish between different groups of disabled people. They tended to group together all the allegedly undesirable traits found in people. They even grouped criminals and the poor with people with disabilities. Karl Pearson, one of the leading figures in the eugenics movement, classified the unfit as "the habitual criminal, the professional tramp, the tuberculous, the insane, the mentally defective, the alcoholic, the diseased from birth or from excess" (cited in Kevles 1985: 33). Pearson was the head of the Department of Applied Statistics which included Galton and the Biometric Laboratories at University College, London.

> This department gathered eugenic information on the inheritance of physical and mental traits including scientific, commercial, and legal ability, but also hermaphroditism, hemophilia, cleft palate, harelip, tuberculosis, diabetes, deaf-mutism, polydactyly (more than five fingers) or brachydactyly (stub fingers), insanity, and mental deficiency.
>
> (1985: 38–39)

Such deviations from the norm were thought of as a disease for the nation. The Eugenics Record Office asserted that "the only way to keep a nation strong mentally and physically is to see that each new generation is derived chiefly from the fitter members of the generation before" (cited in Kevels 1985: 39–40). Thus, the understanding of disability took a new turn whereby disability is shaped as a metaphor. If national citizens are not fit or do not fit into the concept of the nation, then the national body will not be fit. Davis, who opposes the logic of eugenics, argues that such a notion contributes to the body politic: "by that notion a hunchbacked citizenry would make a hunchbacked nation ... nevertheless, the eugenic logic that individual variation would accumulate into a composite national identity was a powerful one" (Davis 2013: 10). This understanding excluded people with disabilities from industry, whereby workers were thought of as interchangeable, and merely sought to create a universal worker. The industrialists believed in uniformity and therefore deviance in physical coherence was not entertained.

3.4 Disability and the industrialized society

The concept of disability transited from feudalism to modern industrial capitalism. Vic Finkelstein debated the shift in the lives of people with disabilities and identifies three phases. In the first phase, he states that people with disabilities congregated at the bottom of the economic pile in the company of poorly paid workers, the unemployed, and the mentally ill. In the second phase, he noticed the emergence of segregated disability institutions following the introduction of new production technology. Thus, "large-scale industry with production lines geared to able-bodied norms" (French 1993: 57) excluded impaired people who previously had been integrated, socially active members of their class and community. Furthermore, the growth of hospital-based medicine encouraged the expansion in the number of professionals whose expert knowledge was disabling. But, paradoxically, public services also helped disabled people to acquire social independence and to take the professional control of their lives. It was this critique that gave birth to the social model (Finkelstein 1980: 11). In the third phase, Finkelstein debates the emergence of the social model and critiques the exclusive structure of society. Finkelstein emphasized the era of industrialization that formed a different set of attitudes for people with disabilities. During the period of industrialization, the historical analysis of disability is not counted. However, the dynamics of the industrial process and the social and political outcomes are deeply connected and have affected the lives of people with disabilities. Agriculture or small-scale industry did not preclude the great majority of people with disabilities. They participated in the production process, whereas fully fledged capitalism complicated the economic base for people with disabilities. In the same context, Oliver argues that "the mode of thought and the problem of the order were added to the impact of the economy" (1990: 27). He adds that

> the evolution of intellectual concepts, from a religious interpretation of reality to a metaphysical and then a scientific one, interacted with the disruption thrown up by the rise of capitalism alter historical perceptions of disability and propagate new medical and institutional methods for subduing deviancy.
>
> (1990: 29)

Every disability scholar has highlighted the fact that the condition of impaired people in pre-industrial society was better than of those in industrialized society.

Brendon Gleeson, an eminent figure in disability studies, has looked at the way in which geographical spaces for people with disabilities were confined in industrialized society. He states that "the historical production of space was a contested process where the exercise of power largely determines who benefits and who loses from the creation of new places and landscapes" (Gleeson 1992 : 65). He advocated for embodied materialism in which he observes disability as a part of a broader process of social embodiment. According to him, the roles and representations of body types varied in time and space. This shift was noticed in a comparison of feudal England and the industrial city. Gleeson believes that among the medieval peasantry, people with disabilities occupied a great space in peasant social space. In that period, if the bodies were affected by diseases such as leprosy, they were excluded due to spiritual significance. They believed that leprosy-like diseases were contagious and did not want to be infected. With the gradual shift from the medieval period to industrial capitalism, this social inclusion was sacrificed:

[O]ne disabling feature of the ... city was the new separation of home and work, a socio-spatial phenomenon which was all but absent in the feudal era ... In addition, industrial workplaces were structured and used in ways that disabled "uncompetitive" workers ... the rise of mechanized forms of production introduced productivity standards that assumed a "normal" (this is to say usually male and non-impaired) worker's body and disabled all others.

(Gleeson 1999: 78)

The labor market exclusion resulted in socio-spatial marginalization through incarceration, home working, and street trading. People with disabilities used to be visible in the Victorian city but were now more engaged in the customary pedestrian activities of shopping, socializing, or circulating. Gleeson adds that "the street was a place of subsistence which also served as a stage that constantly retold the story of their social difference" (1999: 110).

These histories of disability directly emphasize the material implications of the economy for social and political life. Prior to the advent of industrialization era in the late 18th century, people with disabilities were not differentiated from the masses. Needless to say, they were poor but they were grouped with ordinary people and were not excluded. The post-industrialization era saw people with disabilities barred from the workforce and they were even segregated in the state policies that were implemented by professional experts. During the 19th century, many non-statutory services played a vital role in extending the area of disability. In the United Kingdom the passing of the Poor Law Amendment Act of 1834 saw the construction of workhouses for the destitute and institutions for the mentally defective. However, charitable organizations were merely responsible for building segregated institutions for people with disabilities. The development of orthopedics in the 20th century was directly associated with a physical impairment that represents the politicization of clinical knowledge. "Early hospitals like the general institutions in Birmingham were largely preoccupied with deformities of feet and became ever more marginalized after 1850 by the rise of orthopedic surgery in general hospitals" (Barnes 1996: 109). At the same time, techniques such as massage, gymnastics, electrotherapy, hydrotherapy, etc., were introduced to refine the physical and mental body. These continued with fatalistic attitudes against the deviant body:

Many surgeons admitted to a large class of stationary cripples who, as a result of congenital malformations, accidents of childbirth, infantile paralysis or long-standing rickets, were beyond the surgical pale and were capable of help only through special educational and training facilities.

(Cooter 1993: 60)

Such surgical cases were referred to pediatric hospitals, which resulted in an increased clinical interest in curing such crippling conditions. There were not enough beds for impaired children, therefore an alternative model was conceived. According to Colin Barnes, "it was exemplified by Agnes Hunt's charitable convalescent home at Baschurch near Oswestry in Shropshire, which, during the Edwardian Period, pioneered orthopedic hospitals of international renown with a program of surgery, open-therapy, and satellite after care-clinics" (1996: 116). The aftermath of the Second World War (1939–1945) was another reason for the construction of clinical hospitals. Soldiers returned home with locomotor injuries, fractures, gunshot wounds, etc. These hospitals were required to cure them and as a result they established a new power structure that they did not want to lose. In the same context, Cooter (1993) argues that in return for civilian work, orthopedic surgeons promoted an ambitious scheme to recreate the power and glory of their military empire through a national scheme for the cure of crippled children. He says, "the influence of local authorities in medical planning made it possible for the Ministry of Health to co-ordinate this scheme. Consequently, orthopedics turned to the charitable sector in the form of the Central Council for the care of cripples" (1993: 53).

The Central Council, later called the Royal Association for Disability and Rehabilitation, was founded in 1919. Prior to the Second World War, charities covered many areas such as medicine, education, and welfare, but after the foundation of the Central Council they were centralized. The national Council had its roots in the arrangements at Baschurch, and advocated the development of a network of central orthopedic hospitals that were affiliated to a series of local aftercare clinics. The central orthopedic hospitals sought to cure crippled children through the use of skilled surgery to the benefit of their physical disabilities. According to Girdlestone,

> the local after-care clinics supplied a "short-cut" to accurate diagnosis and hospital admission, enabled the surgeon to supervise his handiwork … to realize the results and offered him a wonderful school in which to learn more and more all his life how best to help the crippled child.
>
> (1924: 13)

By 1936, there were 40 orthopedic hospitals in Britain and 400 orthopedic clinics (Anderson 1969: 54). Disability scholars argue that the council had no objective base to establish hospitals but rather they wanted to establish power relations between institutes and people with disabilities and as well as seeking to promote the medical culture. "Childhood impairments were declining during the inter-war period as the incidence of rickets and tuberculosis fell, and orthopedic surgeons increasingly moved on to the management of fracture cases in order to advance their professional ambitions" (Cooter 1993: 45). In the same context, Barnes argues that the network established through collaboration with organizations like the Nottingham District Cripples' Guild was an important precursor of the surveillance medicine that David Armstrong (2002) has dated from the Second World War. The national schemes did not focus on the normal person; rather they supervised "deviant" people without being responsible for the pain that was caused to them.

3.5 Disability and education

The integration/segregation debate regarding the education of the disabled also began around this time and initially focused on where children considered to have special educational needs (SEN) should be educated, either in special or in regular mainstream schools. Disability activists focused on a broader range of political, economic, and social issues to avoid sterile discussions. Eventually, the term inclusion was introduced in the discourse. "Inclusive education is about the education of all children which necessitates serious changes, both in terms of society and its economic, social conditions and relations and in the schools of which they are a part" (Barton 1998: 60). Barton emphasized the social model approach and used it as an essential tool in changing the education system towards a more inclusive one. Barton pointed out that

> [i]dentifying institutional barriers to participation in education—in terms, for example, of the organization and nature of the system of provision, the curriculum, and the pedagogy and assessment practice—this is an urgent and crucial task demanding serious and systematic attention. It is an essential part of the process of engagement that the struggle for inclusive policy and practice involves.
>
> (1998: 61).

However, their attempts did not produce any real changes in education.

The university is considered to be a part of a radical political force that is used to bring about change in the lives of the common people, but it failed to effect change in the lives of people with disabilities. This does not mean that radical ideas about integration and inclusion was not emerging but the constantly opposing forces were preventing such changes. People's social movements did promote inclusion and forced academics to adopt new positive changes. However, the voices of the disabled were still not heard in educational research. But the emergence of disability studies in the UK and the USA within the academy influenced the traditional academic agendas:

> The increased interest in disability in the academy should not be surprising, given that there is now growing recognition that it raises a number of important theoretical and empirical questions at both individual and structural levels that are not easily answered with reference to established wisdom. Disability is both a common personal experience and a global phenomenon, with widespread economic, cultural and political implications for society as a whole.
>
> (Barnes et al. 2002: 2)

From the 1970s onwards, a large number of graduate and postgraduate courses in disability studies were created. Universities such as the University of Bristol, the University of Leeds, and the University of Glasgow showed their interest and organized conferences and seminars in alternate years. The discipline of disability studies was institutionalized within the academy and raised several important concerns. Scholars such as Graham Scambler and Anthony Giddens confirmed that disability studies programs across the world have become more popular and that there is a growing recognition within British sociology that disability is not simply a medical problem. However, Oliver and Barnes (1998) have argued that with notable exceptions the general trend has been toward a more pluralist approach commensurate with orthodox academic concerns rather than the development of a more comprehensive and radical sociopolitical analysis based on social model insights.

It is important to mention the European Union's policy on disability that reflects the notion of the social model of disability: the EU also sees disability as a social construct. The EU social model of disability stresses the environmental barriers that prevent the full participation of people with disabilities in society, and insists that these barriers must be removed (Commission of the European Communities n.d.). In various United Nations (UN) documents, the influence of the social model is visible. The UN Standard Rules on the Equalization of Opportunities for people with disabilities and the Convention on the Rights of Persons with Disabilities are two examples of such perspectives. A social model perspective played a key role in the recent Rethinking Care from Disabled People's Perspectives' initiative sponsored by the World Health Organization's Disability and Rehabilitation team: a two-year project and conference that involved professionals, disabled people, and their families from all over the world (World Health Organization n.d.).

Ever since the Education Act was passed in 1944 in the UK, the idea of educating children in mainstream school environments had been accepted. Schools that could take children with disabilities alongside "normal" children were founded and the idea of integration was endorsed. However, the outmoded special school system had an impact on the nascent education system. Hence, special schools flourished in the post-War period and continued to expand until the early 1990s, despite the publication of the highly influential Warnock Report in 1978 and the implementation thereof through the Education Act 1981 (Oliver 1996: 551). Following the longstanding critique of segregated educational systems for children and students with SEN, the principle of inclusive education was endorsed in official documents both nationally and internationally (Oliver 1996: 556).

In 1995, UNESCO endorsed the approach of special schools by implementing practical and strategic changes which were based on the assertion that "regular schools with this inclusive orientation are the most effective means of combating discriminatory attitudes, creating welcoming communities, building an inclusive society and achieving education for all" (Fletcher 1995: 1). The

Salamanca Statement and Framework for Action on Special Needs Education was introduced in 2000 to speed up progress in getting children with disabilities into mainstream education, but it did not work. According to Oliver and Barnes (2010), by 2007 the number of disabled children in mainstream education had declined by 8%. Mainstream schools were not inclusive and the segregation of disabled children into special schools was common. With few exceptions, dominant discourses emphasized academic success and ableist values. Major concerns revolved around the continued dominance of standards agendas and examination assessment criteria that prioritized outcomes over the process and disregard the appropriateness of an inclusive curriculum (Qualifications and Curriculum Authority 2005).

Disability activists criticize special schools because they do not provide disabled children with the qualifications and skills needed for adulthood. Research indicates that over 25% of disabled adults have no qualifications or marketable skills whatsoever—more than twice that of their non-disabled peers (Office of National Statistics 2005). If we consider the findings of the Salamanca Statement, it can be argued that disabled children's exclusion from all forms of education is commonplace. In most countries, disabled girls are denied the right to education. Attempts to effect change have been made, but progress is slow. It is especially worrying that the world faces a series of unprecedented challenges that undermine any hope of future economic and political stability and progress toward a truly global society. There is now an urgent need for greater attention to be given to the development of a political analysis that is inspired by a desire for transformative change and that constitutes hope at the center of struggles for inclusivity (Barton 1998: 53).

3.6 Disability and globalization

In the late 20th and early 21st centuries the lives of people with disabilities were transformed because national and international politics and policy were affected by the idea of globalization. The political and economic aspects of globalization had implications for disabled people that increased globalized responses to disability. After globalization, the world economy has manifested itself through international trade, direct foreign investment, and global financial flows. Needless to say, it has influenced people's lives but disability scholars are very skeptical about the positive influence of the globalized economy on the lives of people with disabilities. They argue that recent changes in the world economy represent a deepening of internalization, rather than a qualitative shift toward a genuinely global economy where borders are irrelevant. According to Ruigrok and Tudler (1995), The majority of the world's largest firms maintain a distinct national presence, even though they generate significant sales overseas. They argue that the extent of internationalization in the contemporary global economy is no more than, and probably less than, that which existed during the classic gold standard era from the 1870s up to the First World War (Hirst and

Thompson 1999: 89). They believed that international investment was not equal for all; most of it flowed from advanced capitalist economies to other advanced capitalist economies and these investments were regionally based. The nation-state discriminated against people with disabilities by arguing that the global economy plays a vital role in framing the social policy and nation-states have become powerless due to globalization which was a way to avoid taking responsibility for disability issues.

It has already been debated the way 19th-century industrialization created a dominant modern understanding of disability. It is worth quoting Mike Oliver who says that

> whatever the fate of disabled people before the advent of capitalist society ... with its coming they suffered economic and social exclusion. As a consequence of this exclusion, disability was produced in a particular form; as an individual problem requiring medical treatment. Old age (and I would suggest madness and distress) suffered a similar fate.
>
> (1996: 127)

Due to their physical differences, people with disabilities were excluded from the labor market that inextricably associated disability with poverty. Capitalist and capital-driven societies are centrally related to the unemployment of disabled people. It goes without saying that the lives of people with disabilities are worst in developing countries than in developed countries. The Western industrial conceptualization of disability and impairment was rapidly applied to the rest of the world and was imposed upon societies in the southern hemisphere without regard to their particular histories, cultures, traditions, circumstances, or preferences (Coleridge 1993, 56). Industrialized societies created their own particular category of disability, and generated an industry to service it, one that was exported to the developing world. This industry was motivated by the medical model of disability and was associated with the medicalized rehabilitation, segregation, exclusion, and institutionalization of disabled people.

Like industrialization, globalization constructed the form of impairment and disability that was regulated by capitalism, the labor market, and employment conditions and has had similar effects in terms of maintaining exclusion and the link between poverty and disability. Given the prime concerns of the globalized economy, the inclusion of people with disabilities was never prioritized. One of the major differences that can be identified between globalization and industrialization is the shift of multinational companies from the West to the East to mobilize capital which multinational companies could not do in the West. Unskilled and semiskilled manufacturers globalized capital in developing nations and created disabling conditions during the period when Western industrial economies were shifted to the Third World through the processes of globalization.

Governments need to be able to mobilize capital at the international level in order to propels them into competition with each other for investment and to earn profits. Therefore, governments follow policies of low taxation, low public spending, flexible labor markets, and privatization and minimize their economic and social involvement so that it facilitates capital accumulation. Mishra states that

> put simply, by providing capital with an "exit" option, globalization has strengthened the bargaining power of capital very considerably against the government as well as labor ... Thus money and investment capital can vote with their feet if they do not like government policies ... Indeed globalization virtually sounds like the death-knell of the classical social-democratic strategy of full employment, high level of public expenditure, and progressive taxation.
>
> (1999: 6)

If Mishra's argument is taken into consideration, the consequences for disabled people of such constraints on the welfare state are profound. By constructing an unfriendly environment for people with disabilities, the welfare state produces oppressive forms for people with disabilities. But the constant protest from disability activism has opened up the prospect of achieving equality. The intervention by disability activism has compelled the nation-state to reorganize the national architecture and to recreate the new forms of support as well as framing social policy so that it can be beneficial for people with disabilities. However, it has also been noticed that when it comes to implementation of such policy, multinational corporations seek more than just low taxes and cheap labor. They develop infrastructure, skilled labor, and new markets for their goods. The significant inflow of foreign direct investment into advanced capitalist countries challenges the notion that companies primarily pursue overseas investments for the sole purpose of accessing cheap labor. If there is the political will and multilateral agreements are in place, competition between nation-states can be regulated. To meet the challenges of globalization, different welfare states have responded differently. Esping-Anderson argues that "one of the most powerful conclusions in comparative research is that political and institutional mechanisms of interest representation and political consensus-building matter tremendously in terms of managing welfare, employment, and growth objectives" (1996: 6). So, each welfare state has attempted to meet its objectives but their principles varied accordingly. Globalization posed a particular cost to the welfare state that pointed toward a particular set of policy options. Each policy emphasized education for disabled people and paved the way for their high level of employment. However, such policies protected those already employed and tended to reduce the net number of jobs thus creating a division between those in paid employment and those not in it. Yet, combined with education policies premised upon skill acquisition and life-long learning, flexible labor markets can also promote equality of opportunity, eliminating the surplus of unskilled workers and ensuring that inferior, low-paid jobs do not become life cycle traps, but merely stopgaps for or first-entry jobs. This is consistent with New Labour's policies, which are premised upon increasing labor market participation rates and increasing skill levels through educational reforms.

(Holden 1999: 34)

These policies were influenced by the ideas of Reich (1991) who argued that workers must compete with one another to attract international mobile investment. Despite their low wages, workers have to compete with each other to maintain their standards of living. People with disabilities do not even fit into the competition because of their physical differences and the exclusive structure of the labor market. Such policies do not recognize the need for disabled people's full and equal inclusion in education. The way policies are framed makes inclusive education for disabled people look like a distant dream.

However, in the case of Britain's New Labour, the party's emphasis on increasing employment opportunities was welcomed by many people with disabilities. They were always in need of work and expressed their desire to work and campaigned for equality in the labor market. Unfortunately, they were excluded from the labor market which resulted in their oppression. The development of industrial capitalism excluded people with disabilities from the world of work and equal participation in society. "Disabled people have one of the highest rates of unemployment in Western societies like the U.K. Mental service health users tend to have the highest rate among disabled people" (Bird 1999: 90).

Globalization, another name for European rationality that was popularized by Niklas Luhmann (2012), believes in bringing people together, thereby debunking all the pillars of regions, religions, colors, etc. which were separating them, and is also a major discourse of Orientalism. It is hard to believe that it does not have a political effect on the relations between nations and on relations between individuals. In the context of relations between nations, the politics of globalization is considered a structure of power perpetrated by European imperialism. In the context of relations between individuals, the process of globalization affects the lives and cultures of their communities through one of its major tools called global economic forces. A profound transformation can be noticed in the role of the state under the influence of globalization, namely the privatization of the government sector. Government services that were put in place for the benefit of the welfare state are declining. Deborah Stienstra says, "As restructuring reduces the state's role in (public) welfare provisioning ... women, as agents and victims in the private/family are left to pick up the slack" (2013: 117).

Due to the gradual privatization of government services, an increasing number of private companies seeking material gains are leaving disabled/non-capable people as the responsibility of families or under the purview of charities. With respect to the spaces of people with disabilities including women, it is not surprising that globalization has widely affected their lives. The intrusion of multilateral institutions, corporations, and the politicizing of the public/private domain in which they operate seek to exclude them. The private spheres such as the practices of caring, consumption, and religion are politicized so that they are constitutive of the public spheres as envisioned by globalization. The formal spaces of globalization are fundamentally masculinist in their exclusion of the economic, cultural, and political spheres (often casual or informal) that operate in households and communities (Nagar et al. 2002: 260). This disregard for activities such as sweetshop production and domestic work devalues their significance and contributes to the marginalization of both men and women within the framework of global capitalism.

An ideological shift, as Slavoj Žižek (2008) calls it, addresses real problems rather than mystifying us about them, and has occurred in this "society of violence," thereby bringing up new notions of domesticity, masculinity, femininity, disability, and sexuality. Globalization creates a false consciousness in which we come to believe that all are free and equal.

Contrary to this, it also brings the notion that those who are "able" or who can function independently as part of the public sphere and those who are not able or dependent should seek a space in the private sphere, in particular with the family and in the household. Deborah Stienstra opines, "With restructuring in the process of neo-liberal economics and globalization, we see that those who are valorized as 'able' or independent are increasingly found in the private/corporate sector" (2013: 117).

The process of globalization/industrialization values the body in terms of its capacities. Capacities are evaluated in terms of the production of wage labor. In the same context, Nirmala Erevelles (2011) states that labor is the central organizing force in history because human beings do not just live but instead "produce" their lives within specific historical contexts through their relationship to labor which is an understanding of the historical materialism of an individual in opposition to the poststructuralist discourses that see a body wholly constituted within language. In other words, the historical materialist framework reads the subject—its body, consciousness, and meanings as produced by and through labor. In day-to-day life, the oppression and exclusion that people with disabilities experience is an inevitable consequence of particular forms of social development associated with Western capitalism. If we trace the history of the shift from feudalism to capitalism in terms of the labor market, we notice that efficiency and productivity are demanded from individual workers which leads people with disabilities to be dependent on the state. The very politics behind the exclusion of people with disabilities, therefore, is essential for a surplus labor market which is the demand for capital to minimize the costs of production and which calls upon the owners of industries to maintain certain levels of unemployment.

It is the modernized labor force, which is quite distinct from that of ancient times, that defines people's lives and ensures their survival. Michel Foucault argues that, while work has always had a productive function, in the modern era it has taken on two additional functions, "the symbolic function and the function of dressage, or discipline" (1977: 23). Those who could not participate in this complicated social sphere were considered as not being able to adapt to new conditions and did not have the symbolic qualities. They were defined as aberrant. Through this, two separate categories, able and disabled, were established. With their disciplinary attributes the able were understood to be part of mainstream society because they could fit into the structured modern social spheres and could support capitalism's purpose through conducting their bodies. The disabled were perceived as a threat to the social order. Thus, the medicalization of people with disabilities was an attempt to integrate them into mainstream society. They were being rehabilitated and normalized so that they could be productive for modern globalized societies.

Operative disciplinary mechanisms have enabled the exclusionary practices and reinforced them in the global society. Disability politicized by modern labor forces emerged in a new form that has less to do with an individual's impairment. In other words, the unimpaired body is also evaluated as a disabled/deviant body if it fails to conform to new emerging political norms. People with disabilities are not important within this global economy. Within the framework of a discriminatory and oppressive labor market, people with disabilities are categorized as those who cannot work and who are stereotyped as dependent and socially excluded.

It has been noticed that the human rights agenda has worked for the inclusion of people with disabilities at the international level and by pressing the issues of disability constantly it has moved from the margins to the mainstream of society. The UN General Assembly made its first declaration regarding the rights of the disabled person in 1975. Following the declaration, Mark Priestley argues, the UN proclaimed 1981 as the International Year of Disabled Persons (IYDP) and embarked upon the development of a world program of action (2001: 4). In 1985, the Universal Declaration of Human Rights was specifically extended to include disabled people. The UN action plan and the IYDP gave rise to many debates and discussions among disability activists and within the international policy community. Toward the end of the International Decade of Disabled Persons (1983–1992) the UN began work to develop a longer-term strategy under the slogan of a society for all (Department of Economic and Social Affairs Disability, United Nations n.d.). In 1992 the UN declared 3 December an International Day of Disabled Persons. Implementation of the long-term strategy at the national, regional, and global level also coincided with the development of new Rules on the Equalization of Opportunities for Disabled Persons (United Nations 1993). These rules address the participation of people with disabilities in fields such as sport, religion, recreation, etc. The definitions of disability proposed by the social model that believes that disability is created by society are widely accepted by people. "Society creates a handicap when it fails to accommodate the diversity of all its members, and people with disabilities often encounter attitudinal and environmental barriers that prevent their full, equal, and active participation in society" (Department of Economic and Social Affairs Disability, United Nations n.d.).

Following the introduction of the IYDP and the UN rules, countries such as the UK, the USA, and Canada introduced anti-discrimination legislation. Anti-discriminatory practices are often implemented by countries to safeguard the rights and interests of the majority population. Before such measures can be effectively established, it is essential to raise awareness, promote political engagement, or instill a sense of social consciousness within the society or community (ADL n.d.). The self-organization of people with disabilities has acted as a catalyst in these processes. However, it was not until a report published by the European Parliament for the 1996 European Day of Persons with Disabilities that disabled people gained recognition as citizens, consumers, and workers within the EU (Waddington 1996: 76). For disabled people, the concept of dependent living or integrated living was a central theme. They mobilized disabled people by saying that life is just not about getting up in the morning and going to bed at night; rather, it is about the whole of life and it encompasses everything. They demanded control over employment and condemned the provision of segregated services as a violation of human rights. However, all around the globe disabled people find it difficult to overcome barriers in the workplace. Disabled people are disadvantaged in both accessing and sustaining work and other forms of economic activity. It is axiomatic that in a world where work is valorized as an important social contribution, as a defense (however limited) against poverty, and as a source of self-validation, the lack of paid work or wider economic activity is a significant social disadvantage (Roulstone 1998: 211). The lack of access to paid work maintains the connection between disability and poverty in both the majority and minority worlds (Roulstone 1998: 223).

3.7 Disability and modernity

The social model of disability challenged and examined the unequal treatment of individuals with disabilities in various aspects of life, such as education, employment, healthcare, caregiving systems, communities, and within their own homes. This model not only scrutinized these discriminatory practices but also had a significant impact on the development of disability-related policies and attitudes. Discrimination against people with disabilities in education, the workplace, medical institutions, the care system, the community, and at home was interrogated by the social model of disability which dominated the disability discourse and influenced the policies. It set aside the discourse of impairment and critiqued the oppressive forms of capitalism. Modernity tends to produce bodies marked with differences as strangers to society that push against the moral, cognitive, and aesthetic boundaries and challenge the sense of order in society. Modernity tends to homogenize the body and annihilate the differences. The production of "stranger" that was conceived as a threat to social order was constructed by the limits of tolerance and conformity. The category and form of "stranger" were associated with people with disabilities. Anthropophagic (assimilationist) and anthropoemic (exclusionary) strategies have been applied to disabled people throughout the modern period. Anthropophagic strategies are reflected in the community care and anthropoemic strategies are reflected in segregationist policies, and both hinge upon the gaze that views impairment as a disorder. Both strategies were needed to characterize modernity and also to produce the will to order that continuously invalidated the form of impairment. Being impaired was perceived as contrary to the natural order of things, or anomalous to it. In his book, *The Normal and the Pathological*, Georges Canguilhem states that

> every preference for possible order is accompanied, most often implicitly, by the aversion for the opposite order, that which diverges from the preferable in a given area of evaluation is not the indifferent but the repulsive or more exactly, the repulsed, the detestable.
>
> (Canguilhem 1991: 240)

For modernity, the medicalized body is natural and normal and competes with the pathologized body.

> In the context of industrialization and urbanization and, more importantly, the "need"—as Nietzsche might have it—to constitute these social phenomena in regimes of truth, positive philosophy (that developed in the modernity) developed a way of seeing which, like biomedicine itself, was normative and normalizing.
>
> (Canguilhem 1991:56)

Medical science that emerged in the 19th century pathologized and invalidated the phenomenon of impairment. Positive social science, through its disembodied discourse of handicap and (from the 20th century) its disablist concept of impairment and the role of rehabilitation, stamped the exclusion order (Oliver 1996: 45). It suggests that the discursive constitution of impairment is important to the material construction of disabling barriers. An impaired body is understood as repulsive and detestable.

However, in all these discussions and engagements, the social deviance of people with disabilities was never called into question. They were conceptualized as outsiders. People with disabilities recognized that no one could interpret their problems and started to articulate their problems. Disabled people prefer to reinterpret their collective experiences in terms of structural notions of discrimination and oppression rather than interpersonal ones of stigma and stigmatization (Oliver 1996). It was noticed that the articulation of disabled people's problems was the paradigm shift in the knowledge of disability. It was the refusal of people with disabilities to be constituted by the vision of others, and to be objectified and invalidated by the abstract and external corporeality of the eye of power. It questioned the watch tower of modernity and the appropriation of the objectifying gaze. The gaze is deflected by disabled people from impaired bodies to the social body which, hitherto a model of innocence, is now identified as the source of disorder that marks the beginning of an assault on the tyranny of perfection (Glassner 1992: 67). Disabled people argue that disability must be understood as a form of social oppression. It is considered a perspectival shift in which disability is revisualized from the viewpoint of people with impairments. As the intellectual expression of the social movement of disabled people, the social model of disability proposed a theory of disability praxis and a materialist model of emancipation which validated and valorized the intellectual and practical activity of disabled people themselves (Oliver 1990: 187). The collective action of the "strangers" (disabled people) discovered an autonomous point of view and attempted to end the hegemony of the charitable gaze of bourgeois paternalism. It was no longer conceived as the deficit of the body but reconceptualized as a product of the social organization. It was perceived to be a consequence of the social relationships of production in a capitalist society.

The discourse of impairment that is pre-social and the discourse of disability that is socially produced raise the question of the binary nature–culture divide. In the vision of modernity, nature is in flux and its flow can be tamed. It is an act of domination that seeks to control the chaos of images. The vision seeks containment, boundaries, compartments, taxonomies of phenomenal form, angles, homogeneity, stable relationships, and above all the security of binary distinction (Hughes 1999: 92). In the Western discourse, where everything is legitimized by the discourse of logos, the observer or spectator is the God who selects and pronounces truth and falsity, who sorts out what is ugly and what is beautiful, who decides what is valid and what is invalid. The visual field that appears on the screen is an embryo and the eye has to be trained to see and to know this. According to Hughes,

> by abstraction and by reference to a vague sense of the circumstances under which a life is worth living, by a judgment as much aesthetic and emotional as medical, the conclusion is reached and this one is a candidate for termination.
>
> (1999: 95)

The vision of modernity trains the eye, tames the images, produces the philosophy of life, and gives logic to composing the worthlessness of the body.

This is considered the politics of visualization and interpretation. The impairment is produced by what Levin calls an "assertoric gaze," which is explained as "more than any other senses, the eye objectifies and masters"

(1997: 50). This is the look of the hard, certain eye; a vision that is intransigent, mechanical, objective, inflexible, and exclusionary (Hughes 1999: 56). This vision is of the visual culture of modernity. This vision declares that everything else that is tamed is only worth seeing. This gaze is wrapped in discourses of perfection and tragedy. Clinical reason assumes the alignment and coordination of seeing and saying. It is a form of governance (of the fetus) that contains—in an embryo—a system that prescribes a moral border of bodies which is often coded in the language of risk (Hughes 1999: 87). The Holocaust, for instance, represents the intolerance of modernity. The movement of disabled people who celebrate their differences questions the logic of such terrible histories.

The emergence of modernity gave birth to normativity which believed in the binary power of the normal/abnormal. It has been implicated by now that disability scholarship has emphasized the exclusionary practices practiced by normative culture rather than a religious culture whose influence was slowed down by industrialization and modernization. In place of the pathologized embodied individual, environmental and social factors are taken to construct the conditions of disability. The social model of disability gave rise to its normativity and generated new resistance. Disability took a new form in the era of modernity where the religious model of disability was replaced by the social model of disability. The social model of disability colluded with normativity led by modern tendencies and constructed physical difference as a failing, incomplete, inferior, and marked disability embodiment as deeply devalued. Disability embodiment is deeply devalued not because of what it is but because of what it fails to be. It does not get its meaning autonomously but is checked relationally, Disability is constituted in the socially political context. Far from being a bioscientific fact, Mitchell and Snyder argue, "disability is a category constituted, given meaning and expressed through an endless set of cultural, historical, political, and mythological parameters that ambiguously define disabled people as excessive, as contaminatory, as at once malign and helpless" (1997: 3). Normative categories impose strictness to separate the disordering otherness of disability. The anomalous feature of disability reminds the normative healthy body about its vulnerability and potential breakdown. According to Foucault, disability has always been the object of institutionalized discourses of control and containment (1977: 253).

The Self and the Other complement each other to the extent that Otherness becomes an interior attribute of the embodied self, while the sovereign subject of modernity denies the Otherness of the embodied self. While analyzing the problem of the sovereign subject of modernity, Margrit Shildrick states that

> given that explicit privileging of wholeness, independence and integrity demanded of the able-bodied subject, the cultural imaginary is highly invested in fantasies of an invulnerable body, which in the face of a disability that threatens always to claim its identity in the selfsame, produces an anxiety that cannot be allayed.
>
> (Price and Shildrick 2002: 43)

Nowadays few disability scholars label people with disabilities as temporarily able but it needs to be understood that to be temporarily able-bodied is not simply a temporal matter; one must explore the inherent instability of normative embodiment. In this connection, Hannabach says, "after all, the normative body, with its singular gender, race, and sexuality identification, is established only through the active expulsion of embodiments, perceptions, and identifications that exceed narrative and political unity" (2007: 256). They all emphasize the analysis of the psychic content of anxiety that produces a threat to the integrity of the self. In the same context, Kristeva explains that "Freud always maintained that psychic life was double determined by the biological domain and the symbolic domain" (1996: 85). The manifestation of the disabled body continues to have a direct impact that goes beyond a changing signification. Ethics and the politics of modernity could not resist the psychic anxiety that positions disability as an Other. Disability as an Other does not only disturb normative expectations but also destabilizes self-identity.

There have been multiple shifts and reversals in the way in which disability has been defined and perceived. Discussing a single discourse and making that discourse dominant will cancel out a complex mix of interwoven ideas and beliefs that belies the notion of historicist or progressive periodization. Merely talking about history in positivist terms will not provide a constant circulation and recirculation of ideas that are both articulated and hidden with regard to disability. Having said this, representation of the recorded and preserved beliefs also helps to analyze the position of disabled people at a given time. The structure of language in which signifiers are infinitely reinterpretable and the signified changes constantly with reiteration has also to be unraveled to recover a pure origin. Every historical version of disability has one common theme, namely the physical violence against people with disabilities. It is experienced by them at any time. The very real physical violence that is exerted over the bodies of disabled people is considered normal but is paralleled by a less obvious discursive violence that is an intrinsic feature of any binary system of sameness and difference.

The French theorist Henri-Jacques Stiker offers a challenging explanation of why disability is a threat that transcends time and eras. He says that differences in the body signify a threatening disorder. He points out that "aberrancy within the corporeal order is an aberrancy in the social order" (1999: 40). He also indicates an ontological threat that "the disabled are the tear in our being" (1999: 10). His approach to disability rejects the understanding of positivism and implicitly deconstructs contemporary narratives of sociocultural and political progress as they expose historical material relating to disability. He makes us aware of the operation of cultural imaginary that is deeply invested in normative fantasies. David Mitchell writes in the Foreword to Stiker's book, *A History of Disability*, "Stiker seeks simultaneously to demonstrate the presence of disability throughout western history and to unmoor our collective fantasies in the promise of eradication or cure" (1999: ix). In the same context, Shildrick writes that "the success and/or failure of strategies of both integration and exclusion speak precisely to the difference of disability, and its status as the other within" (2009: 46). The disabled body manifests itself in such a way that it disrupts both the social body and the normative selfhood, and it cannot be grasped in its difference because it remains undecidable, neither self nor Other.

The porous nature of disability coincides with the nature of the monstrous body that plays a key role in the construction and reinforcement of the distinction between normal and abnormal and in the imposition of normativity. However, Foucault argues that "disability is not coincident with the monstrous in that it has a place in civil or canon law" (2003: 64). The texts of the modern period approach mental disabilities in the same epistemic frame as human/animal hybrids. It is an overgeneralization to say that all forms of disability are seen in the same way, but coinciding the disabled body with the monstrous body represents the anxiety of undecidability at the level of law. A Foucauldian reading shows the breaks and schisms in history and also shows the emergence of scientific and empirical rationalism that is the result of the post-Cartesian period. Scientific and empirical rationalism emphasizes the elimination of ambiguity and privileges rational action. More importantly, it helps to create a system of normativity that maintains the distinction between normal and pathological embodiment. This new approach toward the body targets the disabled body and attempts to normalize it: "we pass from a technology of power that drives out, excludes, banishes, marginalizes and represses, to a fundamentally positive power that fashions, observes, knows and multiplies itself based on its effects" (Foucault 2003: 48).

The post-Darwinian period that gave birth to eugenics caused few moral misgivings in terms of people with disabilities. Few scholars noticed that the application of eugenic principles was based on contemporary science, but they failed to construe their application as a utilitarian good in its own right. "What drove eugenic practice was always less the putative facts of bioscience than a series of both explicit and implicit value judgments in the realm of both the aesthetic and the moral" (Shildrick 2009: 53). Eugenics mainly attempted to covert the discomfort provoked by corporeal differences and encouraged cultural normativities to operate. Such practices of eugenics revealed the Western fantasy of invulnerability and self-mastery. The directive principles of eugenics tried to cover the illusion of the absolute sovereignty of the embodied self. The policies of integration led by the government could not subdue the anxieties mobilized by the supposedly contaminatory potential of Otherness.

Bodies marked with differences do not provoke anxiety because of their difference as such, but because these bodies are very like other bodies this make them realize that they can also become like other bodies. They do not fit into the boundaries of sameness and difference and spread impurity through the normative categories. For example, the Nazis portrayed bodies marked with differences as useless eaters and dehumanized them as a political act of denying their commonality with the normative majority. Their denial represents the violent action exercised by the sovereign state. The state practices biomedical surgeries, instrumentation, etc., and intends to fix the radical anomalies of the body. Such interventions by the state cover the embodied differences, if not eliminating them entirely. Rosemarie Garland-Thomson states that

> "these procedures benefit not the affected individuals, but rather they expunge the kinds of corporeal human variations that contradict the ideologies that the dominant order depends upon to another truth it insists are unequivocally encoded in bodies ... The medical commitment to health ... has increasingly shifted toward an aggressive intent to fix, regulate or eradicate ostensibly deviant bodies.
>
> (2002: 13)

According to Stiker, people with mental illness are exposed to exclusion and surveillance, while people with physical disabilities are exposed to regimes of recovery and assistance that hint at a state-led act of normalization. It is a political act of sameness that promises greater equality to disabled people provided they are reintegrated into the norms and values of the dominant majority. As he puts it, "Paradoxically, they are designated to be made to disappear, they are spoken to be silenced and further, specificity and aberrance are forbidden" (1999: 136). These interventions are an effective way to evade the fear of strangeness, a fear that is no less apparent in contemporary society. The construction of docile bodies, subject to control, standardization, and predictability, is accomplished as an act of social justice.

The social model of disability that seems to be devaluing the phenomenology of embodied difference perpetuates a historically situated pattern of disavowal. The social model of disability fails to recognize the issues of pain, desire, and affect that are incorporated into the impaired body and at the same time denies the difference of the body. It emphasizes the social and environmental adaptations and does not recognize the fragility and vulnerability of the body or all forms of embodiment. The desire to deny a vulnerability that cannot be hidden generates anxiety in the individual psyche and cultural imaginary. The collapse of specifically different categories of disability into a generalized form of improper embodiment is conventionally set against the normative standard of the body perceived as closed, invulnerable, and separate (Shildrick 2009: 57). The psychoanalytic theory approves the body as a phantasmatic that is an unstable image of integration—in other words that which Jacques Lacan (1977) calls the *corps morcelé* (fragmented body). A disabled body is perceived as a woman's body that is always leaky and anomalous. It breaks the proper boundaries of embodiment and separation, and makes all forms of bodies insecure. As Liz Grosz notes, "female corporeality is characterized as a leaking, uncontrollable, seeping liquid: as formless flow ... lacking not so much or simply the phallus but self-containment ... a formlessness that engulfs all form, a disorder that threatens all order" (1994: 203). In the modernist era, disorder, ambiguity, and uncertainty cause anxiety in Western culture.

Disability is a highly complex and intrinsically ambiguous designation that can never be addressed adequately by positivists. Furthermore, it is impossible to define disability merely through historical narratives, biomedicine, or social constructions. By engaging with multiple cultural and psychic investments, we can articulate the genealogy of the discursive constitution of the disability. The psychoanalytic approach reveals the implicit violence exercised on the disabled body by the so-called normal body. It unravels the incompleteness, precariousness, and open-endedness of the disability, whereas the domain of power/knowledge exposes the politics of the structure of normativity that requires medical institutes to constitute disabled others as pathological subjects. There is no singular explanation and no certainty in the quest for understanding disability.

Western discourses about people with disabilities unravel the enigma of normalcy and question the way religion abhors and ostracizes the body marked with differences. The difference of body is a highly complex and intrinsically ambiguous designation that cannot be fitted into the binary-based models. This chapter represents the way modern technology has institutionalized normal discourse and invalidated the abnormality of the body. The chapter did not intend to show the discriminatory practices against people with disabilities; rather, it intended to show the shift from inclusionary practices to exclusionary practices against disabled bodies. Exploring religio-political discourses, the chapter unraveled the politics of assimilation rather than transformation. It also intended to question the sociocultural imaginary that receives a threat from abnormal bodies and how the historical approaches helped to justify the pretension of an able-bodied society that does not allow people with disabilities to share the public spaces with the able-bodied. In Chapter 4, I will examine the existing disability discourses of India and government policy that have a very discriminatory attitude toward the body marked with differences. I will also examine how disability discourses of the West have affected the disability discourses of India.

Chapter 4

Disability in India

4.1 Disability and the discourse of religion in India

The understanding of disability in India is different from the way that the West has conceptualized disability. The experience of disability in the West is grounded in the Judeo-Christian tradition, whereas the experience of disability in India is largely based on the Brahmanical textual tradition. However, there are similarities between the Western and Indian cultures of social exclusion and the stigmatization of people with disabilities. However, the concept of social inclusion is different in these cultures. According to the Brahmanic textual tradition, in Hindu caste society people were disinherited if they had any form of disability because impairment was seen as an impediment in the performance of one's duties. A person with disabilities cannot work for the wellbeing of the family and cannot perform the rituals on the death of their father. According to Buckingham, "The *Yajjnavalka-smriti*, a dharmasastric text believed to be derived from the *Manusmriti* in about the fourth century AD, is fairly typical of Brahmanic legal texts in its exclusion of those with disabilities from inheritance" (Buckingham 2011: 421).

These texts do not define what it is to be disabled or mad. It is very arbitrary and the problem lies with the way the structure of rituals or duty was defined that do not accommodate certain differences of the body.

In this link between impairment and ritual incapacity, "the Brahmanic tradition has parallels with the tradition of Leviticus which tends to be cited in discussions of western Judeo-Christian cultures of stigmatization" (Bredberg 1999: 194). Johanna Dorman states in her book, *The Blemished Body: Deformity and Disability in the Qumran Scrolls* (2007), that people with disabilities were not allowed to enter the temple, while priests with physical disabilities were not permitted to officiate at rituals. In his book *A Treatise on Hindu Law and Usage* John Mayne (2013) states that the Brahmanic textual tradition was only relevant to the high caste minority of the Indian population. However, India has known diversities for several centuries, and therefore it represents only one among a range of social traditions. It would be unjust if we were to take such instances and generalize the whole human experience of disability in ancient

DOI: 10.4324/9781032722054-4

India. This opinion has been framed because we have access to such texts and historical writings, but we may find another version of the experience of disability if we examine other historical sources such as village traditions, folk tales, stories, and dance. Thus, we might find traces of traditions of reflecting how disabilities of various kinds were thought about, conceptualize, and treated.

Extending the notion of the "disciplined body" that was popularized by Foucault, the paradigm of the history of the colonial body elaborates on the experience of the disabled body. Race, gender, and caste are the major segments of society that limit human capabilities and constitute the understanding of the disabled body.

> As the recent deployment of history in asserting and reclaiming the dignity of the Dalit identity and Dalit women in the Indian Independence movement shows, such themes can be powerful analytic tools in the reconfiguring of domestic and national histories.
>
> (Pawar and Moon 2008: 122)

This is not to say that the history of thinking about disability in India can be reduced to the colonial paradigm of power relations. Indeed, it enhances the value of human beings and contributes to their way of life. Changes in policies and legislation bring a new affirmative action for people with disabilities and represent a shift from the colonial model of disability that is founded upon charity to inclusion through economic and social contribution. It does not completely transform the charity model but questions the traditional forms of exclusion of people with disabilities. Disability history moves ahead with this positive change and can critique the present malaise associated with the body marked with differences. The emergence of subaltern studies has also provided a framework to recover the voices of the marginalized or the voiceless. To legitimate their agency and autonomy, scholars felt the need for historical recognition of marginalized voices. Increased understanding of the historical experience of disability, the contributions of people with disabilities to civic and political life, and the historical roots of stigma and exclusion which continue to limit capability among people with disabilities not only contributes to the capacity of those with disabilities but to society as a whole which benefits from an understanding of exclusion as a construct rather than as a natural or inevitable consequence of disability. The history of disability is also important in the formation of a nation's cultural identity. More than anything else the history of injustice done to people with disabilities legitimizes their claims for greater economic and social participation in India today. However, activism for people with disabilities in India has not yet developed, but the democratization of history provides an opportunity for academic scholars and activists to bring out justice for them and to resist continued marginalization. "Despite growing activism, people with disabilities are yet to claim ownership of historical knowledge about themselves and to assert the validity of their interpretation of such knowledge and material" (Narayan 2008: 170).

Since ancient times, India has followed the tradition of helping the poor and the destitute. Even in feudal times, love for charity and brotherhood persisted. Rulers and the community used to share this onerous responsibility. The Hindu religion has always emphasized the values of compassion, charity, philanthropy, and mutual aid. The prevalent "guide system" of ancient India assisted in promoting such practices for the disadvantaged strata of society. Furthermore, the custom of the joint family, Chowdhary (1981) says, kinship, and other social institutions also provided an added inbuilt mechanism to support such philanthropic activities. The norm of care and protection was perpetuated by society in every possible way.

By unraveling the folklores and myths, one can glimpse the philanthropic activities that were practiced. The classical texts of Hinduism which is practiced by the majority in India and the *Dharmasastras* refer to bodies marked with differences. The references from the Vedas are not well known to the people but they are aware of the projection of disabled characters in epics. In India, attitudes about people with disabilities are still shaped by the discourses of epics; for instance, Vishnu's appearance as a dwarf and the appearance of Buddha and Ashta Vakra as gifted dwarves. The representation of Vishnu is as a deceitful person in this *avatar* (incarnation). Vishnu tricks the demon Bali out of the land usurped by him. Another instance is that of Ashta Vakra, the revered Vedic sage, who suffered from multiple disabilities. He is invited to participate in a large symposium organized by the King Janaka. However, he is ridiculed by the people because of his bodily differences. Therefore, he rejects the king's invitation to participate in the symposium declaring that they have already judged him by his physical appearance. He goes on to say that this audience is not one of scholars and intellectuals but rather a group of traders of hides and skins who know nothing about the soul. Dwarves, the hunchbacked, and people with disabilities are not considered auspicious by most Indian people due to the biased representation of the character Manthara in the *Ramayana*. Manthara is represented as a reason for the exile of Rama and the subsequent battles. Manthara, in the epic, symbolizes evil. At the same time, in the *Mahabharata*, Kubja, who is known to be a physically deformed person, is ridiculed by all but finds salvation when she prays to Lord Shri Krishna. The purpose of the story is to highlight the principle of *bhakti* (devotion). Nonetheless, the disabled person is perceived as an object of ridicule.

It goes without saying that such texts are responsible for creating a value system that defines the way in which people view disability, namely that it makes life miserable and difficult for people with disabilities. Thus, charity for people with disabilities goes unquestioned. "The Rigveda lays stresses on human concern for and services provided to the disabled and the needy people" (Kaushik 1977: 8). The *Mahabharata* reveals that blind people are not eligible to be rulers and are disqualified from taking part in a coronation; thus

Dhritarashtra cannot be king because he is blind. A careful examination of this epic reveals that people with disabilities were shown sympathy. In the same context, Narada asks Yudhishthira about the treatment of people with disabilities who had fought for him:

> Do you maintain the women of those who died for you or who have come to a sad plight while fighting for you on the battlefield? And do you maintain those who are wounded on the battlefield, while fighting for you?
>
> (Bhatt 1963: 93)

It is interesting to note from this that the king was expected to provide sustenance to those disabled in the war and their dependents.

It is also noticed that disability was largely understood as being fearful and ferocious. However, barbaric practices such as the annihilation of people with disabilities never existed in Indian society. "In the recorded history of India, there is no such evidence to suggest that infanticide was a general practice" (Karna 2001: 92). Nonetheless, people with disabilities have always been excluded from or have been treated differently in the sphere of education. Budhayana explains that by "granting food, clothing, and shelter, they [the kings] shall support those who are incapable of transacting legal business, viz., the blind, idiots, those immersed in vice, the incurably disabled, those who neglect their duties and occupations, and so on" (Bhatt 1963: 93). While talking about duties of the king, Manu writes in the *Manusmriti*,

> the king should always give gifts and do other kinds of charities to a lamed Brahmin, to one who is affected by diseases of affliction, to one who is young (an orphan), to him who is very old, and to him who is born in a noble family.
>
> (Karna 2001: 93)

These rules reflect the way that people with disabilities—at least those from the high castes—were protected and cared for.

Although the discourse of disability has been widely debated politically and academically to represent the concerns of the disabled minority, nevertheless people with disabilities do encounter environmental and attitudinal problems in their everyday lives. Therefore, it is important to unravel the discourse of normalcy that lies in the supremacy of people without disabilities. India is no exception in that people with disabilities are still denied their rights and entitlements, and the discourse of normalcy is still practiced. Despite Article 15 of the Constitution of India that guarantees the right of equality for the person with disabilities, the government fails to ensure that people with disabilities are not discriminated against by society. The government does not take the necessary steps to ensure the availability of suitable accommodation for disabled people, who are forced to pay some or all of the costs involved in securing suitable accommodation.

In the National Sample Survey, data was collected from a total of 106,894 individuals with disabilities. Among them, 74,946 were from rural areas, and 31,948 were from urban areas. This data is derived from the central sample of the Survey of Persons with Disabilities conducted during the 76th round of the National Sample Survey (Ministry of Statistics and Programme Implementation n.d.) There is always some problem with the way disability is measured. What is important here is to understand that the census and the NSS are two essential data sources that provide estimates about the lives of people with disabilities. The term "disability" does not refer to a person who is missing a hand or a leg; rather, it refers to those who are unable to access the built environment. People presume that disability is an outcome of impairment. However, it has already been asserted that disability does not lie in the body, because everyone is different. The problem lies with the built environment that is structured in such a way that it can only be accessed by certain bodies. If a person fails to access it, it does not mean that she or he is disabled but rather that the environment was not designed to be accessed by an impaired body. Moreover, society always works for the welfare of the normal body. The term "disability" may also refer to those who have a so-called normal body but who fail to access the built environment for some reason. The population of 20 million people with disabilities living in India who are prevented from getting a fair share of their right to civic amenities represents the failure of the government to provide access to disabled people. The government and local authorities have not yet taken the necessary steps to ensure equality for all. Moreover, such individuals are denied their right to live in a community with the same choices that are available to others. There is hardly any home where the person with disabilities enjoys his or her residential and community support services. They are poorly protected from torture, cruelty, inhumanity, or degrading treatment or punishment. They are frequently subjected to violence and are treated as if this is their due. The parents of disabled children tend to avoid taking them out of their homes due to the community's degrading remarks.

4.2 Disability and education

Educational institutions have failed to provide inclusive education for people with disabilities. The structure of the Indian education system is governed by norms that leave no space for people with disabilities. The problems of people with disabilities are considered their personal issues and they are compelled to adjust to the education system which refuses to adapt itself to their needs. This medical model of disability frustrates the expectations of young disabled students by making them put up with institutional discrimination. Segregated forms of school provisions do not allow people with disabilities to occupy an equal space in the education system. By presenting interviews with a group of disabled children, this chapter will critique the social perceptions of disability in India and will bring out a positive image thereof. It goes without saying that the status and experience of disabled people have changed over time, but that prejudices toward and the systematic segregation of people with disabilities still exist. It is important to ask how society defines and excludes specific individuals or groups. Deeply held fears and prejudices have at particular times in global history led to strong custodial measures being viewed as the most appropriate response for those individuals who were defined as a menace needing total institutional provision, or a burden needing sterilization and even extermination, and as vulnerable thus in need of protection (Wolfensberger 1993; Scull 1982; Ryan and Thomas 1980).

We notice that the confined physical spaces of educational institutions fail to engage people with disabilities. Schools, colleges, or universities are characterized by intense social interactions. They are considered as socializing institutions that instill in young people appropriate ways of thinking and behaving. Education requires the inculcation of particular social and moral values and responsibilities with which people can identify positively irrespective of their class, caste, gender, religion, or body. However, the reality is shocking and alarming as people with disabilities experience a sense of inferiority and lowliness in these physical spaces.

Globally, children with disabilities account for one-third of all children out of school (Mitra and Sambamoorthi 2006: 4022). In developing countries, the numbers are even more staggering, with 90% of all children with disabilities out of school (Buckingham 2011: 423). Although children with disabilities must receive an education, it is also starting to be recognized by educational authorities around the world that the type of education that children with disabilities receive is just as important (Kohama 2012: 2). It has been noticed that the notion of segregated education is entrenched in India and that children with disabilities are often kept apart from their classmates. In developing countries, segregated education takes place in the form of special schools created specifically for the education of students with disabilities, or in completely separate classrooms for students with disabilities (Kohama 2012: 12). Segregated schools represent students with disabilities as a problem in the system, and they are considered an impediment to learning. As result, they often receive different curricula and are taught using different methods that limit the possiblities for non-disabled students and disabled students to come together. Educational institutions are spaces in which students learn to respect differences. However, segregated schools impede the basic principles of education in that they propagate the ideology of dependency and difference.

Integrated education is another form of education that functions in the same way that inclusive education functions but does not have a commitment to the ideology of equity the way that inclusive education does. Integrated education is founded upon the presupposition that students with disabilities will adapt to mainstream education and will comply with the resources provided. It is expected that they will fit in with pre-existing structures and imbibe the ideology of ability. "Integration is often mistaken for inclusion because students are placed in a mainstream classroom, which is a step toward inclusion" (Kumar 1991: 45). Integrating people with disabilities with non-disabled people does not result in inclusion. It is important to unravel the politics of integrated schools that represent able students as superior to disabled students. The concept of inclusive education comes from awareness about disability that believes in "the process of strengthening the capacity of the education system to reach out to all learners" (UNESCO 2009: 8). It involves restructuring the culture, policies, and practices in schools so that they can respond to the diversity of students in their locality. It rests on the principles of equity and directs all teachers and administrative staff members to have a positive attitude toward students with disabilities so that they do not feel discriminated in school. Inclusive education means that all children, regardless of their ability levels, are included in a mainstream classroom, or in the most appropriate or least restrictive environment, that students of all ability levels are taught as equals, and that teachers must adjust their curricula and teaching methodologies so that all students benefit (Kohama 2012: 58). Such a system accepts students with differences and does not compel them to adapt to norms. Studies have shown that "systems that are truly inclusive reduce drop-out rates and repetitions of grades and have higher average levels of achievement compared to systems that are not inclusive" (UNESCO 2012: 16). We need to develop an inclusive education system because a rigid education system impedes learning for a child and every child is capable of learning.

The Indian government has not yet focused on training teachers who can teach people with disabilities. There are very few centers that provide education to special students. Few universities offer bachelor's degree courses in special education. Many schools lack the necessary facilities and user-friendly infrastructures for people with disabilities. Furthermore, there is no financial support for people with disabilities.

Recently the Indian government has taken steps to ameliorate the problems faced by students with disabilities. It has drafted numerous policies designed to protect the welfare of people with disabilities but has failed to actually implement them. The Rights of Persons with Disabilities Bill, 2012, addresses the educational problems faced by people with disabilities and states,

> The appropriate governments and local authorities shall ensure that all educational institutions funded or recognized by them provide inclusive education, and to that end inter alia (1) admit students with disabilities without discrimination and provide them with education and also opportunities for sports, recreation, and leisure activities on an equal basis with others, and (2) make their buildings, campus, and various facilities accessible to a student with disabilities.
>
> (Ministry of Social Justice and Empowerment 2012: 19).

This reflects the failure of local authorities and governments to provide disabled students with accessible buildings and opportunities for recreation.

Inclusive education works toward identifying, challenging, and removing disabling barriers in pursuit of a more equitable system of schooling. In contrast, educational institutions contribute toward maintaining existing social conditions and social relations. What little the government does do, however, and there are very few instances thereof, is to open special segregated schools. We contend that all educational systems need to be restructured in terms of their governance, financing, content, and outcome of provision. Special segregated schooling must be abolished. Inclusive education does not support a limited physical space occupied only by people with disabilities; rather, it believes in bringing all students together.

This necessitates serious changes both in terms of society and the economy. It demands changes in social conditions and relations and in the schools of which they are a part. Therefore,

> an interest in removing disabling barriers is part of a politics of disablement and this is about far more than disabled people; it is about challenging the oppression in all its forms ... it is impossible to confront one type of oppression without confronting them all and, of course, the cultural values that created and sustain them.
>
> (Barton 2006: 60)

We need to ask ourselves the following questions:

- Are schools, colleges, or universities committed to the principle of difference?
- Do they instill the ideology of difference among students?
- Whose interests do these educational systems serve?
- Do they not believe in exclusionary practices?

The educational system requires immediate attention that will improve pedagogy to ensure inclusive education for all.

Part of the disability studies approach involves a serious interest in how we define disability and challenging the disablist assumptions that legitimize forms of professional and commonsense thinking and practice (Schweik 1994: 34). The above-mentioned questions are very important in unraveling the social construction of disability. Language, special needs, and special education differentiate between non-disabled students and disabled students. The continual use of the term "special needs," Ballard (1999) argues, inhibits the development of critical analysis and the culture of special education will continue for as long as the term "special" is part of the vocabulary of education.

Article 24 of the United Nations Convention on the Rights of Persons with Disabilities (CRPD) pertaining to education addresses the right of people with disabilities to access mainstream education. Inclusive education is imperative for people with and without disabilities because it allows people of all ability levels to develop skills and become effective members of a free society (Kohama 2012: 8). It also stresses that the education of people with disabilities is not just a human right but that it is also important to develop the potentiality of all human beings. "Education gives people of all ability levels dignity" (United Nations 2007: 16). Section two of Article 24 specifically discusses education and mandates that people with disabilities should not be excluded from the general education system owing to their disability. People with disabilities must be in a position to access "free and compulsory primary and secondary education in the community within which they live ... including reasonable accommodation for children with disabilities, and providing effective individualized supports in environments that maximize academic and social development" (United Nations 2007: 17). Section three of Article 24 emphasizes the mobility tools that guarantee equal participation in both school and the community. It mandates that students with disabilities should learn and have access to materials in Braille, sign language, and alternative scripts, as well as the necessary mobility aids. Most importantly, it specifies that education should be delivered "in the most appropriate languages and modes and means of communication for the individual" (United Nations 2007: 18). The final two sections of Article 24 discuss tertiary education and the advisability of employing teachers with disabilities who can use Braille and sign language, and who possess alternative forms of communication. The fifth section of Article 24 discusses the importance of making tertiary education or vocational training available to all people with disabilities and emphasizes the importance of ensuring that people with disabilities are not discriminated against in the entry process and throughout these programs (United Nations 2007: 20).

The CRPD was constituted to prevent discrimination against people with disabilities because the policy that was in place and aimed to empower abled people. The introduction of the CRPD proposed a framework to change the education system from a system of segregation and separation to a system of inclusion. Emphasis was placed on using existing infrastructure and knowledge, especially around existing special schools and resource centers, and using them to help, create, and maintain an inclusive system of education (Kohama 2012: 34). There are very few special schools in India. India has opened special schools for blind students and for hearing impaired students. Special school teachers have the in-depth knowledge that is necessary for the early screening and identification of children with disabilities, can serve as training and resource centers for mainstream schools, and can become integrated into an inclusive school as a resource center for children who need to be taken out of the classroom for part of the day because they need extra individualized instruction (UNESCO 1994: 21). By implementing the framework of the CRPD, we can introduce curricula, buildings, pedagogy, assessment procedures, staffing, school ethos, and extracurricular activities that will help people with disabilities. It will also identify the education of girls with disabilities who have been doubly marginalized. Despite the introduction of government policies to build awareness, women with disabilities continue to suffer from a double marginalization both as women and as disabled persons. Female activists and Indian feminism have transformed the structure of patriarchy by introducing the right to education, the right to vote, etc. However, women with disabilities are consistently marginalized. In the 1980s, European and American feminism made an effort to develop a gendered understanding of disability.

> Women's telling of stories of disability and the application of feminist concepts of the social construction of gender to ideas of disability as socially constructed contributed to a new insight into the nature of disabled embodiment as an aspect of women's experience.
>
> (Wendell 1996: 35)

According to Ghai (2002), women with disabilities were not acknowledged as women with a legitimate and equal voice in feminist matters. Moreover, the disability movement also ignored their concerns and rights. The difficulties in accessing education experienced by people with disabilities are compounded for girls and women by the widespread tendency in India, as in many other countries, to give preference to boys' education (Buckingham 2011: 423). "Consequently disability compounds the cultural tendency for physical and economic dependence among Indian women so that women with disabilities, particularly mental disabilities, become easy targets for sexual predation" (Thomas and Thomas 1998: 34).

4.3 Disability and colonialism

It is important to comprehend the framework in which special education policy is created. There are so many factors, such as religion, caste, and beliefs, that influence the policy; however, a country like India represents various sentiments and beliefs of people. Certain critical, structural, and historical facts always play an important role in shaping the course of special education and inclusion in India.

India was a colonial country for almost 150 years, and the first constitution was drafted in 1950. Yet the policies that had been operative since the colonial days continue to hold sway even now. India has not yet found freedom from poverty. It is worse for people with disabilities whose level of income is less than that of any other minority group. People with disabilities need to account for the "conversion handicap" (Sen 1992). "People with disabilities derive a lower level of welfare from a given level of income than the rest of the population, due to additional costs incurred in converting income into well-being" (Kohama 2012: 54). The government turns a blind eye to the fact that people with disabilities can incur extra expenses that normal people do not have to bear. If the medical model is taken into account, people with disabilities need extra medical care and help due to their physical deficiencies. From the perspective of the social model, a lack of social accommodation for people with disability results in their extra expenses. Due to poverty, the people of India encounter innumerable problems. Moreover, the religion and history of India are not conducive to social change. An estimated 80% of the Indian population practices Hinduism which creates a social structure quite different from that of other countries. The caste system of religion has been distorted, and as a result multiple hierarchical concerns around caste have been built into Indian society (Kohama 2012: 12). With the Dalits, the "untouchable" caste, and other marginalized groups in India—females, the poor, children, the elderly, migrants, and people living with HIV/AIDS—the complicated hierarchical structure of Indian society emerges (Kohama 2012: 13). Having argued this, it has also to be recognized that India has made a good effort to establish an inclusive education system after 64 years as a republic. Before that India's policy was regulated and controlled by the British Raj. However, the inclusive policy never aligned with the grounded realities of India. Moreover, there were always problems in implementing the policy. Only a fragment of society benefited from it and a large proportion of the population could not enjoy the benefits promised by the policy.

Prior to India's independence from Britain, efforts to introduce special education in India remained sparse. Archaeologists discovered evidence of the inclusion of people with disabilities in India dating back some 2,000 years ago in the form of adapted toys that made education accessible to children with disabilities (Sharma and Deppeler 2005: 25). Such instances in the form of evidence we receive are part of the "Gurukul system" of India that existed in India for centuries before British rule. The Gurukul system was sensitive to the unique cultural, social, and economic needs of the students and their families and imparted life skills education that recognized the potential of each student (Sharma and Deppeler 2005: 26). However, there is no evidence that documents information about students with disabilities, although structurally, it seems, that system was inclusive. The Gurukul system ended after India came under British rule.

The British implemented their own policy which resulted in the exclusion of minorities and the lower classes which is still prevalent in India today (Kohama 2012: 56). During the post-independence era, the government of India has (on paper) supported various versions of inclusive special education in the policy. The majority of children with disabilities were probably not in school in the initial decades after independence.

In 1835, Thomas Babington Macaulay gave his "Minute on Education" speech, which led to a shift in the history of Indian education. From the traditional Gurukul system in Indian education, India switched to the British style of education. Macaulay, a British politician who was later elected as a member of the governor-general's council, sought to reshape the Indian culture which was only possible by introducing a different system of education. His mission was to create "a class of Indians ... English in taste, in opinion, in morals and intellect" (Indian Institute of Technology Kanpur n.d.: 6). Macaulay blatantly belittled the Indian education system. He goes on to say that the entire native literature of India and Arabia is not worth a single shelf of a good European library (Macaulay's Minute on Education 1835: 9). Macaulay's speech, however, does not include any policy regarding people with disabilities. This is because people with disabilities often were not educated during this period, and also people with disabilities were not considered good enough to be modeled into British-style Indians (Hegarty and Alur 2002: 52).

Prior to independence, there were very limited facilities for people with disabilities that were provided by the private sector or non-governmental organizations. The first special school was opened by Jane Leupot in 1869 with the support of the Church Missionary Society. It was for blind children and was the first school for children with disabilities. Some 14 years later, a school for the deaf was opened in 1883. In 1887, Christian missionaries opened a school for the blind in Amritsar. During the 1800s, all the special schools for people with disabilities accommodated people with physical disabilities; it was not until 1918 that the first school for people with intellectual disabilities was established (Sharma and Deppeler 2005: 567). All these schools made a good attempt to educate people with disabilities but failed to provide them with inclusive education. Such schools were segregated according to the children's disabilities and were not free from the ideology of ability. Undoubtedly, special schools were extended in various parts of the country by 1900. Until the 1970s, these schools were the primary method of service delivery for children with disabilities; most were for children who were blind or visually impaired, and the majority were funded by non-governmental organizations or the private sector.

In the first half of the 20th century, Indian people protested against British rule and people with disabilities did not appear on the agenda of the freedom movement. However, Mahatma Gandhi, the political leader of Indian freedom and leader of the Satyagraha Movement, introduced the concept of "basic education to challenge the British influence over Indian education." Gandhi's idea of education catered to marginalized populations because it focused on handicrafts, which favored the lower castes and people with disabilities, many of whom were used to working with their hands and had not previously done much academic work (Mishra 2011). However, Gandhi also does not seem to have been very conscious of the issue of education for disabled people.

In 1909, an attempt was made to legislate inclusive education in India. Gopal Krishna Gokhle, a professor of English literature, mathematics, and political economy who served, for example, on the Poona Municipal Council, the Bombay Legislative Council, and finally the Imperial Legislative Council, introduced a bill under the Indian Councils Act of 1909 to make primary education compulsory (Metcalf 2006: 135). This bill aimed to provide funding for compulsory education for all but was not supported by the government. By 1940, every action and policy by the government of India contradicted each other. The Sargent Report published by the Central Advisory Board of Education in 1944 suggested that children with disabilities should be incorporated into mainstream education (Hegarty and Alur 2002: 55). The Sargent Report stated that through the politics of mainstreaming every child would be educated regardless of their physical deficiency. The government of India contradicted this suggestion. Throughout the 1940s, the government of India began setting up segregated workshops and trade schools separate from those for students without disabilities to teach children with disabilities skills to enter the workforce (Kalyanpur 2008: 244). Moreover, this decade was marked by a large increase in the amount of money given to the voluntary organization to establish special schools. Most of these segregated schools were expensive and located in urban areas, further marginalizing people with disabilities in rural areas (Kalyanpur 2008: 245).

4.4 Disability and the Constitution of India

India gained its independence in 1947 and the Constitution of India granted inclusive education as a fundamental right for all citizens. It is important to understand that constitutional rights are different from state policies and their legal implications. The rights listed in the Constitution are absolute and completely enforceable. But state policies are completely subjective on a state-by-state basis. Article 45 of the Indian Constitution has the provision for free and compulsory education for children. It states that the state shall endeavor to provide within 10 years from the commencement of this Constitution free and compulsory education for all children until they reach the age of 14 years (Jha 2007: 243). In 1993, Article 45 was reaffirmed with the Supreme Court's judgment on the infamous case *Unnikrishnan vs. State of Andhra Pradesh*. Here, the court ruled that Article 45 must be read in conjunction with Article 21 of the Constitution which states that "no person shall be deprived of his life or personal liberty except according to procedure established by the law" (Legislative Department n.d.). The conjunction of Article 45 and Article 21 ensured that elementary education was deemed imperative for life and personal liberty. As a result of this, a different clause was added to the Constitution of India in 2002. The 86th amendment to the Constitution, section 21A reads, "the State shall provide free and compulsory education to all children of the age of six to fourteen years in such manner as the State may, by law, determine" (Government of India 2005). However, it invited much criticism and some argued that it has age restrictions. Having said this, it was also important to specify the form of education and whether it should be segregated or inclusive.

The 1960s are remembered for a great change in the organization of special education. The Ministry of Social Welfare was charged with the responsibility for weaker and vulnerable sections of society. According to the Salamanca Statement and Framework for Action on Special Needs Education,

They largely focused upon rehabilitation, and not as much on education. Instead of supporting the current education system, the Ministry of Social

Welfare began giving out grants to non-profits that provided education for children with disabilities, inadvertently preventing the inclusion of these children within the public or mainstream sector.

(UNESCO 1994: 19)

Another move that occurred in the history of special education is the Kothari Commission which was established by the government of India in 1964 to draw up a plan of action to improve the education system. But once again the plan created under the Kothari Commission for people with disabilities could not be implemented by the government of India:

We now turn to the education of handicapped children. Their education has to be organized not merely on the humanitarian ground of utility. Proper education generally enables a handicapped child to overcome largely his or her handicap and make him into a useful citizen. Social justice also demands it ... on an overall view of the problem, however, we feel that experimentation with integrated programs is urgently required and every attempt should be made to bring in as many children in integrated programs.

(Hegarty and Alur 2002: 56)

According to Hegarty and Alur (2002), the Kothari Commission's plan could not be implemented because of a split that developed in 1964 within the Ministry of Education and the simultaneous creation of the Ministry of Social Welfare, and the latter's subsequent policy of assistance to voluntary organizations. "The shift in responsibility meant shifting the responsibility for the education training and rehabilitation of people with disabilities and went directly against the Kothari Commission's report and recommendations of inclusive, or at least integrated schooling" (Hegarty and Alur 2002: 54). The Integrated Child Development Scheme (ICDS) of 1974 turned out to be another reason for preventing the implementation of the plan of action of the Kothari Commission. Created by the Ministry of Human Research Development, the ICDS reached out to "vulnerable populations" to provide services such as pre-five-year-old schooling and early intervention, including healthcare, nutrition, and preschool facilities (Kohama 2012: 21). Unfortunately, the ICDS did not include people with disabilities in that category:

Since nothing was specified regarding the needs of Anganwadi workers, the social workers who implemented this scheme on the ground, to specifically reach out and children with disabilities, children with disabilities were not included in early intervention efforts, which would have funneled them into mainstream schooling.

(Hegarty and Alur 2002: 52)

In 1974, the Ministry of Welfare created the Integrated Education of Disabled Children Scheme (IEDC) to provide financial support for books, school uniforms, transportation, special equipment, and aids for children with disabilities. The IEDC intended to include children in mainstream classrooms by making children with disabilities use these aids. But making them adapt to such aid was not enough to bring them into the mainstream structure of society. However, "these plans were supported by UNICEF. Fifty percent of the funding was supposed to go through the state governments, the responsibility was transferred to the department of education in 1992" (Kalyanpur 2008: 245). However, scholars like Sharma and Deppeler note that it was implemented in only 10 out of 29 of the states in India. Sharma and Deppeler (2005) argue that teachers lacked experience and were not aware of the needs of children with disabilities. Furthermore, they state that there was a lack of equipment and teaching aids. By 1979–1980, only 1,881 children from 81 schools all over the country had benefited from this program. Once again, this program and policy could not take the form of inclusive education.

4.5 Disability and the Indian policy

It is important to discuss the National Policy on Education (NPE) that was created in 1986 for children with mild disabilities with the aim of including them in mainstream classrooms, while children with moderate to severe disabilities continued to be placed in segregated schools. This policy contradicted Article 45 of the Indian Constitution which believes in equality in education as a fundamental right for all. Article 45 does not differentiate between mild disabilities and severe disabilities; rather, it views all children as equal regardless of their differences. The NPE had the provision to train every teacher in mainstream schools but this was not implemented until a plan of action was created in 1992.

> The 1992 Program of Action (POA), created to implement the 1986 NPE, broadens the 1986 definition of who should be included in mainstream schooling, that "a child with a disability who can be educated in the general school should not be in the special school."
>
> (Hegarty and Alur 2002: 44)

The plan envisaged equipping children with disabilities with life skills by making them use resource rooms and special schools. But the POA does not define the paradigm of life skills. The POA assumed that schools across India would share their resources with other institutions. However, rather than including or even integrating children with disabilities into their programs, these schools would open resource centers for the unprivileged, providing children with disabilities with learning resources after typical school hours, but not during the normal school day, thereby eliminating the possibility of inclusion for these students.

Prior to the passing of the Right of Education Bill, many policies and programs like the Rehabilitation Council of India Act, the People with Disabilities Act, the District Primary Education Program, and Sarva Sikhsa Abhiyan (SSA—Education for All), were introduced for the betterment of children with disabilities. SSA was not a disability-specific program but rather a disability-inclusive program with specific aspects seeking to open new schools in those locations which lacked schooling facilities and attempted to strengthen the existing social infrastructure through the provision of additional classrooms, toilets, drinking water, maintenance grants, and school improvement grants.

> Existing schools with inadequate teacher strength are provided with additional teachers, while the capacity of existing teachers is being strengthened by extensive training, grants for developing teaching-learning materials and strengthening of the academic support structure at a cluster, block and district level.
>
> (Ministry of Human Resource Development n.d.)

The goal of SSA was to introduce universal education by 2010 for all children aged from six to 14. It failed to reach the goal, but the program is still running.

It is interesting to observe the way the program intends to benefit children with disabilities but utterly fails to achieve it. SSA aims to allocate 1,200 rupees per annum for each child with disabilities. Money has to be spent on assistive devices, on materials in alternative learning formats, or on anything that would help such children to integrate into mainstream classrooms. However, the money is funneled through the district or school level, and it is therefore impossible to ensure that it will be spent on the child with disabilities (World Bank 2009: 58). According to SSA, it should be possible to spend more money on assistive devices for children with disabilities because ownership of assistive devices is considered a fundamental right. Unfortunately, SSA provides these assistive devices with the collaboration of other programs. The outside program poses restrictions on the purchase of assistive devices and considers the right of providing devices to the child with disabilities as charity. One of the programs that SSA collaborates with is the Assistance to Disabled Persons for Purchase/ Fitting of Aids and Appliances program run by the Ministry of Social Justice and Empowerment, which requires that children with a disability have a doctor's note, fall into a particular income bracket, and after the age of 12 can only receive one device every three years. In addition, despite the stated importance of this population, less than 1% of the total funding allocated for SSA is being used for purposes of inclusion (World Bank 2009: 66). SSA also designed a plan for each district to work for children with disabilities and encouraged districts to formulate their plans for children with disabilities. It formulated a "no rejection" policy under which children aged from six to 14 cannot be turned away from the institution even if they have a disability. However, this contradicted the People with Disabilities Act which demanded an appropriate environment for children with disabilities. Under SSA, the government of India and the World Bank attempted to monitor the effectiveness and results stemming from the program. Undoubtedly, this program had good intentions but there was no attempt to remove discrepancies, like those between the data collected by SSA and the data collected by the National Service Scheme, the National Institute for Social Empowerment, and the government of India on inclusive education.

All these policies intended to bring children with disabilities into mainstream education, but they lacked commitment to the cause of the disabled. The Right to Education Bill that was drafted in 2005 by the Ministry of Human Resource Development was not disability-specific but it is important to discuss it in order to understand the specific sections of it that engage with children with disabilities. This bill sought social justice and collective advocacy rather than individual rights. "The International Labor Organization says that when students with disabilities are not promoted as a separate group with separate needs in policies such as the Right to Education Act, that their specific needs are not addressed and met" (Hegarty and Alur 2002: 44). It did not include any specific clauses that addressed the problem of children with disabilities. It included various other clauses that ensured that children with or without disabilities should enjoy the right to education. The Act states that institutions will not bar any child from completing their elementary education irrespective of their economic difficulties, or if they have crossed the upper age limit. Such children will not be admitted into a classroom based on their perceived level of education, but rather they will be admitted into an age-appropriate classroom that contradicts the rule in terms of children with intellectual disabilities. Children with intellectual disabilities will be placed in a classroom based on their perceived level of education. The Right to Education Bill suggests that the government should build schools in areas where children live so that they do not have to make the distance to school an excuse for not attending, or else the government should provide transport facilities to that particular area. The Right to Education Act gives responsibility to state and the government to carry out the entire outline stated in the plan. It does not stop here and makes four more important clauses:

> The teacher cannot be hired on a contractual, month to month basis, allowing for them to be unqualified, but states that teachers must be hired on as permanent staff, giving them full salary and benefits. The bill gave the government five years to implement this change, because of the staggering lack of qualified teachers in India.
>
> (Government of India 2005)

The discriminating attitude toward children with disabilities meant that the bill was not passed until 2009. Every department ignored it and it was not brought up in budget sessions. Finally, it came into effect in 2010. On April 12, 2012, the Supreme Court validated the Act constitutionally. Approximately 25% of all school places were reserved in private schools for Dalit children and other marginalized sections of society. However, this was widely opposed by the private school lobby, which believed that this would dilute the brand value of private schools. The delay in passing the bill represents the politics of marginalizing children with disabilities and it is evident that special education schools lack qualified teachers.

The Inclusion in Education of Children and Youth with Disabilities (IECYD) bill was drafted by the Ministry of Human Resource Development in 2005, the same year that the Right to Education Bill was drafted.

> This action plan envisions that all children with a disability will have access to mainstream education; in order to facilitate this, the government, specifically collaborating between the Rehabilitation Council and the National Council for Teacher's Education, will ensure that there are adequate numbers of teachers trained in inclusive education as well as the proper physical and ideological infrastructure to facilitate inclusions in schools.
>
> (UNICEF n.d.)

This plan had shifted from integration to inclusion of children with disabilities. According to Maya Kalyanpur,

> Whereas under the Scheme of Integrated Education for the Disabled Children (IEDC) as it stands as a present, children with disabilities are placed in a regular school without making any changes in the school to accommodate and support diverse needs, the revised ICEYD will, in contrast, modify the existing physical infrastructures and teaching methodologies to meet the needs of all children, including children with Special Needs.
>
> (2008: 67)

The IECYD includes those children with disabilities who are outside of the 6–14 age range. Through the ICDS, Anganwadi workers will be trained to identify children with disabilities at an early age, so that they can receive early intervention services (UNICEF n.d.). Extending this argument Kalyanpur says that "while the crucial importance of early intervention cannot be overlooked, the IECYD also discusses accommodations for students with a disability in universities, including a mandatory 'disability coordinator' who provides inclusion services for students with disabilities" (2008: 76).

This policy discriminated against students with intellectual disabilities by providing them with home-based training. This plan had the provision of providing accommodation and distance learning for students with disabilities on the assumption that they will learn better with these accommodations.

Scholars who advocate for inclusion point out that while the bill requires the special school to be made into resource centers for people with disabilities and professionals, students will probably still rely on special schools to some extent for education.

(Kalyanpur 2008: 253)

The government realized that students with disabilities have still not benefited from these plans so it reformed the scheme for Integrated Education for Disabled Children (IEDC) and created the Inclusive Education of the Disabled at the Secondary Stage (IEDSS). The IEDC came into effect in 2009 and had the objective to enable children with disabilities "who have completed eight years of elementary education to continue their education at the secondary stage in an inclusive environment in regular schools" (Kalyanpur 2008: 254). The IEDSS was the first policy to recognize the importance of secondary education for children with disabilities. After the 2005 Action Plan, the Ministry of Social Justice and Empowerment's National Policy was created for people with disabilities. "Two policies were created under separate ministries, they are very similar in both the ideologies that they were founded on, as well as the actual changes they are trying to make to the system" (Kalyanpur 2008: 254). This policy intends to bring special schools together as a resource center and to bridge the gap between rural and urban areas by creating more District Disability and Rehabilitation Centres. Such centers will "disseminate information in terms of availability of aids and appliances, ensure the mandated 3% coverage of persons with disabilities in poverty reduction programs, and target girls with disabilities" (Kalyanpur 2008: 255).

The policies discussed above suggest that the government has always attempted to include people with disabilities in mainstream education through its various plans, but in reality these plans were never put into practice. The Kothari Commission or the Right to Education Bill seem to have formulated an inclusive education policy that was never actually implemented. In other words, the government has always exercised discriminatory practices against people with disabilities and has consoled them by drafting these policies although it has never got them into mainstream education. These policies do not take into account the complexity of such children's disabilities and have failed to understand the way in which disability functions. They do not have any definition to measure people with severe disabilities. The government has not yet made any serious attempts to address the problem of people with disabilities, and the demands they make of society. Policies are always framed by certain presumptions rather than taking disabled people's problems into account. People with disabilities have not been asked about their requirements. However, policies to remedy this have been drafted, but the government has not seen fit to implement them.

It is unjust to say that these policies have not benefited children with disabilities, but it is also important to unravel the unequal services being provided in India. These policies do not differentiate between children with disabilities in urban areas and those in rural areas. Moreover, these policies emphasize the provision of extra assistance to children with disabilities. Many children with disabilities live in rural areas.

> The number becomes worrisome in comparison to where the majority of services are offered, which is in urban areas less than 15% of national services for people with disabilities are located in rural areas, and of those most are expensive and/or private.
>
> (Kalyanpur 2008: 57)

It means that disabled people in rural areas do not get much help with their education. They are often confined to their homes. It reflects the discrepancy in services and terms of admission for children with disabilities in schools. In the same context, Kalyanpur, who based her findings on data collated by the national census in 2001, states,

> in terms of education levels, only 11% of children with disabilities between the ages of 5–18 years in urban areas (less than 1% in rural areas) were enrolled in special schools, while 55% of adults with disabilities were illiterate (59% in rural and 40% in urban areas), with only 7% in rural and 18% in urban areas having completed secondary education.
>
> (Kalyanpur 2008: 255)

Kalyanpur points out the discrimination against children with disabilities in rural areas or the least effort being paid by the government to educate children with disabilities in rural areas. As we have already discussed, the discrepancies in the data provided by the national census do not reflect the realities of rural society. Stigma plays a vital role even in rural society and parents do not want to talk about their disabled children.

It can also be said that due to a lack of resources and amenities, parents from rural areas do not send their disabled children to school. This reflects the fact that district and village panchayats (councils) have neglected to build inclusive schools to enable children with disabilities to enter mainstream education.

The abject failure of these policies is reflected in the level of gender inequality among children with disabilities. No policies have been formulated to improve the quality of life of women with disabilities. The national census shows that there is extreme inequity between girls and boys and there are fewer girls with disabilities than boys with disabilities. It is not unusual that there are fewer disabled girls, because selective abortion, female infanticide, and female feticide are part of everyday life in India. These hierarchies have yet not been questioned with the implementation of the legal recourse. The prescriptive gender stereotypes about girls, i.e. that they are meant to serve the men, is still prevalent in Indian society. Families do not want to invest money in the education of girls as it is assumed that they will marry into a husband's family and that the family will take care of the girl. As a result, girls are confined to household work and do not go to school, although education is a basic right granted by the Constitution. "Girls with disabilities have a lower enrolment rate in school than boys with disabilities across many sectors; urban vs. rural, by type of schooling, by the level of schooling, and in primary versus secondary schooling" (Kalyanpur 2008: 250). Girls with disabilities are more vulnerable in their communities than disabled boys. Unfortunately, sociocultural and political-economic factors have led to women and girls with disabilities becoming one of the most marginalized groups in society.

It has also been observed that people with disabilities are discriminated against based on their type of disability. The national census of 2011 did not break down the types of disability according to the Diagnostic and Statistical Manual of Mental Disorders-IV, but rather by the categories "locomotor, multiple, mental retardation (intellectual disability), mental illness, blindness, low vision, hearing and speech" (Ministry of Home Affairs n.d.). Of the 70–110 million people who are disabled in India, their disabilities fall into the following categories: 53% have a locomotor disability; 13% have a visual disability; 10% have an auditory disability; and 4% have an intellectual disability (Ministry of Home Affairs n.d.). People with intellectual disabilities are more marginalized than any other disabled group of people. Due to their intellectual disability, the government fails to categorize them as disabled. Most of the time, they are not even identified as disabled people. The government treats the intellectually disabled body as a diseased body. They become part of the asylum and hospital system, rather than part of the education system. In terms of disability, people with intellectual disabilities have the lowest enrolment rates in school. They are four times less likely to go to school than children with physical disabilities, are the least likely to be employed, and are the least likely to get married. It is not easy to meet the needs of intellectually disabled children in the school setting. The government has made no attempt to transform the structure of the society so as to accommodate such children, who thus are marginalized as they are unable to access any useful assistance that may help them to become part of mainstream education. The government is unwilling to change the curriculum to accommodate these students. Due to stigma, families prefer to confine the disabled children at home rather than sending them to school. As a result, most children with intellectual disabilities remain illiterate.

There are two aspects of government policy that are particularly noteworthy but which contradict one another: (1) its efforts to formulate an inclusive education system; and (2) the failure of government policy in terms of its implementation. It is important to examine the rationale behind the dropping out of mainstream schools by children with disabilities who then enrol in a special school. During a seminar on "Integrated Education for Children with Special Needs: A Matter of Social Justice and Human Rights" held in 2022 in Salamanca, Spain, it was observed that "students repeatedly failed their courses and were asked to leave by teachers or administrators, and many of these students were teased for their 'failure'" (Kohama 2012: 37). Teachers generally do not pay attention to disabled children in class, and instead focus on non-disabled children. They appear not to respond to the problems of disabled children.

These observations do not point out the children's deficiencies; rather, it shows that the system not believe in transformation and inclusion. Normative society does not allow children with disabilities to develop their capabilities and it acts against them. Teachers are unskilled in the use of assistive devices intended for children with disabilities.

Since the enactment of the Rehabilitation Council of India Act of 1992, which set standards for teacher training, there has been a shortage of trained teachers and personnel in schools (Hegarty and Alur 2002: 25). The government needs to understand that each type of disability requires trained teachers in their respective domains. Unfortunately, trained teachers for visually challenged students teach all the groups of disabled students which impedes the inclusion of disabled students. The Project Integrated Education for the Disabled (PIED) found that 45% of children with disabilities can be taught in a mainstream classroom by teachers who have received just one week of training about inclusion:

> These children are those with extremely "mild" disabilities. 30% of the children with disabilities can be taught in a mainstream classroom with teachers trained in inclusion for 1–2 weeks, plus periodic counseling or outside services. These children have mild to moderate disabilities. 15% of children with disabilities can be taught in an inclusive setting with teachers who have about three months of training.
>
> (Kohama 2012: 38)

This shows that children with disabilities can be taught by teachers who have had very little specialist training. A mainstream teacher can also teach them provided that they have invested some time in acquiring the relevant training.

The curriculum plays a vital role in discriminating against children with disabilities. The syllabus is not intended for children with disabilities and is inflexible. There are two main types of curriculum in India: there is a curriculum that is specifically designed for children with disabilities to increase accessibility (e.g., Braille, large print, reading aids, language/communication for deaf children, communication for children with cerebral palsy), and a general curriculum. The general curriculum should be flexible so that it can be adapted for children with disabilities. In terms of testing, India has extremely rigid assessment and examination systems that are borrowed from the British system of education. However, some alternative methods of testing are available to accommodate students with disabilities. Yet the adaptation of tools, mediums, and methodologies of assessment are all grey areas.

Issues like accessibility and funding are two important aspects that impede inclusive education. The education system can never be inclusive if it does not change the architecture of schools/colleges or universities. "In India, most of the school buildings are already built, and building modifications are expensive in a country that already has resource-starved programs" (Hegarty and Alur 2002: 139). Corruption is another issue that hinders inclusive education. Allocated funding does not reach those in need and special schools require more funding in proportion to other schools.

It is very important that the negative paradigm surrounding people with disabilities is changed. "Education for all" can only be achieved in India by changing our attitudes and by internalizing the fact that problem does not lie with the body but outside of the body, i.e., in the environment. Non-governmental organizations are making a large impact in transforming the education system. Policies need to be implemented that can bring change to the lives of people with disabilities. Therefore, the government of India needs to consolidate its responsibility for education. It is the accountability of the government to ensure that all citizens are well informed about these policies and schemes. This does not only include teachers, administrators, lawyers, and students, but also farmers, shopkeepers, homemakers, etc. Information can be disseminated by mounting advertising campaigns.

School is a space where children's subjectivity is produced, regulated, and even resisted. The body as the site of cultural and political activity is constituted and reconstituted by the disciplining discourses of schooling that penetrate the level of the body. Henry Giroux (1992) argues in *Border Crossings: Cultural Workers and the Politics of Education*, that practices are directed by pedagogy and represent the body as the site of cultural struggle over "social forms such as language, ideologies, significations, and narratives, in order to create borderlands in which diverse cultural resources allow for the fashioning of new identities within existing configurations of power" (Giroux 1992: 28). The constitution of the body has been theorized in terms of race, class, caste, and gender, but the subjectivity of the body being constituted in schools goes unnoticed. It reflects the historical practices that maintain two educational systems: one for children with disabilities and one for everyone else. This book has already examined the discriminatory practices perpetuated in schools that propagate inequality in the pedagogic system. These discriminating policies are the reason that disabled people struggle to find employment in a highly competitive market economy. Therefore, the lives of people with disabilities are miserable and economically challenging.

Disability is not an inherent, fixed condition, but rather a social construct and cultural interpretation of physical and cognitive differences. It emerges through a comparison of different bodies, revealing the ways in which these variations shape and often perpetuate unequal social relations and institutions. In essence, disability is a product of societal norms and expectations, and it reflects the power dynamics that influence our interactions and the structures that govern our lives.

Disability studies questions the structure under which policy is formulated. Drafted policies are the effect of thinking derived from the perspectives of humanism and historical materialism that do not believe the body/subject as indeterminate, multiple, and contextual. Disability studies argues for the articulation of desire as crucial to a transformative pedagogy.

This chapter has primarily focused on the continuing discursive exclusion of people with disabilities in Indian society, and it is argued that along with attempts at the formal integration of disabled people into the rights, obligations, and expectations of the normative citizenship, a counter-trend of segregation is equally in play. Disabled people continue to endure broad cultural discrimination and alienation, not so much because of their differences (which may of course be hidden) but because their form of living in the body lays bare the psycho-social imaginary that sustains the modernist understanding of what it is to be a subject. There are many standard demands for the rights of disabled people and a more thorough inclusion of their specific interests in cultural production. But we need to investigate the factors that impede the evolution of equitable conditions. The government and local authorities need to take measures to ensure the full development, advancement, and empowerment of women and girls with disabilities, to guarantee them the ability to exercise their human rights on an equal basis with others. It is an indisputable fact that in India women and girls with disabilities are mistreated by their families in particular and by society in general, reflected, for example, in their caste-based social exclusion in Punjab and the practice of forced hysterectomies for intellectually disabled women in Pune. Disabled people have the right to access all means of support to enable them to exercise their legal capacity in accordance with their wishes and preferences. The legal capacity of people with disabilities should not be questioned or denied, irrespective of the degree and extent of the support sought (Ministry of Social Justice and Empowerment 2012: 9). Even universities have been found to exhibit intolerance in accommodating disabled students and teachers. The national and state disaster management authority should take appropriate measures to ensure the inclusion of people with disabilities in its disaster management activities as defined under S 2(e) of the Disaster Management Act, 2005 (Act No 53 of 2005) during the occurrence of any "disaster" as defined under S 2(d) of the Disaster Management Act, 2005, for the safety and protection of the person with disabilities (Ministry of Social Justice and Empowerment 2012: 15). Some years ago it was reported that the victims of the Hyderabad bomb blast were not being taken care of properly (*The Hindu*, April 1, 2013). The discriminatory and exclusionary practices are quite visible in public spaces like shopping malls. Many spaces are not accessible to disabled bodies. Here, we should also consider the conventions that protect both the disabled and the non-disabled and question the hierarchization between the abled body and disabled body. The discursive construction and maintenance of the stereotypes of disability have effectively devalued disabled bodies and positioned them as Others. The difference between corporeality as a binary of embodied selfhood poses a threat to and produces anxiety among disabled people.

Disability as a sociocultural political category has been critically analyzed in terms of the rights of disabled people since the 1970s. Before that, disability was never part of a serious study. The Indian government made many attempts to improve the status of disabled people through a range of policy and legislative measures. A massive endeavor was made in the areas of health, education, employment, accessible environments, and social security to minimize the trauma which is experienced by disabled people due to their impaired bodies and their interaction with the inaccessible built environment. But what is to be noticed here is the inherent and perpetuated prejudiced thinking which considers disability as a personal problem of an individual. The attempts which were made to improve the status of disabled people in society hardly helped, in that they did not seek to minimize the stigma associated with disabled bodies. Attitudinal barriers which make disabled people feel excluded in terms of their participation in society need to be broken down. Moreover, attempts to provide access for disabled individuals to the built environment also failed, because of the very problem of understanding the nature of disability. The discourse of disability is still woven around the belief that a positive action is a form of charity and welfare which is why the least attention is paid to analyzing the experience, culture, and history of disabled people and perpetuating the prejudiced notion about disability as a natural property of a body. The various modes of representation, namely literature, media, and cinema, have continued to project disabled people as hapless and helpless creatures who need assistance and sympathy. In order to understand disability, we need to critique a rhetorical narrative that was hardly done. What we need to engage with is how disability functions and how it is discursively formed. Disability is now no more than a purely person-centered medical/clinical problem. However, as a result of research done in the area of disability studies it has emerged as a human rights issue and an integral part of a serious sociopolitical issue. So, what we need to do is to attempt to contest disability as sociocultural political category and conceptualize it by debating the existing definitions and critiquing narratives which will unravel the epistemological and ontological status of conceptual categories that are taken for granted. In Chapter 5 we will examine the established notions of normality, abnormality, ability, and able-bodiedness, difference and deficit, health and sickness, strength and weakness, dependence, independence, and interdependence.

4.6 Disability and identity

Between 1872 and 1931, censuses inquired about disability, but this question was omitted in the censuses conducted in 1941, 1951, 1961, 1971, and 1991. In 1981, the census began gathering information on three specific types of disabilities, and in 2001, it expanded to include five types of disabilities. Following years of advocacy and efforts by disability rights groups and activists, the 2011 census included questions related to eight different types of disabilities, and this reflects the attitudinal barriers in acknowledging the disabled identity. Following widespread protests by disability activists it became mandatory to include the issue of disability. The protest movements by disability activists brought the issue to the fore. The fifth National Family Health Survey conducted between 2019 and 2021 incorporated questions pertaining to disabilities for the very first time. These questions aimed to capture five primary categories of disabilities, namely locomotor, visual, hearing, speech, and mental impairments, alongside an "others" category. However, it is important to note that this marked a reduction from the eight disability categories recognized in the 2011 census, and was far less comprehensive than the 21 categories acknowledged by the Rights of Persons with Disabilities Act. Regrettably, individuals with intellectual and learning disabilities, as well as those living with chronic neurological conditions and blood disorders, were not addressed as distinct categories in spite of their unique requirements and heightened vulnerabilities. As disability scholars have argued, historically disabled people have been invisible physically and metaphorically. Issues of gender, caste, poverty, etc., have been addressed more widely in India than the issue of disability. Disability, in India, represents horror and tragedy. The impaired body is very much unwanted; this is reflected in our Indian culture in which an individual feels reluctant to donate any of their organs after their death. It is important to note the prevalent practices in India and their perspectives toward the disabled body. In the recorded history of India, there is no evidence to suggest that the infanticide of disabled children was a general practice. In most cases, abnormality has been equated with the possession of special supernatural powers, and the status of the disabled may be unpredictably high. Even if the disabled are vilified or sanctified, the outcomes are in one sense similar: they are viewed primarily in terms of their disability and are stereotyped accordingly. Whatever their status, they have been separated from ordinary people because they are physically different from them. Both perceptions may be visualized as a means of alienating the disabled.

By exploring the religious discourse, we see how people with disabilities are excluded from mainstream cultural practices. Undoubtedly colonialism had a part to play in the government's policy and services meant for people with disabilities are implemented appropriately. Good education and better employment prospects can transform the lives of people with disabilities. Sociocultural practices do not respect the bodily differences that can result in discrimination against people with disabilities.

Chapter 5

Disability and Indian English Fiction

In the previous chapter, we discussed the issues of rights and education for people with disabilities. We observed that the Indian government has failed to implement many of the drafted policies for people with disabilities. These policies could not be implemented because the government assumes that people with disabilities do not contribute to society, whereas able-bodied persons contribute to the process. Disability also finds some space in Indian English fiction. However, rarely does one come across a novel that offers a faithful and detailed portrayal of the disabled character(s) and the issues related to their disability. Usually the disabled characters play a minor role in the narrative and therefore offer only a shallow portrayal of their lived experiences. To illustrate the relationship between disability and Indian English fiction and to critique its representation in the literature, I have selected three novels, *Trying to Grow* by Firdous Kanga, *Fireproof* by Raj Kamal Jha, and *Animal's People* by Indira Sinha, because they depict the prejudiced attitudes of society toward people with disabilities. The chapter questions the depiction of people with disabilities as Others.

5.1 Disability and anomalous bodies

Disabled or anomalous bodies have been subjected to multiple interpretations and responses for millennia. As was discussed in Chapters 1 and 2 in this volume, disabled bodies are generally associated with omens, considered embarrassing freaks and curiosities, and more often than not are the subject of mockery. They are conceptualized as too abnormal or pathological to uphold systems of power and authority. David Wright and Anne Diggy discuss in their book *From Idiocy to Mental Deficiency: Historical Perspectives on People with Learning Disabilities* (1996) that people with disabilities are subjected to institutional care and control. However, new emerging discourses about people with disabilities have challenged this notion and have begun to explore the experiences of an oppressed minority.

The present study, in the divergent strand, attempts to explore the complex relationship between the biological and social worlds. *The New Disability History: American Perspectives* (2001), edited by Paul Langmore and Lauri Umansky, opens up a new discussion by conceptualizing the disabled body as a

DOI: 10.4324/9781032722054-5

cultural signifier and questioning former the understanding of people with disabilities as being entrusted to charity and social care. This chapter will explore the ways in which disabled bodies have been perceived and represented in the Indian English novels under review and the changing perceptions represented therein. It goes without saying that historically the relationship between the normal and the deviant is has varied. This chapter will address the problems faced by people with disabilities who are considered aberrant, and in particular it will articulate their broader social, political, and cultural values. It questions the way literature legitimizes cultural definitions of normality, competence, and superiority. To understand this wide range of issues, there is a need to address the issues of difference and how Indian society has given value to human life.

People with disabilities are thought of as disadvantaged citizens. They do not enjoy the advantages of social and economic equality and are deprived of an identity group. Sunny Taylor, a disability activist, says that "while issues regarding racial, gender and sexual orientation equality are all the forefront of political and social theory, disabled people are almost left out of these conversations" (Taylor 2004: 55). The presupposition that they are the victims of bad luck or that their disabilities are the result of *karmas* (actions) that they have done in their previous lives discriminates them from their identity group. Taylor adds, "Unlike sexism and racism, which are perceived to be significant social problems, disability falls under the social radar, and disablism is not recognized as a damaging or even particularly serious form of prejudice" (2004: 56). People with disabilities who think that they can enjoy their lives are often viewed as presumptuous and offensive. This chapter will question these prejudiced assumptions and will examine the stereotypical representations of people with disabilities.

The selected novels, *Trying to Grow*, *Animal's People*, and *Fireproof*, represent the blurred relationship between deformity and disability which is another concern of this study. Undoubtedly, the words disability and deformity carry different connotations but there are no clear-cut distinctions between them (Turner and Stag 2006: 2). There are various interpretations of the term deformity. It is generally understood in aesthetic terms and connotes the opposite of beauty or deviation from normal appearance. The disability that fails to match the competence and capabilities of bodies deemed normal becomes synonymous with deformity. Therefore, the definition of and issues concerned with disability have widened. It is important to note that disability incorporates a vast array of experiences that do not invite straightforward categorization. In the same context, Garland says that "[f]acial scarring may be disability of appearance only, causing no physical difficulty but may yet have socially disabling consequences" (2006: 2).

The three novels chosen for this study feature impaired characters and the nature of their impairment differs, which will be briefly discussed later. Deformity frequently becomes a major psychological problem rather than causing physical pain. The novels address the problem of a society that cancels out disabled people's rights in everyday life not because they have problems with their bodies but because they are different. In the early modern period, the concept of disability was subsumed under other categories, notably deformity and monstrosity. Before dealing with the issues of deformity, monstrosity, and disability as represented in the selected novels, the *inexpressibility* of physical pain has to be discussed with a special reference to two of the novels, *Trying to Grow* and *Fireproof*.

5.2 Disability and the discourse of pain

Physical pain is a very important phenomenon of the body that constitutes the individuality of the subject. Pain often accompanies people with disabilities who feel it in their everyday lives. The social model of disability does not consider the body as a problem; rather, it finds the environment responsible for the outcome of disability. Pain is exclusively related to the physical body, not to the social barriers. Pain becomes an important tool with which to question the understanding of the social model of disability and addresses the problem of disability which has to be incorporated to understand disabled people's benefits and rights. In the introduction to her book, *The Body in Pain*, Elaine Scarry describes how physical pain disturbs the social realm more than the individual body. She uses torture and warfare as examples of pain that have a huge impact on her theory. She states,

> Pain is a purely physical experience of negation, an immediate sensory rendering of something being against one, and one of something one must be against. Even though it occurs within oneself, it is at once identified as "not oneself, not me," as something so alien that it must right now be gotten rid of.
>
> (1985: 52)

Pain unmakes the world precisely because it usually lodges the source of suffering in the social realm. Society presumes that pain lies merely in the body. However, pain is not only the outcome of the impairment; in fact, society inflects the pain which goes unnoticed by the social realm. In the case of people with disabilities, disability and suffering has to do with the impairment that has to be realized by the people. Only identifying the pain of people with disabilities will decrease the pain and will allow people with disabilities to work in society.

Trying to Grow is a novel about a young man who was born in Bombay, India. He would never grow more than four feet. His mother, Sera, calls him Brit because he has brittle bones. Because he is frail he is not allowed to visit places or to go outside alone. His parents try their best to cure him, but they fail. He strikes up a friendship with Cyrus. The novel is about Brit's experiences of society and his love of and desire for Cyrus. The aim of selecting this novel is to represent society's prejudiced attitudes toward people with disabilities in terms of disabled people's choices, desires, and agency. This novel explores the enigma of pain and how society oppresses people with disabilities by infantilizing and stereotyping them. It provides a glimpse of society's behavior toward people with disabilities.

Brit, the protagonist and first-person narrator of *Trying to Grow*, discusses his physical pain which he conceals from his family members. There are various reasons to explore the fundamental nature of pain and its bond with disability. Brit's family members are unaware of his pain not because they are not concerned about his pain but rather because Brit does not want to tell them about his pain. He is scared that he will not be allowed to live his life according to his own choices or that he will become an object of sympathy. He is not allowed to play outside and is not permitted to use his legs like other children because his bones are brittle. He is worried that if he discloses his pain it might hamper his freedom. Brit is upset when he is going to meet the headmaster for his examination. He does not talk about it to any of his family members. Sera feels very bad and asks Brit's father Sam, "have you noticed he has not said a word since he woke? What if he does not answer the question they ask him" (Kanga 1991: 52). Sam does not bother to ask Brit what is wrong and comes to the conclusion that he may be in pain. Sam says, "Do you think something might be hurting him? You know how he keeps his pain like some precious secret" (Kanga 1991: 52). This is the problem that afflicts many people with disabilities: people think that their pain in the body and that it upsets them, which is why they hide it. Brit admits,

> I did not speak about pain as long as I could take it; that way I did not have to admit something broken inside me. When my secret was out a cyclone hit my life raining tears, grief, guilt, defeat.
>
> (Kanga 1991: 52–53)

However, it cannot be argued that pain does not become a tool with which to seek the sympathy or help of people unnecessarily because the pain comes with the doubt of whether or not it exists. Pain comes into our midst as something that cannot be denied and that cannot be confirmed (Scarry 1985: 4). People with disabilities face this challenge too; their pain can be noticed or it can be denied.

People living with pain are represented as non-human beings or they are constituted as human beings who are *worthy of dying*. A newborn baby in the novel *Fireproof* is expected to die so that it can be relieved from chronic pain. In the name of pain, pity and disqualification of the lives of people with disabilities are justified, and violence is carried out to relieve them from pain. The belief that all disabled people experience pain and that all pains lead to suffering runs through popular discourses to create entrenched ways of knowing pain and disability. Therefore, there is a need to examine these ways of knowing and experiencing pain. There is a need to question the cultural discourses that project pain as a devastating experience that resists exploring the alternative explanations for pain. Do we not need to think about what kind of pain is allowed to be felt? One may argue that is it viable to live with pain. We are required to think about that pain so that we can challenge the oppression that attempts to annihilate the body with pain, not to overcome it. Medical institutions appear to be unwilling to keep people in pain and to look after them. Alyson Patsavas (2014) argues that when cultural discourses construct pain as the cause of the feeling of devastation, they oversimplify complex cultural, historical, and political phenomena. More than that, they prevent the body in pain from examining the structural conditioning that makes experiences of chronic pain tragic.

Knowledge production about pain situates it within discursive systems of power and privilege. The structural condition that devalues the body in pain must be critiqued. It goes without saying that the process through which knowledge about pain is produced in mainstream representation and the knowledge is circulated through able-bodied assumptions. Carrie Sandhal (2005) points out that the subject positions from which we produce knowledge matters. She explains that power dynamics that are inherent to the process of knowledge production do not privilege experience as a source of knowledge. Standpoint epistemology offers a way to understand marginalized positionalities that exposes systems of oppression. Sandra Harding (1986) argues that knowledge has to be grounded in experience which is why women's experience and their movements are better than neutral knowledge. The novels under study do not directly talk about the experiences of people with disabilities; rather, they implicitly question the socially situated experience of disability and attempt to expose ableist values regarding bodies marked with differences.

Pain presents a different approach to viewing the body against the norm. People with disabilities are often assisted by prosthetic devices, for example, a wheelchair, which is understood as a device of empowerment. It is not viewed as a potential source of pain. Leo Bersani argues that "Pain remaps the body's erotic sites, redistributing the erogenous zones, breaking up the monopoly of the genitals, and smashing the repressive and aggressive edifice of the ego. Rare is the theoretical account where physical suffering remains harmful for long" (1987: 123). In this context, Tobin Siebers says that "the ideology of ability requires that any sign of disability be viewed exclusively as awakening new and magical opportunities for ability" (2010: 63). Prostheses stand in the same logic that intends to extend the ideology of ability and attempts to erase the idea of the difference. However, pain is a reality that will always resist ideological construction of ability and will address the injustice continued with people with disabilities.

5.3 Disability and social attitudes

Fireproof shows how a normal body defines the non-normal body as ugly, dirty, impure, contaminated, or sick. *Fireproof* is set around the Godhra Massacre and reflects on some of the worst communal violence to have taken place in India since partition in 1947. The chief narrator is Jay, the father of a new-born baby who is severely deformed. A mysterious lady named Miss Glass suggests to him that he should take his son away from the crowds and save his life. The novel revolves around the way in which people react when they see a severely deformed baby and at the same time the narrator describes the painful events that have taken place in the Godhra Massacre. People describe his baby thus: "he is a bit different from other babies" (Jha 2006: 64); "it is some kind of an animal" (Jha 2006: 254). Throughout the novel, Jay has to listen to such adverse comments that are the result of "his son being different." Jay feels a certain nervousness about the way people behave toward him, their avoidance of eye contact, and the distance they keep.

According to Young (2000), people with disabilities are clearly structured by the interactive dynamics of desire, the pulse of attraction and aversion, and people's experience of bodies and embodiment. Modern rational scientific dis-course proposes and legitimizes the superiority of able-privileged groups. Young goes on to say that 19th- and early 20th-century scientific, aesthetic, and moral culture explicitly constructed some groups as ugly or degenerated bodies, in contrast to the purity and respectability of neutral, rational subjects. Needless to say, postmodern critics such as Kristeva, Derrida, Lacan, and Deleuze have critiqued the rationalist notions of Descartes and humanism and have ques-tioned the philosophical construction of the subject as self-present, knowing, and unique, and have propounded the material reality of the body as fluid. Iri-garay says in the same reference that with all its animation removed and placed in that abstract transcendent subject, nature is frozen into discrete, inert, solid objects, each identifiable as one and the same thing, which can be counted, measured, possessed, accumulated and traded (1985: 26–28). In *Fireproof*, viewing the deformed body is just not identifying it as a non-normal body but is an example of the gaze of modern scientific reason. The view of the deformed baby by the "normal" characters in the novel can be translated as a normalizing gaze that assesses its object according to some hierarchical standard. Such a view can never be understood as a mere observation. According to the logic of identity, the scientific subject measures an object according to the scales that reduce the plurality of attributes to unity. In relation to the norm, the general attributes of certain subjects are devalued and defined as deviant.

One of the major reasons for the oppression of people with disabilities in society has been the production of aversion to the body marked with differ-ences. It is not only limited to disabled people but is a reaction to the oppres-sed, e.g. blacks, Latinos, Asians, gays, lesbians, and elderly people. They constantly experience avoidance from those whose discursive consciousness aims to treat others with respect and as equals. But we should not reduce the oppression of every group to the same level. Each oppressed group has its own distinct history and identity. It goes without saying that they all share the same status as despised, ugly, leaky bodies which are actually crucial elements of their oppression. Both *Trying to Grow* and *Fireproof* represent the expression of aversion shown by characters during encounters between a non-normal body and a normal body. Certain descriptions about the body of Brit and a newborn baby represent the abnormalcy of the body. This chapter will examine how the normal body reacts to the non-normal body. In *Trying to Grow* the doctor sympathizes with Brit's mother, Sera, and displays a kind attitude toward Brit: "I am afraid I have bad news for you, Sera. Your boy is born with bones brittle as glass" (Kanga 1991: 28), and when Sera smiles and takes this event very lightly, the doctor says, "This is no laughing matter, I assure you. Your son was born with broken femur" (Kanga 1991: 28). Sera responds to him very calmly and says, "then he must use a wheelchair" (Kanga 1991: 28). The doctor is frightened by Sera's attitude and sees it as a sign of madness. For the doctor, the birth of a non-normal baby has to be taken seriously not because he or she will encounter problems due to an inaccessible environment or unbearable pain but because he or she is not normal. Sera's attitude breaks the codifying behavior of society. The doctor advises Sera to provide special care and attention to the baby and says, "call me if you need to talk."

> "I won't need to talk, thank you," said Sera, and the doctor fled, his coat flying behind him. The doctor's suggestion adheres to the exclusionary norms. This is because he asks the mother to take the problem seriously. The doctor, here, functions as a mechanism of a state apparatus that believes in normalizing the differences. Sam whispered into her ear, "you are so brave. When Dolly asked me about her brother, I couldn't speak. I just gave a thumbs-down sign. Darling, darling, are you sure you aren't just putting down a brave act?"
>
> (Kanga 1991: 29)

Sam and the doctor symbolize the agent of normative structure who are averse to the non-normal body. The birth of a deformed baby in the novel *Fireproof* astonishes his father and his adverse attitude is very clear, as shown when he says, "Hold it, why do I sound so bitter? Head nurse had nothing to do with the baby" (Kanga 1991: 21). It is very unfortunate that the birth of a non-normal body is thought of as unnatural.

> It was *my* sperm, it was my wife's egg, it was my wife's womb, it was our nine months and Head Nurse was just a hard-working woman trying to do her job and maybe she was not standing there in judgment, she was only being considerate and her words and gestures were innocent and well-meaning. Which my eyes had seen and my ears had heard, but which I had persuaded myself to turn and twist to sound harsh and brutal. Maybe because it was *I* who was the bitter one. The half-crazed father, frightened and insecure.
>
> (Kanga 1991: 21)

Such examples reflect the adverse attitude of people toward people with disabilities. There is an urge for "perfection" in Sam and Jay's minds that is based upon the discourse of a "normal" body.

What is the rationale behind objectifying the body marked with differences and aversion toward a certain body? Julia Kristeva's seminal book *Powers of Horror* (1982) offers a critique of normal behavior and attitudes. Her concept of "abject" helps us to examine the various shapes that the semiotic/symbolic threshold takes under specific social and historical conditions. Kristeva shows her interest in the effects on subjectivity and meaning when the symbolic does not function. Kristeva suggests that in the the preoedipal stage, our unconscious drives play a significant role in shaping how we form our sense of self through our desires and interactions with the objects around us. This process influences how we desire, protect, and interact with things, contributing to the development of our identity.

The preoedipal process of driving organization opposes the oedipal episode that is structured by the father of the law. There are two heterogeneous aspects of language that are semiotic and symbolic. According to Stacey Keltner,

> The semiotic and symbolic are two modalities of the signifying process that are never experienced as separate but are theoretically separable as two tendencies within signification. The term semiotic is employed in its original etymological sense as a "distinctive mark, trace, index, precursory sign, proof, engraved or written sign or imprint, trace, figuration."
>
> (2011: 22)

The heterogeneous nature of the semiotic does not contribute to meaning in the same way that the symbolic does. The symbolic that may be specified as social gives coherence to subjects, objects, and others. The symbolic process makes a distinction between consciousness and unconsciousness. The idea of the abject emerges before the formation of the ego. The abject refers to the human reaction (horror, vomit) to a threatened breakdown in meaning caused by the loss of the distinction between subject and object or self and other. The primary example of what causes such a reaction is the corpse (which traumatically reminds us of our own materiality); however, other items can elicit the same reaction, e.g., an open wound, faeces, sewage, even the skin that forms on the surface of warm milk (Felluga n.d.). It is the feeling of disgust and loathing that the subject has when it encounters something that is marked as "primal repression" of the subject. It is at the same time fascinating but meaningless and repulsive in an irrational and unrepresentable way. In *Fireproof*, the encounter with a deformed baby fills normal people with disgust. They all scream and suggest that his father throw him out. A nurse tells the father that the baby's life is not worth living, which is actually the primal repression of the nurse. The disgust of the people toward deformed babies represents the hidden insecurity of the able-bodied, and it also shows that the normative order needs to overcome the supposed threat of disability. The hospital staff become aware of the fluid materiality of their corporeality. A deformed baby poses the risk of a return that would disrupt the originary subject.

Kristeva has formulated this theory in the contrast to Lacan's object of desire or the "objet petit a." Whereas the "object petit a" allows a subject to coordinate to his or her desires, thus allowing the symbolic order of meaning and intersubjective community to persist, the abject is radically excluded and as Kristeva explains draws one toward the place where the meaning collapses. What Kristeva thinks about the abject is that it is neither object and nor subject. As Kristeva states in *Power of Horrors*, "abjection preserves what existed in the archaism of pre-objectal relationship, in the immemorial with which a body becomes separated from another body in order to be" (1982: 10). The theory of abjection conceptualizes the form of disability as fear and loathing for the non-disabled self because it exposes the border between the non-disabled self and the disabled self and threatens to dissolve the subject by dissolving the border. At the same time, the disabled self is fascinating, bringing out an obsessed attraction.

The townspeople's comments about the deformed baby—"We have never seen anything like this" (Jha 2006: 39)—reflect the ambiguous experience of a normal subject of deformity and disability. A normal subject cannot cut himself/herself off from it and at the same time it acknowledges the threat felt at the sight of the abnormal. The abject is "what disturbs identity, system, order. What does not respect borders, positions, rules. The in-between, the ambiguous, the composite" (Kristeva 1982: 4). The border between a non-disabled body and a disabled body is very fragile because a non-disabled self experiences the distinctness of a disabled self as a loss and lacks a name or reference for it. In *Fireproof*, people view themselves as having a disabled self within them. They discuss this and say that they themselves are disabled. This refers to the disruption of the identity.

In the age of glocalization, physical experience has become very important to define an individual's identity. Newspapers, magazines, and television all play a vital role in shaping and fashioning the body. It has promoted a consumer culture that constitutes a new conception of self. It de-prioritizes the concept of citizenship, democracy, duty, work, honor, reputation, and morals. Previously, identity formation was more important than personal appearance. Physical looks get more attention than what an individual does. The expression of an individual's identity is shaped by his or her appearance. Once, a person's outward appearance used to indicate their social role, but now it is used to project the inner self of an individual. Anthony Giddens states,

> Under the condition of high modernity, the body has become a self-reflexive project, integral to our sense of who we are. While in pre-modern societies, modifications and adornments of the body were governed by traditional, ritualized meanings, the body in modernity has been secularized and is more frequently treated as a phenomenon to be fashioned as an

expression of an individual's identity, rather than in accordance with some traditionally given system of meaning.

(1991: 99–102)

The consumer culture draws one's attention to designing one's body. The exclusion of people with disabilities is also founded upon their appearance that does not fit in with the concept of normal beauty. The emergence of consumer culture has a de-individualized self of disabled people. It is seen as something that is fragmentary, decentered, and constantly mutating. The world of postmodern fashion discards various guises and eases with the capacity of an individual's adaptation to it. However, mini-narratives have mapped their own graphics in the globe of postmodernity. It breaks the liner and meta-narratives and frames a different range of styles. The various guises that one adopts, Llewelyn Negrin (2008) says, are expressive of a self that exists independently of them; the self is defined through the masquerade—there is no self apart from the masquerade. In *Trying to Grow*, Brit is told to use a chair to move his body even though he is capable of getting around by himself and does not need anyone to assist him.

The form of Brit's body is conceptualized as a disabled person who always needs the assistance of people to enable him to carry out his daily tasks. People pity him because he is disabled. Ruby often talks to him because she finds him an object of interest. In our society, there is an expectation that individuals with physical differences, like Brit and babies with deformities, will be seen as objects of curiosity, pity, and compassion. Society's expectations are a form of masquerade that glosses over the real issues of normal people's felt horror when encountering people with disabilities.

5.4 Disability and the ideology of ability

The postmodern culture leads to the paradoxical nature of the postmodern body, where on the one hand we have various guises, and on the other we have the rhetoric of individualism that grows ever stronger. Brit's fierce sense of individuality, for example, can be pitted against the various guises people want him to adopt so that they feel happy that he is a weakling, dependent upon their pity, and their sense of being "normal" in contrast to his "deformity." We attempt to read a person's appearance as a sign of individual character but it does not evade the question of ambiguous nature disguised in that appearance. Jean Baudrillard says in his book, *Symbolic Exchange and Death*, that signs are free-floating; they do not signify anything beyond themselves (1993: 92). Negrin argues that "items of dress no longer signal attributes such as the class, occupation, or ethnicity of the wearer, but have to a large extent, been stripped of their meanings, as they are pastiched together in unexpected combinations" (2008: 9). There is no certain look that can be identified as supreme because the more authentic it looks the more it signifies another look.

The discourse of identity in terms of bodily appearance for people with disabilities has been debated since the advent of disability studies. Needless to say, the question of identity collapses the hierarchical social order and dispenses with the ascribed social roles. As Zygmunt Bauman argues,

> identity as such is a modern invention. To say that modernity led to the disembedding of identity is to assert a pleonasm, since at no time did identity become a problem: it was a problem from its birth … precisely because of that experience of under-determination and free-floatingness which came to be articulated ex post facto as "disembeddedment."
>
> (1997: 18–19)

The age of modernity is concerned with fixing and stabilizing identity, but as Bauman points out, the post-modern age is concerned with avoiding fixation and the stability of identity. Negrin suggests that fashioning was important to tackle the problem of identity. In the case of women, they had only room for their self-realization because they were prevented from practicing their self-realization in a public place. They exercised their creativity by beautifying their appearance and home.

Body appearance matters in such a way that a person can also assume the identity of an animal. As the theory of representation and structuralists claim that the form of the body constitutes the identity of the person rather than the substance of the body, it does not mean that biological matters of the body do not bear any relevance but rather that the cultural identity of the body is founded upon the physiological structure of the body. Situating this argument in the context of stereotypical representation of people with disabilities in literature, especially with respect to the three novels under study, we can examine how bodies marked with differences are often compared to those of animals. Just because the morphology of certain people resembles that of animals, is it ethical to categorize them as animals? In other words, is the structure of human identity so narrow that it cannot attach to people with disabilities? Who do we need to make any comparison of people with disabilities with any animal or with anything? It is not being argued that animal identity is derogatory or that associating animal identity with people with disabilities is insulting but we need to understand that associating animal identity with people with disabilities is intended to insult the form of disability. In our popular culture, we often observe that people with disabilities are referred to as monkeys, dogs, chickens, penguins, etc. Indira Sinha's well-known novel, *Animal's People*, represents how people with disabilities are stereotyped and negatively interjected with a certain comparison that is not pleasant or positive for them.

Animal's People is set against the background of Bhopal, a district in Madhya Pradesh state where the Bhopal disaster took place in 1984. The narrator of the novel is a victim of the catastrophic chemical leak in Bhopal whose spine does not function properly and he walks with the help of his hands and feet. He is called Animal. The novel discusses the pathetic situation of people due to the Bhopal disaster. Sinha shows how the influence of the West has, in fact, contributed to the disaster. The novel looks at how the American company exploited the Indians and infers that the chemical disaster was the result of industrialization. What is important in the novel is that it examines the dualistic structure permeating the normative culture that emphasizes the radical discontinuity between able-bodied and disabled bodies. It is time to reconsider how popular culture inadvertently supports the marginalization of those considered different, overlooking the crucial dialogue about the harmful dynamics between able-bodied individuals and those with disabilities. *Animal's People* does not actually propagate the stereotypical representation of people with disabilities; instead, it critiques them. In other words, the text has imbibed the attitudes of people and their behavior towards people with disabilities. This text shows that so-called able bodies view people with disabilities as a burden and justifies the domination of normal people over people with disabilities.

There are so many interconnections between the oppression of animals and the oppression of people with disabilities, but my focus is to critique the oppression of people with disabilities and to question the way people with disabilities are caged under an oppressive value system that dictates that certain bodies are able and others are disabled. The story of the novel is recorded in Hindi by Animal himself and has been then translated into English. In the opening of the novel, Animal narrates how a girl and boy sitting under a tree call him an animal and mock him. He often encounters abusive language about his body. Zafar and his group are working for the welfare of the people of Khaufpur. Zafar tells Animal that people cannot be bothered to help sick and poor people. Zafar looks at his back and says, "You yourself are a poison victim ... You queue all day to be seen, the doctor will not examine you because to touch a disabled person would pollute him" (Sinha 2007: 24). Sometimes Animal becomes impatient and attacks and bites people. Their comments such as "*Jaanvar, jungle Jaanvar*" which roughly translates as "animal, wild animal" reflects their mean-spiritedness. It is an insult to Animal. Animal is mocked because of his inability to stand upright like a normal human being. Identifying Animal as a monkey is akin to the separation of the body marked by differences from other people, and has negative and derogatory connotations. Sunaura Taylor (2013) says, "In sideshow culture, disability oppression crashed head-on into racism, sexism, classism, and speciesism." She adds that medical discourses also make such comparisons as elephantiasis, ape-hand syndrome, lobster-claw syndrome, pigeon chest, goosebumps, chicken pox, phocomelia, etc.

> In medical history, gender and racial lines were also often clearly delineated as markers of normalcy and deviance, creating a standard of human physiology that normalized whiteness and often animalized people of color, while simultaneously pathologizing those who physiologically and culturally defied accepted gender dichotomies and roles.
>
> (Taylor 2013: 56)

Clearly, the medical model produces the ideology of the able-bodied that complicates the lives of people with disabilities.

5.5 Disability and the discourse of the non-human being

In *Animal's People* the protagonist Animal is mocked because he cannot walk like a normal person and the fact that he is compared to monkeys is a form of discrimination against him. People in normalized society treat animals as an object of entertainment that are made to serve them. This is the result of unquestioned history and culture that has engendered, gendered, and radicalized ideology in our consciousness. By comparing a man with an animal, people with disabilities are categorized as the ultimate other. Before meeting Zafar, Animal has no work. He used to roam around the village. But after meeting Zafar, he is assigned new work through which he can make a livelihood and can also be helpful to Zafar. The shift in the life of Animal, after meeting Zafar, raises the question of the way the ability of people is valued or it questions the structure of capitalism that values certain capabilities and dismisses other capabilities. Before dealing with the question of capitalism and ethics of difference, it is argued that every life is worth living despite a person having arthrogryposis, blindness, autism, dyslexia, quadriplegia, deafness, etc.

The problems that Animal faces are the result of his difference from other individuals. His difference is identified with animals and that excludes him from the community of normal people. Animals are denigrated because of their difference; that is one predominant reason for their dependency. Some people argue that animals do not develop mental powers and social instincts. Darwin rejected this argument upon which human uniqueness is founded, and he accepted that there are developments of social instincts and mental power in other animals, "the difference in mind between man and the higher animals, great as it is, certainly is one of degree and not of kind" (1989: 130). Ethnologists like Barbara Noske and Norman Whiten confirm the cognitive abilities of non-humans. The logic of dependency can be dismissed with the argument that humans and non-humans coexist together. It is not argued here that there are no differences between humans and non-humans, but rather that both need each other for their existence. Evolutionary biology and community ecology solidly endorse and elaborate on the difference and continuity between humans and non-humans. The theory of "common descent" upholds the view that all forms of life are derived from a single or at most a few common ancestors. The theory of common descent, states Ronnie Hawkins (1998), offers an elegant explanation for the groupings of organisms by degrees of similarity that had been employed by systematists from Aristotle through Linnaeus, combining evidence from such disparate fields as paleontology, comparative anatomy, embryology, animal behavior, and biogeography. Some of the leading scientists agreed with his theory of Darwin because as Ernst Mayr says, "it tied the whole world organic world together, finally making comprehensible the great diversity of planetary life" (1982: 435). What Mayr adds is helpful to understand the way molecular biology appreciated the relatedness of all life forms:

> All organisms possess a historically evolved genetic program, coded in the DNA of the nucleus (or RNA in some viruses), a characteristic uniting all living things, from single-celled prokaryotes to plants, animals, and fungi, and distinguishing them, along with the similarities of their biochemical processes and their complex capacities for self-organization, maintenance, and reproduction, from the nonliving entities around them.
>
> (1988: 16)

To bring this argument is to show the demise of anthropocentrism on which the domination of the body marked with differences and non-humans is founded upon. Undoubtedly, evolutionary sights from such theories necessitate the responsibility of humans towards non-humans or bodies marked with differences but normative culture remains intact.

Animal's contribution to his superior's work and consequently also to society is remarkable. He helps people, gathering valuable information and delivering it to Zafar. Before meeting Zafar, he used to live a miserable life with his dog, Jara, and an old nun called Ma Franci. He is quite bitter about the Bhopal disaster. He narrates frankly the harrowing experiences of the Khaufpuris to the journalist. He is aware of what is happening in the minds of people, in their psychological domain of experience. "People see the outside, but it's inside where the real things happen, no one looks in there, maybe they don't dare" (Sinha 2007: 11). He wants to see an improvement in the pathetic condition of the people and spies on Elli Barber who hopes to open a free clinic in Khaufpur so that the poison victims can avail themselves of the medical facilities. But people do not trust her, and Animal tries to find out the reason why for Zafar. The narrative of Animal counts the struggle of people against the system and politicians; indeed, he does not have "just an ear but an eye for meaning" (Sinha 2007: 35). Ali Faqri suggests to him, "If you act powerless, you are powerless, the way to get what you want is to demand it" (Sinha 2007: 19). He gets courage from his instructions and fights against poverty and starvation. Nisha calls him "a true human being" (Sinha 2007: 364). Nisha acknowledges his ability to acquire new languages and new things. Animal lives a life of dignity and respect. This is because Zafar values him and uses his experience for his work. He applauds his work and never undervalues his capacities. Zafar coexists with him but does not exploit animals. With the logic of help or dependency, people start exploiting people with disabilities. The social contract theory that is founded upon the logic of mutual advantage has failed to provide justice to people with disabilities. It presupposes that people are equal in terms of their mental and physical power in the state of nature. It fails to notice that there is asymmetry among human beings. We cannot put man, woman, or animal in the same category. Martha Nussbaum (2007) argues in her seminal book, *Frontiers of Justice*, that justice will only be possible if cooperation exists without advantage, and that human cooperation should be predominated upon love, compassion, and respect. The representation of society in this novel indicates that we have yet to reach that stage of justice.

People with disabilities are victimized by the limited interpretation of the concept of independence. As Sunaura Taylor says, "Independence is more about choice and civil rights than it is about pure self-sufficiency" (2013: 37). Paul Longmore (2003) says in the same context that it is interdependence, not independence, and community, not physical autonomy, which should be supported and recognized as essential for sustaining a just society. *Animal's People* questions the normative rhetoric that emphasizes independence and self-sufficiency. Ma Franci is a character in the novel who works in the orphanage where Animal grew up. She is very kind to every child and is a mother figure for Animal. After the accident, she loses her understanding of the language and feels that everyone is speaking nonsense. Despite her inability to understand language, she goes from door to door and helps the sick and injured persons. Another important character of the novel is Zafar who has left his study and work and is seen helping the citizens of Khaufpur. He comes across many problems and difficulties, but he is determined to help people appalled by the company. Nisha, Zafar's fiancée, is a very kind-hearted woman who never feels exasperated by the odd behavior of Animal and accepts him as a family member, and he also does not have any issues with them. What Sinha advocates here with the voices of these characters is that interpersonal dependence is relative. It is suggested that we are all dependent on one another. Michel Oliver, a disability theorist, argues that

> Professional tends to define independence in terms of self-care activities such as washing, dressing, toileting, cooking, and eating without assistance. Disabled people, however, define independence differently, seeing it as the ability to be in control of and make decisions about one's life, rather than doing things alone one's life, rather than doing things alone or without help.
>
> (1991: 91)

Being independent does not infer physical self-sufficiency; rather, it welcomes choices for the people so that they can make their own decisions.

People with disabilities are seen as a burden on society. Their impairment is viewed as the reason for their dependency. The newborn baby in the novel *Fireproof* is socially excluded because of his impairment; his father feels that he will be a burden on him throughout his life. In the novel *Animal's People*, Animal is not seen as a burden on Nisha's family and works interdependently. It is not the impairment that becomes the reason for burden but rather the impaired system of social services that hardly facilitates accessibility to people with disabilities. Dependence exacerbates exploitation. The able body gets the excuse to exploit disabled people. People argue that it is nature that offers an opportunity to use animals in the same way that big animals eat small animals. It is a natural lifecycle for survival. People fail to understand the inequalities among living beings. Nature should not be used as a rhetorical tool to exploit non-human beings. Through the lens of animal studies, we can ask whether is it justified to kill animals or to exploit fewer humans (people with disabilities are categorized sometimes as non-humans). Nicolette Hahn argues in her book, *The Righteous Porkchop*, that "it is normal and natural for animals to eat other animals, and since we humans are part of nature, it's very normal for humans to be eating animals" (2009: 45). A very pertinent question that Sunaura Taylor asks regarding the moral obligation of the human being toward non-humans is: can we ignore the fact that humans mete out violence on other humans too? It goes without saying that it is natural that big animals eat small animals and they have to do it for their survival. But a question of ethics can also be raised. Is it ethical to kill or exploit animals or non-humans? The characters in *Animal's People* are ethical toward each other, and they do not exploit anyone. Disability oppression is considered natural and the superiority of the able body is thought to be natural. Appealing to nature for the justification of disability oppression strengthens the conservative power structure that has been intact throughout history. We should recognize the subjectivity of others and should make ethical choices. Impairment is not naturally a bad thing. Can one argue that stairs are more natural than ramps? Can one justify the logic of not providing lifts in the buildings? Disability activists argue that it is mere politics of independency that justifies slavery, colonization, patriarchy, disability oppression, etc. History tells us that women were dominated in the name of their dependency on men. It was argued that slaves were dependent on their masters. Independency becomes a rhetorical tool to exploit women, animals, and disabled people in the name of help, concern, and care. Their dependency is a cause of the difference in the body. It is universally accepted that there are differences in society. People with disabilities have not been considered as differentiated masses; rather, everyone is ethically responsible to acknowledge their differences. They are differentially oppressed by our actions. Certain alterations in our actions may lead to the betterment of disabled others. Zafar is living in the same society where the American company has exploited the poor people of Khaufpur and left them helpless. But the action of Zafar has left some hope for the people of Khaufpur and has dramatically improved the situation of Animal. Zafar uses euphemisms such as "specially abled" (Sinha 2007: 23) which is in common use nowadays. Zafar employs him to spy on the "government, munsipal" (Sinha 2007: 27). Zafar tells him to report anything unusual that goes on at Khaufpur. Zafar appreciates Animal's speech, "An Animal must use its mouth, no other tools does it have" (Sinha 2007: 26). We notice here that disrespected and poverty-stricken disabled Animal is called "Zamispond, jeera-jeera seven" (Sinha 2007: 94). His status improves in Khaufpur and he earns his livelihood and maintains his dignity and self-sufficiency. Although the actions of doctors, nurses, and the common people in the novel, *Fireproof*, have left the father of the newborn baby apprehensive, the actions of the dwarf, another character in the novel, make Jay feel emotional about his baby and he finds himself in a better situation. In the novel, *Trying to Grow*, Brit was not allowed to play outside and was not permitted to be friends with anyone. Later, Cyrus befriends him; as a result, Brit lives a life of happiness and does not confine himself to his room. What is contended here is not to live a normal life but rather how certain modifications in our stylized actions may help us to build a friendly environment for people with disabilities or any minority identity people. The help received from Cyrus and Zafar, respectively, makes the lives of Brit and Animal easier for them.

Animal's People advocates to cut across any hierarchies that fail to provide space to anyone, be that a man or woman, or an able body or a disabled body. It breaks down the caste and class hierarchies, and the narrative style that Animal uses reveals the gaps and silences in the dominant discourses. Sinha uses it deliberately so that the government's failure can be brought to the notice of the people. She uses Animal as a narrator to portray the effect of the tragedy, that even after 20 years, people still have breathing problems. Animal's various skills question the paradigm of ability and shatter the innate hierarchies of ability/disability. Animal is not projected as a Hindu, a Muslim, a Brahmin, or a Christian that represents his belief in humanity rather than in any religion. Animal questions all the religious dogmas. Somraj Tryambak Punekar, the father of Nisha, advocates non-violence and runs a "poison relief committee" to help those "still coughing their lungs up so many years after that night" (Sinha 2007: 33). He feels that the company is guilty and instructs people to utilize the facilities provided by Elli's free clinic. When Elli declares before everybody, "I'm not ashamed to be American, there is plenty to be proud of in America, there is good and bad like everywhere else … I'm here to help" (Sinha 2007: 158) slowly people start coming to her clinic. Somaraj gets the feeling that Elli wants to treat people voluntarily. He fights against the oppressive order and defies the caste and class divisions. Nisha carries the values of her father and fights for justice for the victims. She does not discriminate against Animal because of his poverty and his differences. She provides him with shelter and a means of making a livelihood. She overlooks the distinctions created by religion and plans to settle down with her fiancée Zafar who is a Muslim, near the coast of Ratnagiri. Nisha actively participates in the protests and raises her voice against the politicians and defective legal order. The representation of Nisha and Ma Franci questions the gender ideology and resists the patriarchal codes. Elli is an outsider who works for the people who are suffering. Her efforts make us think about the barriers created by caste, class, gender, and country. She sets an example that everyone should stand up against the oppressive and unjust order. Ma Franci is loved by Hindus and Muslims alike. She is another example who breaches the barriers of insider/outsider. Like other women, Pyare Bai, Devika, and Huriya Bai, Ma Franci does not hesitate to protest against the injustice and in one instance a member of her group slaps a senior cop and says,

'We are flames, not flowers. With our brooms, we will beat the Kampani ... sweep them out for Khaufpur ... India ... [our] existence" (Sinha 2007: 311). Sinha represents different familial ideologies that are against "modern" women. By depicting these characters, she demonstrates the responsibility of women and speaks on behalf of them so that they can be part of the reconfiguration of the global ethic that recognizes the value of freedom and justice, and encourages civil society to care for the body marked with differences.

There are certain instances where the ideology of ability prevails. Animal listens to certain people who are both hostile and friendly to him. He listens to strange voices and stories that advise Animal in order to save him from getting into fights. In one instance, Elli asks Animal about his deformity, and the strange voices tell him that "[s]he will change your life!" (Sinha 2007: 72). Such instances make him feel that disability is something unwanted and there are ways to be cured. Animal plays Kabbadi and defeats his opponents. Taking part in sport is a physiological practice promoted by ability ideology to overcome his disability. However, it cannot be said that Sinha represents the dualism of ability/disability. The representations of Zafar, Nisha, Animal, Ma Franci, Elli, and Somraj insist on collective action to construct a democratic society that may give equal opportunity to everyone regardless of their class, caste, religion, or body. Sinha opposes the deceptions and silences propagated by oppressive structures. Zafar's actions (i.e., his care of Animal) carry forward the movement of transformation wherein the belief in brotherhood and equality lies.

5.6 Disability and subjectivity

The intervention of postmodern and post-structural philosophy questions the transcendental rationality that does not appreciate the multiplicity of the subjects. Postmodern feminist N. Katherine Hayles (1999) contends that everything we know in nature is a human construct. Hayle urges us to reject any kind of objectivism and to acknowledge that positionalities, language, history, culture, disciplinary tradition, gender, class, race, and other contextual factors have relevance. It affects us because we are involved with it, not because we are aloof from it. She emphasizes the acknowledgment of interactivity to understand the way the knowable world represents the privilege of the patriarchal structure. Acknowledgment of interactivity shatters the illusion of "metaphysics of presence"—a philosophical position that maintains that each body has an essence that is ontologically (or definitionally) prior to its actions and attributes and considers this essence the primary means of determining value established by transcendent rationality (Butler 1990: 23–31). Appreciation of interactivity make us think about the particulars of actual existence. Hayles argues that

> [i]nteraction is possible only because we are embodied, and the precise conditions of our embodiment—which for humans include that portion of the electromagnetic spectrum which we utilize for sight, as well as our

upright posture, grasping hands, binocular vision, and so forth, in conjunction with our individual and cultural contexts—have everything to do with the nature of those interactions and thus with how we construct our knowledge of the world.

(1999: 56)

Embodying this approach allows us to think that every being is an embodied being and constructs different worlds through their embodied interactions with their surroundings. Hayles' philosophy of interactivity does not allow us to exterminate other bodies because extermination of the other bodies stops the articulation of certain rich experiences and varieties.

Postmodernist philosophy dismantles the notion of the transcendental subject that recognizes the multiplicity of subjects within the sphere of nature. Donna Haraway states in her well-known book *Simians, Cyborgs, and Women: The Reinvention of Nature* (2003) that we are experiencing breakdowns of the strict boundaries. The interaction of different organisms like human and machine, human and animal, etc. dismisses the illusion of a unified rational subject. We do not have to feel frightened and find it irrational rather it helps break down the maze of dualism that privileges an able body. "Cyborg imagery embodies a dream, not of a common language, but of a powerful infidel heteroglossia allowing all that has been 'other' to speak" (Haraway 2003: 81).

The concept of "cyborg imagery" decenters the positionality of the transcendental subject and as result the hegemony of the able body is deconstructed through which other subjectivities are ignored. Zafar acknowledges Animal's subjectivity and allows him to make decisions in the broader framework of public action, social practices, and habits. Zafar dismantles any power relationship among individual and social groups. By recognizing and respecting the differences between Animal and other groups, Zafar undermines any oppression. Animal does not assimilate himself with other groups and feels comfortable with his sense of identity with animals because his appearance is similar to that of an animal. Zafar frames a social group where different cultural forms, practices, and ways of life are welcomed. He believes in improving the structure that oppresses people. He is fighting against the Western system that has ruined the lives of many people. It appears that Zafar has imbibed Young's theory that "[c]auses [for oppression] are embedded in the unquestioned norm, habits, and symbols, in the assumption underlying institutional rules and the collective consequence of following those rules" (1990: 41). An analysis of the oppression produced by the medical people or various characters in *Fireproof* reveals that it is not their intention to hurt Jay with their feverish comments about his deformed baby or to discriminate against the deformed baby; rather, their discriminatory acts are driven by the normative ideology. They do not, in fact, see themselves as the agents of oppression. The normative ideology does not make them aware that they are marginalizing certain embodied beings.

Iris Young (2011) describes five kinds of oppression applied to human groups in her book *Justice and the Politics of Difference*: exploitation, marginalization, powerlessness, cultural imperialism, and violence. People with disabilities are exploited not only in terms of their space and rights but also in the way their labor goes unnoticed. Moreover, marginalization, a manifestation of the mind/ nature dualism that historically has led to exclusion from full citizenship, if not from the means of making a living altogether, of all those whose reason was questionable or not fully developed could be seen to apply to poor people, women, the mad and the feebleminded and children (Young 2011: 54).

People with disabilities are essentially powerless in the able society. Brit refuses to meet Wagha Baba but his father forces him to go. In many ways, Brit sees himself as a tool in the hands of his family because of his brittle bones. Every decision is made by his family on behalf of Brit who can make decisions but is deprived of them. According to Young, cultural imperialism means to experience how the dominant meanings of society render the particular perspectives of one's own group invisible at the same time as they stereotype one's group and mark out it as the Other. On the opening page of the novel, *Animal's People*, Sinha represents the perspectives of normal people toward Animal, how they define Animal as a monkey, and stereotype the entire groups of disabled people. It goes without saying that people with disabilities do experience violence. It goes unnoticed because people with disabilities are characterized as non-human or subhuman. Young states that "politics of difference confronts this fear and aims for an understanding of group difference as indeed ambiguous, relational, shifting, without clear borders, as no longer otherness, exclusive opposition, but specificity variation, heterogeneity" (Young 2011: 170–171).

Literary discourses show that the built hierarchy represents a territory that binarizes ability/disability and at the same time oppose the normative spaces through their rhetoric. The metaphor being part of a rhetoric helps people to understand the thoughts of others. *Moving Violation* is a memoir by John Hockenberry (1996) in which he writes that metaphor in art can be used as a tool to bring about a revolution. He is a man with a disability who shares his experiences and enlightens us through different cultural definitions of the words. Each word has cultural baggage and has been framed and filtered by the cultural institution. Discourse about disability has also been infected by medical institutions that inscribe and control the experiences of people with disabilities. The novels selected for this study lay bare some of the rhetoric upon which cultural understanding of disability has been predicated. They also represent some of the uses of language that offer a more inclusive view of the human experience. Enabling usage of rhetoric has the potential to constitute certain bodies as disabled as well as able depending upon the context. The rhetorical nature of narrative does not contribute to making something less real or less true but rather has the power to bring about a revolution.

They also help to bridge the gap and to challenge the binaries. It is worth quoting the Canadian author and disability activist Catherine Frazee who writes about the metaphor that forms ideas of normal and abnormal, in this case the "normal body"—a phrase I adopt here because it is widely understood, even if it is rooted in values I do not share:

> The normal body expresses itself very much like on good prose. Its sentences are correctly formed, having all of the necessary components; subject, verb-in-agreement, modestly arranged participles, and punctuation conforming to elaborate rituals of form and syntax. Like language, the body can be complex, but if it is constructed according to the norm, it works largely because everyone agrees about what the norm is. But my body does not speak in sentences laid end-to-end and stacked in sturdy paragraphs. My not-so-normal body speaks in poetry, not prose-in sparing words, in careful disarray.
>
> (2000: 90)

This quotation lays bare the use of metaphors that becomes part of body politics. The metaphor works as a bridge that carries the meaning from one thing to another. Aristotle rightly states in his famous book *Rhetoric* (1984) that "we learn above all from metaphors." A metaphor creates new knowledge; it can never be reduced to mere words, but rather it implicates new meaning.

In *Fireproof*, a girl shouts at the infant baby, "Look, what's he got inside the bag, look, look, it is some kind of an *animal* ... it stinks, it looks like a *monkey*" (Jha 2006: 254 and 255; emphasis added). The girl uses the words "monkey" and "animal" as metaphors, and she uses them unconsciously. In *Animal's People*, the orphanage children start calling the narrator *jaanvar* (animal) unconsciously. Through this process, the metaphor is neutralized to such an extent that it starts to function literally. The use of the words animal, *jaanvar*, *andha* (blind), and *kana* (one-eyed) is not a form of disinterestedness; rather, it carries constructed sociocultural meanings. One can argue that metaphor plays a vital role in an individual's social and cultural existence. Metaphor connects people with their experiences. We understand metaphor because we share the same experience. According to Lakoff and Johnson, "Metaphor imposes a structure on real life, through the creation of new correspondences in experience" (2003: 91). Here, metaphor is taken to extend into the body. It constructs the body. The word *jaanvar* is imposed on people with disabilities and constitutes them as an animal. It explains how we live in the world and share our experiences. People with disabilities are looked upon as animals. Novelists represent the assumption that people have in terms of people with disabilities. Moreover, the metaphor also challenges the assumptions. It goes without saying that there is no fixed, scientific, and true knowledge about the language. Richard Gwyn (1999) says that the study and pursuit of metaphor is a means of questioning the assumptions, descriptions, and definitions of a literalistic and constricting outlook on reality. Adding to that Donna Haraway says, "Metaphors are tools and tropes ... the point is to learn to remember that we might have been otherwise, and might yet be, as a matter of the embodied fact" (2003: 123). They suggest that society and reality are very flexible and malleable. Metaphors turn out to be a way to critique the existing epistemology about people with disabilities and make us aware of the embedded cultural meaning in the language that looks down on the existence of the body marked with differences.

A pertinent question that needs to be asked is why metaphors about disability always hide the individual's humanity? Why do they always represent them as natural and scientific? Why are they constantly associated with negative meaning? One may say that it is a politics of ideology of ability that needs its definition in the binary opposition of disability. Needless to say, those who define it have not experienced disability. A girl in the novel, *Fireproof*, has not experienced how it feels to be treated as an animal. Orphanage children are not necessarily aware of the diversity of disability. They are ignorant about the violence that they commit. As the story develops, Animal stops feeling that he is a human being and is proud to be an animal. Undoubtedly, his feelings are the result of the normalizing structure of the society that aims to capitalize on the body and ignores the differences among the people. His narration highlights the existence of extraordinary bodies and the embodiment of diverse bodies and represents alternative subjectivities. Animal challenges the singular, dominant, and totalizing views of embodiment and experience. By accepting the metaphor Animal ironically questions the normative assumptions inherent within the dominant discourse.

Words such as "retarded," "deformed," and "crippled" are used in novels to describe abnormal, mental, or physical states. As Raymond Gibbs writes, "There are important links between people's recurring bodily experiences, their metaphorical projections of these image schemas to better understand many abstract concepts, and the language used to talk about these concepts" (1994: 135). Here, Gibbs suggests that there is a connection between the body and metaphor. They are made real by the process of internalization. Throughout the novel, *Trying to Grow*, the main character is called Brit due to his brittle bones. Discourse about Brit is written by his brittle bones. It is not that the body and thought are not embodied together, but rather that the peculiar nature of the body shapes the real possibility of conceptualization and categorization.

The question of language is important here to focus on the processes and conditions of being disabled. Language constitutes the cognitive understanding of the world and indicates our values, meaning, and knowledge. Language does not act as a mirror that is able to reflect an independent object world; instead, it is better understood as a tool that we use to achieve our purposes (Rorty 1980: 89). Words like "animal" do not depict the world of the narrator, but rather they constitute it. Language can be thought of as a resource that "lends form" to ourselves and the world out of the contingent and disorderly flow of everyday talk and practice (Shotter 1993: 78). However, if language fails to reflect an independent objective world then it is also not true that it directly represents a pre-existent *I*. It constitutes the *I* and it is brought into being through the process of signification. People with disabilities are constituted through the regulatory power of discourse. The disabled person is not outside of language; instead, he or she is signified as an animal.

The contrast between an eternal metaphysical self and a contingent linguistic self has been explored through debates about essentialism and anti-essentialism (Hall 1990: 92). Essentialists believe that identity exists and can be expressed through symbolic representation. Such arguments strongly believe in an essence of masculine identity based on similarity of experience and expressed through representation of men in film, magazines, and literature. Anti-essentialists argue that identity is a process of becoming built from points of similarity and difference. There is no such essence of identity that is meant to be discovered, but rather a cultural identity of a person is constantly being produced within the vectors of resemblance and distinction. Animal's self-identity as a *jaanvar* is not an essence but a continually shifting description of people. He possesses an identity of especially abled when Nisha and Zafar realize his importance in their struggle for the justice of the village people. In his first meeting with Zafar, the narrator, Animal, introduces himself as an animal and denies possessing the identity of a human. "My name is Animal … I'm not a fucking human being, I've no wish to be one" (Sinha 2007: 23). Zafar dislikes teasing disabled people. Animal is identified as a specially abled person because he is different from the other villagers who cannot do what he can do. "It means okay you don't walk on two legs like most people, but you have skills and talents that they don't" (Sinha 2007: 23). His identity as an animal lies in his resemblance to an animal and in his difference from human beings who are considered respectable and dignified. The meaning of identity categories is held to be subject to continual deferral through the never-ending processes of supplementarity or difference (Derrida 1967: 87). Meaning has no end and remains unfinished, although strategically positioning identity makes meaning possible. An anti-essentialist position, Hall argues, points to the political nature of identity as production and to the possibility of multiple, shifting, and fragmented identities which can be articulated together in a variety of ways (1990: 65).

The issue of sexuality is a major theme in all three novels under study, and they explore how the sexual subjectivity of people with disabilities is denied in our contemporary society. Animal and Brit do not express their erotic desires; their desire is accompanied by a certain anxiety. The society in which Brit and Animal live refuses to recognize them as sexual subjects. The differential embodiment of them becomes a practical concern for society and it prohibits their sexuality. Brit, every day, confronts rejection and pity that makes him express his masculinity through the varied expression of sexuality that is treated as an act of a juvenile. Brit is frustrated with the feeling that there is no one who realizes his masculinity. His non-normative body is assumed to be the nonstandard for sexual agency and disqualifies him from the discourses of pleasure associated with sexuality. The question that I raise here is the denial of any form of sexuality that is both radically anomalous and resistant to the normative form of sexuality. The exclusion of people with disabilities from the very notion of sexual subjectivity begs two questions: (1) why is the body marked with differences politically and culturally devalued? And (2) what is so much at stake in the cultural imaginary that closes down the possibility of expressing alternative forms of sexuality?

The anomalous embodiment of Animal and Brit poses a putative threat to normative sexual relations. Consider the fact that Brit and Animal are mere manifestations of different forms of disability. Their embodiment is visibly anomalous and challenges the normative expectations of the human body. People staring at Animal in disgust and Brit not being allowed to roam around the city presuppose that differential embodiment may threaten the boundaries of what Kristeva calls "the self's clean and proper body" (1982: 71). Shildrick contends that while the prevailing belief in the self-contained body as the foundation of individual autonomy has been firmly established since Descartes, most people actively employ both conscious and subconscious methods to shield themselves from perceived threats of intrusion or overwhelming influence by other bodies. The inhabitants of Khaufpur village feel that their sovereign self may disintegrate if it encounters the Animal other. Zafar and Nisha's suggestion to Animal that he should behave like a normal person is an attempt to negotiate within a strict set of normative rules and regulations. Brit's desire for Cyrus is represented as a locus of anxiety that, undoubtedly, disturbs the normativities of everyday life.

> I wanted Cyrus: his mocking mouth, his quiet eyes, his thigh and hair and cock. Now, if he were someone else, someone who thought life was the food you ate and the movies you saw and not the winds that blew inside your head; or someone who got out of a taxi without thanking the driver; or someone who blew his nose into his hand instead of his hanky, then I wouldn't have given a damn if he looked like Shashi Kapoor or Sean Connery or whoever; not if he had cock that would have made him blue movie star.
>
> (Kanga 1991: 155)

The paradox of sexuality is that it protects the disciplinary mechanism and at the same time breaches it. The invisible forces of pleasure are less controllable and not only oppose the disciplinary mechanism but also find an alternative way to let it out. The desire of Brit for Cyrus represents his repressed sexual feelings that become uncontrollable. The interaction of Cyrus and Brit represents the limitations of normative standards of embodiment. The uncertain nature of people with disabilities disrupts the normal arena of sexuality and the anxiety that it produces registers not only negative but also generates ambiguous nature of the desire. It can be strongly argued that the desire of people with disabilities must be respected and should always be provided with proper structure to get it manifested.

We noticed the way people with disabilities are subjected to the discourse of sympathy, pity, and horror. They are constituted as Others to maintain the normative order. By associating pain with people with disabilities, their suffering is ignored. Dominant discourses of pain frame pain as a problem that renders life unworthy of living. It goes without saying that there are very few novels that deal with the issue of disability, but the novels were chosen for this study unravel the discourse of desire with respect to people with disabilities. The theory of Kristeva helped in formulating the productivity of any form of anomalous embodiment and questioning the boundaries of the self's clean and proper body. We experience that people with disabilities are generally associated with animals, and this association implies people's stereotypical attitudes toward people with disabilities. In the next chapter, the cinematic texts will be analyzed to investigate the attitudes of people against women with disabilities and will engage with their autonomy and sexuality.

Chapter 6

Disability and Hindi Cinema

Cinema is an important medium through which stereotypical images of marginalized social groups are constructed and circulated. We need to identify them and deconstruct stereotypical images of disabled figures to examine the shifts in social attitudes toward marginalized groups. Cinema as a powerful medium also reflects the attitudes about people with disabilities that are embedded in society. It influences people to such an extent that people naturalize attitudes built into cinematic images. It is also very important, therefore, to analyze how cinema has repeatedly produced negative images of people with disabilities. By deconstructing the cinematic images, we can figure out the socioeconomic and political factors that prevail behind the typical presentations of stereotypes.

Many Hindi movies like *Koshish* (1972), *Majboor* (1974), *Amar Akbar Anthony* (1977) portray people with disabilities as objects of pity and as a burden on our society. Joyojeet Pal highlights three particular trends in cinema: "disability as punitive, disability as dependence, disability as disequilibrium and disability as maladjustment" (2012: 6). Such descriptions of disability reinforce the understanding of the medical model that defines disability as an individual problem. Constructed images are presumed by audiences as self-evident and truthful in what they reveal about impairment, whereas such images fail to represent reality and are trapped in the views of social constructionists. It is a sociopolitical and economic context of a particular nation that prevails upon the cultural images of marginalized social groups.

I have chosen the movies *Lafangey Parindey* (*Cheeky Birds*) (2010) and *Black* (2005) for this study to question the stereotypical images of women with disabilities and at the same time to extrapolate the normative oppression that always resists the desire for the liberation of subjugated voices. Moving on from the stereotypical representation of women with disabilities, this chapter will question the notion of ability and will engage with the issues of masculinity and nationalism that resist the emergence of the body marked with differences. It will contest the representation of disability as an object of pathology and disability identity constructed as the "other" of the normal self. Needless to say, most movies strengthen the social construction of normality and thus abnormality is constructed as a means of social, national, and political order. We

DOI: 10.4324/9781032722054-6

seldom find Hindi movies in which sign language is celebrated. A person who has never encountered the lives of the deaf will find deaf people strange and unacceptable. To look at the representation of disability, we also need to investigate the way in which ability is represented. The two categories, ability and disability, complement each other.

Indian movies reflect on the experience of disability in India that is historically distinct from the Western Judeo-Christian tradition. Post-colonialism, the exclusion and stigmatization of people with disabilities in India had similarities with that of people with disabilities in the West. Post-independence movies such as *Koshish (Effort)*, *Satte pe Satta (Seven on Seven)*, *and Aankhen (Eyes)*, projected people with disabilities as beggars which we do not observe in the ancient texts.

6.1 Disability discourse in *Lafangey Parindey*

The movies selected for this study represent disability as a pathological subject and try to normalize those figures. Pinky Palker, a major character in the movie *Lafangey Parindey*, dreams of winning a television talent show that offers 50 lakhs in prize money. Despite her lowly surroundings, she becomes a roller skater but unfortunately she is knocked down and blinded in a freak car accident caused by One-Shot-Nandu with whom she later falls in love. The rest of the film is about the romance between Nandu and Pinky, and Pinky's struggle to *overcome* her disability. She is assisted in her efforts by Nandu who has given up boxing to impress her. What has to be noticed here is the way disability is viewed in Pinky's surroundings and by Pinky herself. By following Nandu's suggestions, which is a form of normative technology, she tries to overcome her disability. It goes without saying that Pinky's conscious attempt to normalize her body demonstrates the stigma associated with disability.

Normalization is a process that attempts to erase the marks that differentiate the body as abnormal or disabled and it communicates the values of the body politicized in a particular society. Normalization assures us that the appearance of the particular body should not be distinct because of its difference and its presence should not be felt as a stranger. According to Erving Goffman,

> When a stranger comes into our presence, then, first appearances are likely to enable us to anticipate his category and attributes, his "social identity"— to use a term that is better than "social status" because personal attributes such as "honesty" are involved, as well as structural ones, like "occupation."
> (Goffman 1963: 29)

Pinky, who has occupied a disabled identity, has to transform her body so that it can meet the normative expectations that her surroundings anticipate from her. Her skating coach expresses his unwillingness to work with her. There is a tendency to isolate disabled characters from their able-bodied peers as well as from each other. Pinky's family and friends anticipate that she cannot be normal or, in other words, she can never be a roller skating champion. In the film Pinky represents an abnormal and wretched human being whose life is marked by a lack of success. Society is not aware that it has made a *demand* for a normal life that actually produces violence on the body of Pinky. It raises an active question about the *demands* that society makes and does not bother whether these demands can be fulfilled or not. These demands push aside the question of how the body *is* but rather bring forth the question of how the body *ought to be*. And if a person fails to meet those demands, they are reduced in our minds, as Goffman says, from a whole and usual person to a tainted and discounted one. Such attributes given to a body are called stigma which produces a discrediting effect. Pinky qualifies for a different set of attributes that may not be needed in her surroundings, but she shares the same language of relationships which she used to share before she possessed a disabled identity. There is a need to highlight the importance of the language of relationships rather than attributes which are not really needed. "An attribute that stigmatizes one type of possessor can confirm the usualness of another, and therefore is neither creditable nor discreditable as a thing in itself" (Goffman 1963: 67). The attitudes that her friends have toward Pinky respond to the language of sympathy and pity and undoubtedly they also correspond to a stigmatized identity. Pinky attempts to correct her condition by devoting much of her time to overcoming her shortcomings and attempts to meet her society's demands and expectations. It is not only her dream to win the talent show that helps her to make these attempts but also her desire to look like a normal person is another strategy provided by the model of normalization. In the representation of Pinky's character in the movie *Lafangey Parindey*, it can be noticed that she feels uneasy about her acquisition of a new stigmatized self and wants to discard it.

Goffman often uses disability as an example of stigmas in his book, *Stigma: Notes on the Management of Spoiled Identity* (1963), which has influenced disability studies scholars to understand the way people with disabilities have been socially devalued. Goffman reflects on the social and psychological burdens that people with disabilities bear. Susan Wendell (1996) questions Goffman's understanding of the generalizations made about people with disabilities. She believes that he misses an important difference between people with disabilities and other stigmatized people. She states, "Most stigmatized people are members of stigmatized groups that have subcultures within which the stigma may be made irrelevant or at least ameliorated by the group's own values" (Wendell 1996: 59). Most (but not all) people with disabilities grow up with non-disabled people and/or are constantly surrounded by them, absorbing their values and assumptions; they have little or no contact with subcultures that de-stigmatize or value their difference positively from the point of view of the non-disabled (Zola 1993: 167). The stigma attached to women with disabilities is more intense and effective than that to men with disabilities because they live in a patriarchal culture. Moreover, women as a category are already ostracized.

Social norms are more oppressive for them because of the dominance of patriarchal ideologies and practices.

Social norms signify forms of social behavior that are based on sets of more or less implicit social rules that exist independently of individuals and exercise a coercive influence. Social norms are prescriptive; they chart out principles that are used to judge or direct human conduct. It makes the body comply with the usual level of attainment and performance. Hacking says that the word "normal" became the most powerful ideological tool of the 20th century (1999: 78). The normal body is constituted through the exclusion of others, i.e., criminals, mad people, disabled people, etc. The practices of exclusion delegitimize certain bodies and their behaviors. The next question that arises is what role does power play in the practice of inclusive living? Foucault's (2003) analysis of power is important to understand the way power is administered on human bodies to calculate and manage both individuals and the population. The main role of power is to ensure life and put it into order. It subjugates the bodies in positive and productive ways. "The emergent bio-power brought life and its mechanism into the realm of explicit calculations and made knowledge-power an agent of transformation of human life" (Drinkwater 2005: 232). In the movie *Black*, Michelle's parents appoint Balraj to educate Michelle and teach her how to live and behave in society. Michelle, who is deaf and blind, does not often follow what her teacher dictates to her. The modern form of bio-power bears the responsibility to produce her body as docile and productive for the normative society, which is why Balraj as a state apparatus conducts her body. As with all forms of disciplinary processes deployed by Balraj, the question of right and wrong is suspended in favor of an understanding of power as productive. Michelle's life is managed and valued even though it is against her will. Here, we notice the paradoxical situation; the bio-power that claims to be productive turns out to be repressive which is witnessed in the resistance of Michelle who constantly rejects Balraj's instructions. The constant resistance of Michelle to putative norms makes us aware of the limitations for people with disabilities posed by the boundaries of normative structures. Pinky, who eventually adopts a disabled identity, is also trained by Nandu to perform as a non-disabled body.

> Power is a mode of action which does not act directly or immediately on others. Instead, it acts upon their actions: an action upon an action, on existing actions or on those which may arise in the present or the future.
>
> (Foucault 1982: 220)

Power acts on the actions of Michelle and Pinky so that they can be useful to society. Society and the individual complement each other. The modern government is concerned with the wellbeing of the population in general and of the individual in particular. Therefore, it manages the lives of people in such a way that they can be productive for society. It aims to channelize the individual so that they fit into a uniformed structure of the normative that does not open the space for differences. New disciplines like statistics, demography, epidemiology, and biology have emerged to make the analysis of the process of life possible on the level of populations and to govern individuals through practices of correction, exclusion, normalization, therapeutics, and optimization. Such practices are enabled by bio-politics and oppress people with disabilities. The voices of people with disabilities, who have been disabled by society because they have not been heard by society, are silenced and their voices are acknowledged as rejected knowledge. The perspective of disability represents the human condition as a condition of dependency and human dependency contradicts the ideologies of rational autonomous agency of modernity. Michelle and Pinky both seek generous support from society and want to live with their disabled conditions that were rejected by the agents of modernity who believe in self-dependency and autonomous positions. The very definition of self-independent and autonomy fulfills the dream of bio-politics and silences the voices from below. Being independent and autonomous is to live with one's choices rather than to comply with what modern normative belief propagates. Pinky and Michelle are left with no choices and voices but they have to adopt what Nandu and Balraj teach them and they have to listen to what they say.

The violence and oppression which Pinky and Michelle experience go unnoticed by society. The Hindi movies *Lafangey Parindey* and *Black* help us to understand the way violence is generated and perpetuated by society. The corporeality of disability is never understood as natural as the corporeality of the non-disability has been understood. The corporeality of disability has been heavily affected by social processes and power relations. The cinematic representation of Michelle and Pinky draws our attention to the actualized violence perpetrated against women with disabilities, namely the violation of their bodies in the form of murder, medical mutilation, abortion, and enforced sterilization. We need to consider the feelings of disgust and pity that are provoked by women with disabilities. In the movie *Black*, Michelle is not allowed to play in public and the way her behavior has been represented shows people's feelings of disgust. There are many instances in which her parents leave the dining table because she does not eat *normally*. In the movie *Lafangey Parindey*, the way in which Pinky's friends communicate with her and help her is due to her disability. The word *bechari* (poor girl) is used repeatedly of Pinky, which shows her friends' sense of pity and sympathy for her. In public discourse, disability may be rendered invisible. "The normal mind cannot encompass a difference so profoundly embedded in its/our sense of the 'normal' and its silenced Others (those who are not part of the taken-for-granted everyday world of the dominant cultures" (Meekosha 1998: 162). The problems and difficulties of Pinky and Michelle are articulated by Nandu and Balraj, respectively. Silencing of the disabled subjects represents the domination of the non-disabled over the disabled and the objectification of the disabled body. Feminists' concerns for the body have encompassed the heterogeneity of discourses and issues.

Undoubtedly, the patriarchal structure does not function for women with disabilities in the same way as it functions for men with disabilities. Traditionally, women's bodies have been perceived as subordinate and male bodies as superior. Moreover, the public space for women with disabilities is narrow, and disability studies contests this to overcome the binaries of nature/culture, sex/gender, and private/public so that the body should not be discriminated against just because it belongs to a different sex. Pinky and Michelle belong to a different sex—they are women—which turns out to be a major reason for silencing their lived and subjective experiences and their suffering, pain, rejection, loss, grief, desire, joy and achievements go unnoticed. Voicing the subjective and lived experiences of disabled people poses a threat to male hegemony and it may constitute women-centered worlds and spaces. There is much debate that assumes that such celebration may lead to essentialism and biological reductionism. Another debate assumes that biology is not destiny, because culture is the determining factor. The particular cultural forms determine the configuration of the bodies. This position may also lead to another form of one-dimensional and essentialist explanations. Seen in this way, "the body has been forced to vacate its residence on the nature side of the nature-culture duality and take up residence within culture" (Garland-Thomson 1997: 14).

Medicine, media, fitness industries, health, and fashion are the major tools that turn women with disabilities into objectified bodies. The male gaze is one example that represents how women with disabilities are oppressed and objectified. It is not that disability is the only phenomenon that is stared at by other people—all bodies invite an ocular response from the gazer but bodies with differences intensify the interest of those who stare and the act of staring is a way of getting to know the body more. Women with disabilities have always been sensitive to participation in larger events such as ring ceremonies, weddings, etc. They feel that people will stare at and comment on them. They also feel responsible for making social gatherings uncomfortable through their bodily presence. As a result, they are reluctant to move out of their domestic spaces. Similarly, people with disabilities astonish normal people with their presence. The appearance of Pinky in the final round of the talent show astonishes the judges and their eyes are riveted on her body. It is not so much because of her wonderful performance but because of the public appearance of a blind girl. There is a general belief that a woman with disabilities can never perform as well as a non-disabled girl and dazzle with her talent. The performance of a blind girl, undoubtedly, surprises everyone but she is also appreciated because of her poor background. It is beyond our imagination that a girl who is blind and belongs to the poor strata of society can ever access the public spaces in such a way that is not possible even for an able-bodied person. Furthermore, their astonishment has to be analyzed as their fascinated belief and uneasy identification. Such an appearance makes us think that the person looks so much like us and yet is so different from us. Such sights confuse us so that we compel ourselves to affirm our shared humanity and challenge our complacent understandings. The exclusion of people with disabilities is also because such sights intrude on our routine visual landscapes and, of course, compel our attention, often obscuring the personhood of the bearer. The uneasiness that is produced by the appearance of the body marked with differences in the normal life of normal people represents the inability of the people to understand the disruption of what is expected. Socioeconomic resources and the built environment do not allow people with disabilities to be ordinary. Shilpa Phadke (2010) says that it is unnecessary to point out that men have more access than women, and that the rich have more access than the poor, adding that women with disabilities who belong to the lower castes and classes have the least access to things than any other marginalized community, or indeed that the very aspiration of becoming a global city is based on the exclusion of those who do not fit into it. People with disabilities are thought to pose a risk to non-disabled people and are unproductive for society, and this rationale results in the exclusion of people with disabilities.

6.2 Disability and body

The world in which we live has taken a somatic turn which means that the current era is obsessed with the body and that much of that obsession is directed at the female body. Various critics have claimed that the panoptic gaze of contemporary culture is distinctively gendered (Garland-Thomson 2005: 15). The interiorizing gaze affects female bodies much more than it does male bodies. Joan Copjec states, "The panoptic gaze defines perfectly the situation of the woman under patriarchy" (1994: 54). Sandra Bartky explains:

> The woman who checks her make-up half a dozen times a day to see if her foundation has caked or her mascara run, who worries that wind or rain may spoil her hairdo, who looks frequently to see if her stocking has bagged at the ankle, or who, feeling fat, monitors everything she eats, has become, just as surely as the inmate of the Panopticon, a self-policing subject, a self-committed to a relentless self-surveillance. This self-surveillance is a form of obedience to patriarchy.
>
> (1990: 80)

If a so-called able-bodied woman has to comply with patriarchal norms to serve the interests of men, women with disabilities who are imagined as asexual will undergo much persecution and social ostracism.

The unfriendly glances that Pinky and Michelle encounter in their everyday lives is a form of non-verbal behavior that is designed to enforce social hierarchies and make them feel inferior and unwanted by society. It forces them to submit their selves to the hegemonic structure of the normative and subjectifies them in such a way that they can regulate their behavior and bodies. The constant hostility that they meet reflects the undesirability of disabled bodies in public spaces and makes it impossible for them to cohabit space with people.

Phadke (2010) continues here by saying that cities are not relentlessly unfriendly but rather shift from being friendly to unfriendly depending on various contextual and situational factors, including among other things temporality, crowds, lighting, and availability of infrastructure and amenities such as transport and toilets. Moving away from all these difficulties, if women with disabilities loiter in unfriendly spaces, they are exploited. Their bodies are viewed as property. The exploitation of their bodies allows for the sale of commodities and they are used to market products as diverse as soft drinks and cars: here sexual desire is being sold. Women are often willing accomplices in these processes of appropriation (Meekosha 1998: 169). In various classical arts, we come to witness the women's bodies featured as dismembered parts. It is not related to disability but such representation is the eroticization of the body parts. The viewer is invited to imagine and fantasize about the whole from the perfect parts. Disability in these arts is not simply a reflection of societal values; it is also a politically charged commodity that is bought by the audience. Cinema is one of the powerful cultural tools that plays a major role in the perpetuation of mainstream society's regard for people with disabilities and "more often than not the images borne in those movies have differed sharply from the realities of the physically disabled experience" (Norden 1995: 132).

The literature on the representation of disability in the cinema tends to focus on an examination of how disability has been constituted and the role of the disabled in cinema. There is also a need to examine how an able body is described or visualized in film. To understand the question of disability, one needs to focus on representations that privilege ability. Disability and ability actually complement each other in terms of the marginalization of disabled people. It goes without saying that a woman has never been the parameter to chart out the feature of ability. Ability is the term that is often used interchangeably with masculinity and muscularity. To understand what ability is, it is important to examine the way masculinity has been defined and examined and has set a model to be followed by the rest. In the movie *Lafangey Parindey*, Nandu exposes his body to make the audience want to imitate him in developing an able muscular body. The character of Nandu is also important to understand the way masculinity has been constructed and is circulated in public to define the ideology of femininity. The rhetoric of masculinity that is constantly used about Nandu's body foregrounds the social construction of the gendered identities subjecting fragile and docile bodies. The phantasmatic exhibition of Nandu's body represents the construction of ability/masculinity by the cultural environment rather than by biology or nature, which is why it is important that the representation of ability/masculinity/muscularity should be open to question that has for so long applied to women and their femininity. Robert Connell coined the term "hegemonic masculinity" to describe those white, heterosexual, competitive, individualist, and aggressive men in the paid labor force who dominate the moral, cultural and financial landscape (1995: 77). Rebecca Feasey defines the hegemonic male as "a strong, successful, capable and authoritative man who derives his reputation from the workplace and his self-esteem from the public sphere" (2008: 3). Kimmel says in the same reference that the hegemonic male is "a man in power, a man with power, and a man of power" (2004: 184). In one incident, a young boy expresses a desire to be like Nandu. He says to Nandu that he wants to build up muscle and become a boxer like him. This represents the circulation of such images that are intended to be followed and to suppress the other bodies in the margins. It also exhibits the model of masculinity that is an ideal image of the male against which all men have to be judged, tested, and qualified. In fact, "hegemonic masculinity has become the standard in psychological evaluations, sociological research … self-help, and advice literature for teaching young men to become real men" (2004: 184). The relationship between advanced capitalism and the existing ideologies in our country has not been properly established so such references create problems of understanding. In our society, there is pressure for people who are seen as different to conform to masculine norms in order to attain political influence, wealth, or social status.

in the same way that Nandu represents the type of hegemonic male who enjoys and maintains the hierarchy. Being able, explicitly, means "not being disabled" irrespective of the sex, age, ethnicity, class, caste, race, or sexual orientation of the able body in question. Therefore, it may be concluded that the idea of anti-disability lies at the heart of any contemporary historical conception of ableism, so that ability is defined more by what one is not rather than who one is.

Lafangey Parindey is in two parts. The first part is about the life of Pinky who wants to be the best roller skater in India, while the second part focuses on Nandu who is a boxer and aspires to be a *bhai* (master). The space in which Pinky lives is mainly meant for a woman and is feminized in such a way that when working with her Nandu feels insulted. He directly denies dancing with Pinky and feels ashamed of the dancing profession. It is against his dignity, in other words, this space does not provide the platform where he can practice his masculinity. Society has long been accustomed to the gendering of the public and private spheres, and the "hegemonic model of masculinity remains dependent on the demarcation of such gendered spaces" (Feasey 2008: 153). The masculinization of the public sphere has no room for women; a woman has to practice masculinity to locate herself there. The representation of masculinity can be seen to exploit the experience of women with disabilities. Indeed, it is the mobility of the able body's experience and their desire to inhabit the public sphere that silences the experience of women and women with disabilities. Rather than constructing the softer and more reflexive notion of masculinity, the cultural environment is empowering and strengthening the traditional notion of masculinity. The celebration of Nandu's character and the masculine projection of his character is just another way of maintaining the patriarchal rule. To encourage masculinities that transcend the narrow hegemonic stereotype means enabling these men to draw on traditionally masculine and feminine characteristics and allowing them to move freely between public and private spheres. Perhaps, then, we can talk about hegemonic masculinity as something that men should pity and fear rather than something they should be seen to aspire to. The lived experience of masculinity is more complex and fluctuating than those representations of manhood/ableism and the male role is depicted in the cinema. However, this becomes a way to define norms and conventions that consider the role of ability and disability as appropriate and inappropriate.

The emergence of neoliberal culture has complicated the life of the body marked with differences and empowered the ability culture by opening up the cultural field to all manner of diverse cosmopolitan currents. The neoliberalization of culture supports the leitmotif of bourgeois urban culture. Deborah Tudor says that neoliberal culture rests upon the transference of authority from official sources to private experts in fields ranging from psychology (self-help) to fashion, weight loss, and career planning (2011: 59). It makes the individual responsible for their personal and professional welfare or loss. The culture was solidified in such a way that an individual has to bear the sole responsibility for his or her problems, and society and environment have nothing to do with their anxiety and failure. In this process of shifting from individuals embedded in social class to untethered self-disciplined individuals, neoliberalism revoked but also reinvigorated white patriarchy (Tudor 2011: 59). It also contributes to the construction of the subject. Rose says that current critiques of postwar social citizenship have given rise to new ways of understanding individuals as subjects of freedom, whereby "freedom is now understood in terms of the capacity/responsibility of the autonomous individual to determine the course of one's own existence through acts of choice" (2003: 84). Such moves by society have left the individual to be independent and have questioned the language of dependency. Our society enables non-disabled people to deploy new strategies to discriminate against people with disabilities. It does not aim to reconfigure the environment to ensure accessibility and accommodation for people with disabilities, but rather emphasizes the voluntary compliance and incentive of the people. Nandu appears as an agent of neoliberal culture who teaches Pinky to be self-independent and to comply with individualistic norms. The strategies that Nandu deploys in the dance practice raise many important questions to understand the way neoliberal culture discriminates against people with disabilities. Thus, do workplace barriers have nothing to do with attitudinal problems? Pinky's struggle to become a good roller skater goes unnoticed by her community. It is her blindness that determines her frustration, while the problems she faces with her communities have no significance. The representation of Pinky's character overlooks these core issues that examine the problem of women with disabilities. At the beginning of the movie, Pinky says that she does not want to live in this society and is exasperated by her surroundings. She feels trapped by the attitudinal barriers that resist her liberation. She is not free to make decisions and choices; her family becomes the first to resist her. She is made to realize that she is a woman and has no right to go outside her home. In one instance, Pinky's mother raises the issue of marriage with her, which is one of the very pertinent issues that foster the patriarchal structure. She asks, "Is this what you will serve to your husband?" Such questions actually interpellate the subject and reinforce their gendered identity. Disability can never be imagined without contemplating the phenomenon of patriarchy. A woman is already disabled in the patriarchal society; she has not necessarily experienced the impairment. The eventually disabled identity of Pinky complicates her life more severely. Nandu manipulates and controls her body according to the wishes and convenience of neoliberal culture. Such strategies that promote individualism deployed by neoliberal culture reorganize the framework of hegemonic masculinity. The narrative of the movie shows the representation of women but largely in an invisible way and gives more visibility to male authority. Pinky is nearly the sole disabled face on the screen, and bears a double burden of representation, as female and disabled. Pinky is depicted as a skilled roller skater who is a good communicator. At first she rejects Nandu's help and says that she does not want anyone's sympathy. All these character traits indicate a confident, accomplished, intelligent girl who does not want to be dominated by anyone. But as the story progresses, she complies with Nandu's instructions and submits herself to him. The movie leaves a message that disability can be rectified at the cost of the "will of the individual" and also suggests that a weak woman can achieve her goals with the help of an enlightened man. So, apart from the stereotypical notion regarding disability strengthened by the movie, it also represents the compromise of neoliberalism with feminist ideals. It does not cancel out the fact that Pinky's body is not exhibited as an object; rather it shows that the objectification of her body constitutes another way that women with disabilities under neoliberalism bear masculinity. The inscribed values in our society are reiterated only by the objectification of the body of women with disabilities. The discourse constructed around the bodies of women with disabilities enables individual theory and ignores the social issues and political classes. The individual is blamed for their faults and the discourse attempts to discount the critique of operating oppressive cultural and social institutions. The hidden agenda of neoliberalism is to eliminate the social aspects of critique and to enforce the able norm in the appropriation of the disabled body. If we dismiss the notion of social structures, then it is pointless to analyze stereotypes and gendered images in dialectic with each other.

Viewing *Lafangey Parindey* through the lens of disability makes one conclude that the movie has represented the positive side of disability and the disabled body can speak about his or her experiences in the public sphere. However, a closer reading of the movie shows how women with disabilities are regarded as subordinate figures and whose appearance remains sexualized. This power relationship between women with disabilities and non-disabled people creates no public space for women with disabilities. The narrative suppresses alternative value systems and foregrounds hegemonic value systems.

6.3 Disability and the discourse of pleasure

Since the 1990s, people with disabilities in India have begun to question their marginalization and isolation, and to speak for civil rights refusing to tolerate exclusion. The exclusion of people with disabilities in terms of sexuality is seldom discussed. According to Anne Finger, "It is easier for us to talk about—and formulate—strategies of discrimination in employment, education, and housing than talk about our exclusion from sexuality and reproduction" (1990: 9). It is a disturbing issue not only for non-disabled people but also for people with disabilities who avoid talking about it. The voices and experiences of disabled people are absent when it comes to the issue of sexuality. Robert Murphy, a disabled anthropologist, states, "The sexual problems of the disabled are aggravated by a widespread view that they are either malignantly sexual, like libidinous dwarfs, or more commonly completely asexual, an attribute frequently applied to the elderly as well" (1987: 83). Activists feel unwilling to engage with disabled people's sexuality thinking of it as a lower concern than other issues such as health and education. Even families ignore the issue of sex. The trend that Hindi movies have followed has been dominated by the notion that people with disabilities are asexual. Hindi movies such as *Koshish* (*Effort*) (1972), *Dushman* (*Enemy*) (1979), *Dhoop Chhaon* (*Sunlight and Shade*) (1977), *Jaydaad* (*Property*) (1989) have represented disabled protagonists as asexual. Very few Hindi movies project disabled characters as hypersexual. The recent movie *Margarita with a Straw* may be an exception. In the context of India, across the diversity of cultures, people with disabilities predominantly occupy a place as asexual. The oppressive structure of heterosexuality operates differently for able-bodied women and disabled women. Homogenizing the oppression of heterosexuality will bring injustice to women with disabilities. The pressure through which heterosexual practices operate on women with disabilities has a different form of subjection in comparison to able-bodied women. They are often not considered "woman enough" which is why they are particularly at risk of (hetero)sexual abuse.

The current shift in Hindi cinema represents women with disabilities as sexual agents and has rectified the stereotypical image of women with disabilities but fails to rupture the structure of normativity. The representation of women with disabilities challenges imposed asexual identity and campaigns for the issues of sex and love. *Lafangey Parindey* and *Black* shift beyond the strategies deployed to change the discriminatory practices in education and employment, and bring our attention to the exclusion of women with disabilities in the arena of sexuality. These movies do not explicitly explore sexual politics but implicitly question the normal cultural understanding of sexuality in relation to women with disabilities. Both Pinky and Michelle fight against the social stigma associated with sexuality and disability. As a blind girl Pinky practices with Nandu and develops feelings for him. She wants to start a romance with Nandu but Nandu fails to understand this. It is not that Nandu is unsympathetic about her blindness, but rather as a heterosexual agent he is dominated by the notion that the impaired body is asexual and this prevents him from developing feelings for her. Prejudice and stereotype play a critical role and disables their relations. In the sphere of sex and love, the prejudiced assumptions that people with disabilities are asexual and that is much stimulated by medical institutes become dominant and inescapable in the relationship of Nandu and Pinky. The stereotype of disability often concentrates on asexuality. The dependency of people with disabilities subjects them to infantilization. The infantilization of sexuality of women with disability is the cultural negation of their right to be sexual beings. Nandu's rejection of her love makes Pinky face the humiliation and discriminatory practices organized by the dominant heterosexual norm. What disability studies aim to do is to explore the multifaceted realm of disability and sexuality by deconstructing the narratives, voices, and perspectives of able-bodied society. There is a need to reframe the discourse around sexuality. The denial of Pinky's love in the larger framework of heterosexuality compels her to fit into the norm, which is why Pinky dresses beautifully to tempt Nandu and attempts to overcome her blindness. Before we delve into the discussion of the normalization of disabled sexuality, we must analyze sexuality in terms of disability.

Sexuality is not only limited to sex and sexual practices, but also refers to a person's sexual orientation or identity, preferences, desire, and eroticism. Sexuality is a term that refers to both internal and external phenomena in both the realm of the psyche and the material world.

> Sexuality is experienced and expressed in thoughts, fantasies, desires, beliefs, attitudes and values, behaviors, practices, roles, and relationships ... sexuality is influenced by the interaction of biological, psychological, social, economic, political, cultural, ethical, legal, historical, religious and spiritual factors.
>
> (Menon 2007: 4)

Sex and sexuality are often linked to physical beauty and youth, and the issue of pleasure in terms of disabled people's sexuality is ignored, vilified, and exploited. One of the major institutions, namely the media, is silent on sexual pleasure for people with disabilities. It does not ignore the fact that the media has prioritized sexual pleasure for the able-bodied. The expression of sexual pleasure for people with disabilities is conspicuously absent in mainstream media because it does not fit into the targeted market profile, and therefore the representation of sexual pleasure for people with disabilities aims to fit them into the market profile and has exploited sexual pleasure for gain. "Sex is portrayed as a privilege of the white, heterosexual, young, single, and non-disabled. Sexual pleasure is held out as a reward for buying the right product and targeted to markets with the most disposable income" (Tepper 2000: 285). Sexuality that is already marginalized in society occupies a space in the media institutions, not as a source of pleasure but rather to benefit the capitalist market. Hindi movies do not view disabled people as acceptable candidates for sexual expression; they are regarded as being in need of protection. The need to project them as sexual subjects is created by the capitalist market. The new dresses and cosmetics that Pinky uses to tempt Nandu represent the way the neoliberal market sexualizes the woman's body and unconsciously pushes people to participate in the capitalist market. In both movies, there are very few discussions about sexuality. In one instance, Pinky's friend dismisses her beauty and says *"Oye ma'am, tu koi Aishwayra Rai hai kya? Ki koi tujhpe line marega?"* ("Oh girl, do you think you're Aishwarya Rai? Who's going to die for you?"). These are the common views that are expressed by people to mock disabled people's attitudes and non-disabled people boast about their looks. However, the standard of beauty always lies with a normal person. The comparison of Pinky to Aishwarya Rai (a celebrated Indian actress primarily known for her work on Hindi and Tamil movies) is a nod toward the societal understanding of the kind of beauty that is associated with a normal person. It can never be imagined in terms of a non-able bodied person. Therefore, we tend to undermine the beauty and at the same time the sexuality of people with disabilities. We are preoccupied with the notion that sexuality is integral element of the able-bodied. "The non-disabled world has found it difficult to grapple with the idea that these 'damaged bodies' could have sexual feelings, the mere thought that they may engage in sexual behavior is considered unwholesome, repulsive and comical" (Greengross 1976: 2).

Generally, women develop an understanding of their sexuality and explore their relationships with others at a young age. But that is a very exceptional case in terms of women with disabilities if they anticipate their relationships with others. Any institution, predominantly the family, is unlikely to educate them about their sexual identity. They are prohibited to think or even talk about sex. Even as a child Michelle was never told by her teacher that would one day be able to have intercourse and be a wife and mother. Her sexual needs were considered either non-existent or inferior.

The sexuality of people with disabilities traverses normalistic social expectations that are derived from some facet of disabled people's physiology. Simone de Beauvoir's (2010) claim that "one is not born, but rather becomes, a woman," explains the instability of gender identity that is tenuously constituted in time. The sexual identity of people with disabilities follows the same logic and is instituted through a stylized repetition of acts. Their bodily gestures and movements that are socialized by the sociocultural process constitute the illusion of an abiding disabled self. The various acts through which Pinky precedes her life destabilize her identity. Her disabled (sexual) self is instituted through acts that are internally discontinuous. It has to be understood that the body is a historical construct rather than being a biological entity. The body of Pinky is assumed to be disabled because she is blind. Therefore, various physiological and biological causalities that structure her bodily existence are seldom noticed, and meaning associated with her embodied existence that is derived from the context of lived experience is valued. An individual is not the effect of natural fact, but rather is a product of a historical situation. It does not mean that the naturality and materiality of the body are denied, but it is reconceived as the body comes to bear cultural meanings. Merleau-Ponty in his book *The Phenomenological Perception* reflects on "the body in its sexual being" and claims that the "body is a historical situation rather than a natural fact" (1962: 172). Merleau-Ponty and de Beauvoir understand the body as an active process that embodies certain cultural and historical possibilities, it is a complicated process through which an individual is appropriated. In the context of the sexual bodies of people with disabilities, it is not be incorrect to say that their sexuality is appropriated to facilitate the sexuality of the normal able body because the cultural and historical meanings attached to the sexuality of people with disabilities permeates the possibility of strengthening the normative sexuality. Normative sexuality has to be organized to open the space for normal people which is only possible when non-normal sexuality comes with a different baggage of cultural and historical meanings. Pinky and Michelle are not allowed to carry emotional baggage because they would not be considered normal sexual beings. Our task is to examine in what ways the bodies of people with disabilities are constructed through specific corporeal acts, and what possibilities exist for the cultural transformation of the bodies of people with disabilities through such acts.

It goes without saying that body is a historical idea but to maintain that historical idea, a set of possibilities has to be continually realized. Butler says that the body is a historical idea which means that the body comes into being through concrete and historically mediated expression in the world. "The body is not merely matter but a continual and incessant materializing of possibilities ... One is not simply a body, but, in some very key sense, one does one's body and, indeed, one does one's body differently from one's contemporaries and from one's embodied predecessors and successors as well" (Butler 1988: 521).

The question that arises here is what is it that makes the body a historical situation? A historical situation is a manner of doing—it is reproduced and dramatized. Doing the disabled body makes the embodied agent exterior and they become open to being perceived by others. The embodiment of the body represents a set of strategies or what Foucault calls "a stylistic of existence (1977: 23)." Like gender, disability is a corporeal style that is both intentional and performative. Performative style has very little to do with the materiality of the body; it is dramatic and non-referential. The disabled body is a cultural interpretation and signification of the materiality of the body. To be disabled is to become disabled, and a disabled person has to compel the body to conform to a historical idea of disability. People with disabilities have to induce cultural signs of disability to materialize themselves. Disability turns out to be a performance with clear punitive consequences, so when Michelle fails to perform adequately she is punished for it. Michelle is not only punished to correct herself but rather she sometimes even fails to perform an "act of disability." Michelle's acts create the idea of disability and without those acts there would not be disability at all. Therefore, disability is a construction that does not reveal its genesis, and furthermore those acts are naturalized and thought of as the essence of disabled people. Some of Pinky's acts render her as a normal subject because she does not repeat acts that she usually performs while walking on the road and while talking to Nandu. Her corporeal styles materialize the historical possibilities. These corporeal styles are of "punitively regulated cultural fictions that are alternatively embodied and disguised under duress" (Butler 1993: 523). The body is only known by the way it appears, and it is renewed and revised over time. It is not a predetermined and foreclosed structure; rather, it is a legacy of sedimented acts. Being in a historical situation emphasizes the fact that the body suffers from a certain cultural construction.

It is the repetition of the act that produces the norm and invariably maintains the identity of the body. This repetition re-enacts and re-experiences a set of meanings that are already culturally established. They are legitimatized only through the repetitions of rituals. There are few poststructuralists who assume that performative acts are imposed and inscribed upon the individual, but that the body is not passive to the extent that cultural codes can be scripted contentedly. It does not also mean that embodied disabled bodies pre-exist the cultural conventions which actualize the signifying bodies. They are brought onto the stage with an already written script and they enact it in various ways. The disabled body performs its given role in a culturally restricted corporeal space, and it enacts interpretations that have already prescribed directives.

Disability is a reality that has to be understood by normal people too and they have to meditate upon the way that such a reality is performative. Performative means that it is only real to the extent it is performed. It is not the body of Pinky and Michelle that makes them disabled, but rather it is their performance. They perform those acts that conform to an expected disabled identity and sometimes these acts also contend with expectations. We expect that a disabled identity performs in a certain way and when certain performances frustrate our expectations that are based on the perception of the disabled body, punitive actions are played on them because they are not allowed to break the normalistic code of society. They are left with no options— they must either to conform to the disabled identity or to the normal/able identity.

Performance and expressiveness of the body not only construct the identity of the disabled body but also interpellate the disabled subject. Louis Althusser's famous interpellation, "hey, you there!" helps us to understand the way the subject gets interpellated into the discourse. Disabled subjects are no exception to this rule and they also recognize themselves in this call. There are many instances in the movie *Black* in which Michelle is called to turn toward Balraj to become the agent of the law. Althusser's theory of interpellation makes it clear that we are living in the ideological framework that actually determines the becoming of subjects. The performative call of Michelle's teacher that "hey, you should not do this" directs Michelle to follow the structure of hetero-normativity. For Michelle this call is a process of making her follow the cultural practices. Through the internalization of ideology a subject is constituted. "Ideology is about how humans imagine their place, their role, and their relationships within the social realm, as ideas, operate in social practices" (Althusser 1971: 162). There are multiple ideological apparatuses such as educational institutions, families, cultural organizations that administer social practices. It is social practices that govern the subject's possible activities. Through these processes, the state maintains its sovereignty because it conducts the behavior of its subject. Michelle's teacher works as a state apparatus and at the same time deploys the technique of the state's repressive apparatus by using physical violence to normalize her. Needless to say, the ideology of the able body is the one that hegemonizes the culture. When the ideological state apparatus sometimes fails to properly inculcate the normal behaviors into the child, the repressive state apparatus comes into play and denies the rights of the disabled child/individual. However, the line between the ideological state apparatus and the repressive state apparatus is not well defined. We never know when the ideological state apparatus has been taken over by the repressive state apparatus but acts of reprimand and illicit violence produced on disabled bodies can be counted as the function of the repressive state apparatus. But the theory of Althusser opens up the space for disabled subjects' resistance and social transformation. Althusser's theory reflects how disabled subjects are being exploited under the framework of normative ideology. The theory of ideology and interpellation shows that the subject is an effect of ideology. The subject is the one who has internalized the ideology that means that the disabled subject has given consent for exploitation and at the same time his theory explains how they are free too. According to Althusser, "The individual is interpellated as a (free) subject so that he shall submit freely" (1971: 182). We find here the paradox that Althusser's subject is free and at the same time he has submitted to normal ideology. The subject finds their agency only when the ruling system breaks or contradicts itself.

Another problem that crops up in the recent debate on disability studies is the question of the autonomy of women with disabilities. This book has examined the rights, education, and lives of women with disabilities, but the question of autonomy has not received much impetus and has remained ignored, not because it never concerns us but rather because the question of the autonomy of women with disabilities challenges the cultural hegemony of the able-bodied up to the macro level. The autonomy of women with disabilities raises a number of questions, such as the position of women with disabilities in the family in particular and in society in general, gender stereotypes, personal relationships, and the way society reconceptualizes the question of autonomy as such. The question of autonomy is important to understand that given the way society has been organized, the autonomy of women can hardly be noticed, and may disorganize the sociocultural orientations. We often come across a situation in which women with disabilities have to compromise their autonomy and have to submit to an oppressive structure; in other words, being disabled has given sufficient reason for a woman to compromise their autonomy. We have the ideal of autonomy from which women with disabilities are alienated. In fact, in India, women with disabilities are generally not allowed to experience their autonomy and agentiality.

Autonomy is not meant for women with disabilities—it is for the able-bodied. It has already been theorized that being able-bodied is akin to being muscular and masculine or, in other words, being a person who is autonomous and can be a so-called man. There are very few opportunities open to women with disabilities; they are dependent on others for their work. People are supposed to "be like a man" for what they believe or value, including the simple assertion of their self-interest. The maxim "be like a man!" has no serious meaning but it reflects the mood of society that believes that a man has the autonomy to do something. Autonomy for women has never been imagined. For personal and social ties, a woman bears more responsibility than a man. Moral and social codes are much more intense for women than they are for men. The constructed social and moral codes for women restrict not only their autonomy but also make them live like slaves. They sacrifice their choices and desires in the name of being good women. The concept of good and bad assures the man's autonomy and strengthens the patriarchal culture. Popular culture still presupposes that women have to preserve the relationship, for example, marriage, that autonomy-seeking men want to abandon. If that is a form in which a woman lives, we can imagine the life of a woman with disabilities and the circumstances she has to go through. Sociocultural spaces have been monopolized by the able-bodied, and it is not easy for women with disabilities to contest these problems.

Movies like *Lafangey Parindey* and *Black* represent the oppression of able-bodied culture whereby women with disabilities cannot live with their differences. Thus, neither Pinky nor Michelle can act or perform an action independently. Their autonomy has been taken away from them, regardless of their capacity to act and perform independently. The normative culture does not allow them to initiate an action freely and autonomously. Pinky's dreams would have never been possible without Nandu's help, and Michelle would have never known what life is without the assistance of her teacher. Being autonomous does not cancel out the concept of assistance and support for women with disabilities—it has to be provided to them when they require it. However, most of the time, their choices are neglected and they sympathize with the help and care. Pinky's friend does not allow her to go out alone and most of the time she is accompanied by her friends. She feels comfortable in crossing the roads and while doing her skating practice but her friends keep on channelizing her. The problem does not lie in the understanding of the friends but rather in the male-dominated structure that presupposes that women with disabilities are dependent upon non-disabled people and the male-biased culture that presumes that they do not have the autonomy to act and perform their actions willingly. In the context of women with disabilities, the able-bodied person dominates them. Domination is exerted not by choice but by force. Michelle has no voice till she is cured. Every act is governed by her teacher. What is most striking is the stagnant cultural understanding of autonomy that resists the need to change. Society does not need a change in the cultural understanding of autonomy because it avoids the risk of disruption in inter-personal relationships.

6.4 Disability and autonomy

Historically, autonomy has been associated with the able-bodied. The con-stituent traits of autonomy that are manifested through someone's actions and lives are publicly esteemed much more often in the able-bodied than in people with disabilities. Why does a concept like autonomy irrevocably shape the paradigms of male-identified traits? Can it ever be freed from patriarchal con-straints? There is a need to bring out new paradigms of autonomy that feature disabled people. There is also a need for a systematic rethinking that collects the narratives of women with disabilities. A new appropriation of the concept of autonomy through the lens of disability studies actually requires these nar-ratives to question the normative constraints. It attempts to voice the situations of women with disabilities paradigmatically or distinctively. Such collected narratives will express and refashion their deepest commitments and sense of self. Such narratives have never appeared to wish to continue the patriarchal constraints. The historical link between autonomy and men has to be under-mined. Pinky and Michelle challenge the uniform relationship between auton-omy and men. That Pinky and Michelle resist Nandu and Balraj represents a shift in the autonomy of men. The growing diversity of disabled women's lives further challenges it. Women with disabilities are coming out of the closet to occupy the public spaces and make people realize that autonomy is no longer straightforwardly oriented toward the able-bodied or alien to women with dis-abilities. One may argue that both Pinky and Michelle could have challenged the normative paradigms of autonomy because they were accompanied by the agents of normative structure. But what needs to be noticed is their resistance and their celebration of their bodies. They do not lament that they are disabled; rather, they choose to stand and fight against the oppressive culture of the able-bodied. They question the stereotypical disabled traits and at the same time abrogate the stereotypical able-bodied traits and are never ashamed of their bodies. Thus, Pinky was not allowed to go outside and continue her skate dance practice. However, she ignored her surroundings and continued her dance practice. Pinky is against the traditional ideal of autonomy.

In our Indian culture, independence and outspokenness are features of autonomy but that is only for males—these traits cannot be internalized by females. They will be considered uncivilized and *poohar aurat* (those who do not know how to behave in public). The corrective method deployed by Pinky and Michelle's families is an attempt to socialize them with feminine traits. Disabled people's socialization does not promote autonomy competency more effectively; in contrast, able-bodied socialization does, which is why the able-bodied have far greater opportunities than disabled bodies. The situation for women with disabilities is worse especially when it comes to acting and performing autonomously. Such modes of action and living have, in the past, been closed to most women because they required resources that were unavailable to women such as political power, financial independence, or the freedom to travel unmolested in public space—to jog safely, for example, through Central Park in New York.

Undoubtedly, autonomy was not given to women with disabilities because they have to be within the marginalized space. If they become autonomous, the authority of the able-bodied will evaporate. The space occupied by the able-bodied will be threatened. The misunderstanding that prevails in the case of autonomy is that it will break the relationship. For example, if a child rebels, the parental value will come into question. But strictly speaking, the notion that autonomy that is unqualified disrupts the social relationship is false. The capacity that constitutes autonomy does not disrupt the social relationship. In a few cases, the actual exercise of the capacity disrupts the social relationship. Marilyn Friedman says that "the differences that arise between people as a result of one party's autonomous rejection of values or commitments that the other party still holds may lead one party to draw away from or reject the other" (Friedman 2005: 41). Therefore, it is not autonomy that disrupts the social relationship, but rather people do so.

Autonomy or any issue facing women with disabilities must be viewed differently, i.e., disabled people are one homogenous group with no gender distinction. Traditionally, there has been a tendency to generalize the issues facing people with disabilities. Disability movements and feminist agendas overlooked the reality of being a disabled woman and having a physical disability. However, recent research has questioned the homogenization of issues of disability and has added to that list of oppressions, a third, that of being a black disabled woman with physical disabilities. Treating disabled women as a unitary group will again overlook many factors such as types of disability, race, sexuality, caste, and class. These are the factors that influence individual experiences and they may differ from the experiences of other disabled women. Moreover, people can use their common experiences to develop a political analysis that creates bonds and builds positive strengths.

One of the roles of a woman is to bear children; throughout her life, she is conceptualized as a daughter, wife, or mother. Undoubtedly, feminist movements have challenged the institution of the family since it specializes in socialization and has been responsible for the oppression of women. They have questioned the role of women as nurturers and have defined it as a politics of patriarchal society that seeks to exploit them. The cultural conditioning of a woman's body, however, remains strong in our society which is why ignoring the effects of social, political, and economic structures which serve to control the daily lives of women will lead us to misjudge the role that sex plays. These are the stereotypical roles that persist in our day-to-day lives. But for women with disabilities, society presupposes that disability will prevent them from taking up such traditionally defined roles. Women who adhere to traditional gender roles might view it as ordinary, but for those barred from these roles, meeting these standards can mark a significant achievement. Falling short of fulfilling these roles could become a source of disappointment for them.

Pinky is horrified when she finds out that it was Nandu who caused the accident. Pinky is happy that she has the respect of her friends and that the boy of her dreams, Nandu, is with her. She dreams of being a perfect partner for him and wants to marry him, but this actually results in making her perform prescribed gender roles. Sometimes she regrets her blindness and pushes herself to prove that she is a "normal" woman. She feels proud to be out in public with Nandu. She has overcome the feeling of being blind and is looking forward to living a perfect life married to a man and rearing his children. This shows that the ideological construction of family institutions can create a sense of achievement for a woman. Pinky attempts to occupy a position in "no woman's land" which pushes her to choose very traditional feminine roles that aspire to notions of normality. In the case of Michelle, her parents want her to occupy a space in "no woman's land." Throughout her childhood, she tries to avoid being confined by the prescriptions of femininity, but later she fails to fight against repressive gender roles. Evidently, it would have been difficult for both Pinky and Michelle to live as disabled women without conforming to conventional gender roles. Such conventional gender roles obscure the question of autonomy and constitute them as disabled women. Society's rejection of women with disabilities makes them feel less worthy and incomplete. Society creates stereotypes of passivity and childlike dependency for them that results in the alienation of women with disabilities in the ideal space of autonomy. To avoid that embarrassment and pain to able-bodied society, one has to comply with the goal of normality.

The constitution of disabled subjects includes body image as a factor through which they influence their self-image. In our Indian society, women are defined by their physical appearances; statements such as she is beautiful, she looks like an actress, or her skin glows endorse the view of women as ornamental objects. Their beauty is objectified which helps in conceptualizing gendered images. There are many instances in the movie *Lafangey Parindey* that reflects how Pinky attempts to change her physical appearance. The comment by Pinky's friend, "*Tu koi Aishwarya Rai hai kya?*" ("Do you think you're Aishwarya Rai?") represents society's view on how a woman should look. It suggests that a good-looking woman, which is a demand of gendered society, is young, slim, and non-disabled. The non-conformity of women with disabilities labels them as defective women. A normative society that emphasizes feminine attractiveness imposes the restrictions on women with disabilities to take care of their bodily functions. The resistance of women with disabilities against the dominant notion of normal appearances seems to be very difficult for them. Representations of beautiful images by the media that expect a woman to look beautiful are internalized by women with disabilities, which is why they find their bodies defective and feel embarrassed in society.

> Specialists trained to treat one or other of our body parts have contributed to our dismembered body image. Value judgments are assigned to our "good" parts and "bad" parts, health is seen as a virtue, disease as evil and ugly.
>
> (Browne et al. 2004: 246)

Nasa Begum adds,

> With very little attention given to the positive aspects of a person's appearance and a tendency to reduce the body to a sexual object, disabled women learn very early on that their bodies can be objects which are manipulative and controlled by others.
>
> (1997: 23)

Michelle's teacher makes her aware of what it means to look beautiful. Thereafter Michelle feels that because she is disabled she is defective and that a disabled body is undesirable in society. She starts believing that her body is her enemy and that she has no control over it; that is why she changes the way she perceives her body image. The body image of women with disability is negative which affirms feelings of inferiority and worthlessness. In contrast, the body image of the able-bodied is positive which helps them to build confidence and self-esteem.

In India, the body of a woman with disabilities is de-eroticized. Undoubtedly, disability is a cultural phenomenon that is rooted in our senses; therefore, one has to contemplate how a disability becomes a part of the senses such as vision, touch, and hearing, and how it disrupts and distorts the sensory fields. Such questions engage with the nature of the subject, and one learns more about the observer than about the observed. The interaction between an able body and a disabled body disrupts the visual, auditory, and perceptual fields. The major cause of this disruption is the maintained modern binary of abled and disabled. It is a desire that accounts to split bodies into two immutable categories that are able and disabled, normal and abnormal, whole and incomplete. According to leading psychoanalysts such as Sigmund Freud, cultures perform an act of splitting. These violent cleavages of consciousness are as primitive as our thought processes can be. From childhood, an infant splits the good parent from the bad parent. However, the parent is the same. If the child is happy with the parent then the parent is good, and if the child is unhappy with the parent then the parent is bad. During the early phase of infancy, the child learns to combine these split images into a single parent who is sometimes good and sometimes not. "The residue of Spaltung, a Freudian term, remains in our inner life, personal and collective, to produce monsters and evil stepmothers as well as noble princes and fairy godmothers" (Davis 1995: 147). In the same process, cultural norms try to split bodies into good and bad parts. There are cultural norms that are good and bad. We experience that if someone is too short or too tall, too fat or too thin, her/his body will be thought of as bad. In India, certain body parts are thought of as bad; for example, underarms, left hands, sexual organs, etc.

With the rise of the factory in the post-industrial age, the label of disability as negative has been intensified. Disability is now much more dysfunctional because it is very difficult for people with disabilities to keep to factory norms and to work in the production process. After the accident, Pinky is unable to carry on working and loses her job. Her body now cannot be manipulated for productivity. The post-industrial era has changed the way we split up bodies. Even the different sorts of impairments have different signs and meanings and they can never be clubbed together. Moreover, some impairments have negative connotations and some have positive connotations; for example, some people would say that it is better to be deaf than to be blind. Certain values have been attached to certain body parts, so if they lose the capacity that is assigned to them through impairment, then they lose value too. Value is not just about the individual body parts but also what that body produces with the help of those body parts. A woman with disabilities is often less productive in society, which is why she is valued less than another able-bodied women. It goes without saying that the ideology behind the myths of being beautiful or valuable and ugly or non-valuable has endured since the pre-industrial age. Such ideologies are perpetuated by the media, literature, and cinema.

The concept of the "Other" has to be investigated to understand the position of women with disabilities. Simone de Beauvoir uses the term "Other" in her book *The Second Sex* (2010) to explain the male view of women. She explicates that men are considered essential and women as inessential, that man possesses the position of Subject in our society and woman as his Other. Making people Other means grouping them as our *object* of experience and they never become the *subject* of our experience. They become symbolic of something else which we want to reject or which we fear and do not want to be associated with it. Non-disabled men view people with disabilities as Other because they symbolize them as imperfect, impure, and uncontrollable. It is important for non-disabled people to view people with disabilities as Other to validate their experiences and suit their needs. One may argue that non-disabled people may also be Other for people with disabilities, but othering for the non-disabled is minor. However, people with disabilities often categorize other disabled groups as Other, and women with disabilities are generally considered Other by men with disabilities. Men with disabilities have the privilege of being men in a male-oriented society; society despises men with disabilities because their bodies are marked with differences. Men with disabilities are valued more than women with disabilities, who suffer due to hierarchies of power and value in institutions. Institutions do not distribute the power equally to all disabled groups. The disabled people who symbolize heroic control against all the odds and who overcome their bodily incapacity receive public attention and are awarded. Women with disabilities lack the availability of facilities and opportunities which makes them live a life of an Other who is hardly noticed by society. However, this sort of challenge leads to erasing the differences between people with disabilities and grouping them with the norm of non-disabled people. They seek public attention because they perform on the beats of physical strength and endurance. Society receives a false impression by noticing the heroism of people with disabilities and inspires other people with disabilities to overcome their disability while ignoring their limitations and other economic, social, and cultural factors that do not help them to perform heroic acts. Both *Lafangey Parindey* and *Black* show their main characters performing heroic acts in difficult situations and overcoming their disabilities. When these movies end, the audience applauds for reaffirming that it is possible to overcome disability. It signifies that people with disabilities can control their bodies and can attempt to assume a non-disabled identity. In addition, it connotes disability as a disease that reduces or consumes the energy and stamina of people. However, it overlooks the other disabled groups who fail to perform heroic acts because they belong to a different set of sociocultural and economic backgrounds. Michelle's parents are very rich, and therefore they can afford a teacher and a special training room. She can go to school and can attend public meetings. Michelle's father is very influential which helps her to be with non-disabled people without encountering any social problems. Pinky's situation is very similar. She has her friends to help her. There is a chance that the image of a disabled hero may minimize the Otherness of some people with disabilities; however, that is an ideal for most people with disabilities that can never be met and one that will result in increasing the Otherness of the majority of disabled groups.

The exclusion of women with disabilities is a result of the self-perpetuating social system in which they are not allowed to socialize with non-disabled people. They are prevented from making their own mark on culture. Even society prevents non-disabled people from identifying with people with disabilities or identifying themselves as potentially disabled which contributes to people with disabilities becoming a symbolic "Other." The consequence of being an Other is that they are sometimes subjected to physical and sexual abuse. They are subjected to a high level of abuse and assault that goes unnoticed, and is not even recognized as abuse by the people who regard them as Other. They take it for granted and assume that physical and verbal abuse corresponds to their physical body, and that it is common and does not affect their self-esteem. To understand how this sort of abuse affects them, one has to be aware of the subjectivity of people with disabilities. The struggle and feelings of people with disabilities are not counted as shared cultural understanding of human experience. This tends to make them feel that they are invisible in society or sometime hyper-visible which is constructed by their heroic acts. Their experience is not integrated into the culture which limits their possibility of living a good life. They do not know how to communicate or behave in society with their bodies marked with differences. Nicholas Watson has observed, "The experiences of impairment and disability are both public and intimate. It is only through people's stories and biographies that the understanding that unites the public and the private into a coherent entity can come into being" (2002: 5). Untold narratives create an abyss between people with disabilities and non-disabled people, and being disabled is like entering a new world.

Disability must be viewed as a form of difference. "Otherness" and stigma are two common aspects of disability that defy the question of value. The next question that can be posed is what is so different about people with disabilities? We are all different. Race, culture, gender, and ethnicity are also forms of differences that individuals possess. To defend this argument, one may say that the disability category masks all the differences, while other categories mask fewer differences. Needless to say, the disability category does not mask gender differences but it does so in the case of class, race, sexual identity, age, etc. Society attempts to erase these differences and emphasizes similarities to people without disabilities. It is a political attempt to ignore disability as a reality and to reduce the human qualities of people with disabilities. It does not directly challenge the non-disabled paradigm of humanity. Just as women emphasize their similarities to men moving into traditionally male arenas of power, Susan Wendell (1996) argues, it does not directly challenge the male paradigm of humanity, although both may produce a gradual change in the paradigms. Moreover, the constitution of the Other is an important need of the Subject, and the Subject wants the Other to carry the Subject's fears and rejected qualities. Therefore, the assimilation of people with disabilities with people without disabilities is hard to achieve. However, most people with disabilities do not want to assimilate themselves with non-disabled groups. One prominent rationale is that assimilation creates a strong sense of sympathy and solidarity. The second rationale is that until social values are changed radically they feel that they may always be devalued because of their bodies marked with differences. Michelle's teacher eventually becomes disabled and he does not want to be with non-disabled groups. Even Michelle was not accepted at school because of their inability to overcome her disability. Disabled people know that they can resist the non-disabled paradigm of humanity and the ideal image of the body by standing outside the "normal" boundary. Values that are highly esteemed in non-disabled cultures, such as the value of independence from the help of others, can be more safely questioned and debated in a context where the stereotype of all people with disabilities as dependent and incompetent is known to be false. They want to preserve their culture which is quite true in terms of the Deaf community. They do not want to be assimilated into hearing society to preserve the culture that Deaf people have created. They have a way of understanding and knowledge that are not available to people without disabilities. There is a very touching scene in the movie *Black*, in which after 20 days of teaching, Debraj manages to teach Michelle some words and etiquette but he finds it difficult to teach the meaning of certain words to her. When Michelle's father returns home, Debraj packs his bag and walks toward the door. But he finds that Michelle continues the insolent behaviour which frustrates him and he pushes her into the water fountain. Michelle feels the touch of the water and starts to understand the meaning of the word. She is in a position to recognize her parents and vocalize a few words. In a scene in *Lafangey Parindey*, Nandu feels guilty about making Pinky blind and swears to teach her dance. But Pinky fails to feel about her surroundings. Nandu takes her to a lonely place and dumps her head into the water and leaves her after a few seconds. That is a life lesson for Pinky. A person has to be desperate if he or she wants to achieve their goals, just as one is desperate to breathe in the absence of air. After that, he took her to his place where he practices fighting and builds a new set through which she feels her surroundings through touch and smell. Pinky and Michelle as people with disabilities have a different way of knowing the world which is very tough for people without disabilities. Their way of behaving and approaching the world differs from that of people without disabilities. It is quite justified to say that people with disabilities must resist their assimilation with the non-disabled group till the non-disabled society cultivates a proper space for them and transforms the structure of society to receive them as human beings. Society needs to pay more attention to disability as a reality of the human condition than to the symbolic association with disability.

In the preceding arguments, I questioned the fixity of subjectivity and constituting discourses of disability. What follows in the case of disability is the issue of intercorporeality, which is a relevant concept for understanding the embodied experiences in a globalized society. The term intercorporeality is important to understand the way a body marked with differences crosses the boundaries and the body enacts the very means through which embodied subjects are both constituted and undone. Merleau-Ponty, a famous phenomenologist, believes that through bodies we can share and extend our bodily experiences: "I cannot conceive myself as nothing but a bit of the world, a mere object of biological, psychological or sociological investigation" 1962: ix). It opens up new opportunities for intercorporeal practices. The term intercorporeality is an attempt to understand the social nature of the body and the bodily nature of the social relationship. "The experience of being embodied is never a private affair, but is always mediated by our continual interactions with other human and nonhuman bodies" (Weiss 1999: 5). It also suggests that our relationship with others is our intersubjectivity toward something that is bodily and tangible. Locating intercorporeality in disability studies represents the corporeal encounter of people with disabilities and people without disabilities that does not erase the radical and irreducible differences, but challenges the boundaries between the self and the other.

The movies *Lafangey Parindey* and *Black* implicitly reflect on the issues of intercorporeality and represent the interaction between women with disabilities and their care attendants that displaces the limits of their assumedly contained sovereign selves. Nandu and Balraj both care for Pinky and Michelle in their own ways. This exposes the problematic foundation of independent living models that assert a normative encounter between autonomous and sovereign selves. It opens a way to reconsider the sociopolitical implication of the relational ethics of intercorporeality. The interaction between Pinky and Nandu and between Michelle and Balraj is not dissimilar to the way Nandu and Balraj used to meet with others. In relation, both Nandu and Pinky and Balraj and Michelle experience the leaking of their identities. They form an assemblage through such interaction, and that assemblage has ethical implications for how we come to understand our bodies. People with disabilities are engaged with many assemblages, for example the human-animal assemblages, the assemblages of dogs, monkeys, birds, etc., human-machine assemblages, assemblages of wheelchairs, ventilators, etc., and disabled/abled assemblages, assemblages of friends, teachers, care attendant, etc. It does not mean that people with disabilities are unique and different from others, but rather it reflects upon the relational ethics that has repercussions for all human beings. The concept of assemblage questions the formation of a normative sovereign able body that eludes us regarding not getting affected by the presence of 'Others'. Gibson thinks that the assemblage of disabled/abled makes a strong contribution to reconceptualizing the pragmatism of care. She argues that such an approach to the care assemblage complicates the usual ways in which the attendant is considered an employee and as such is expected to be a detached tool (2006: 192). This does not only complicate the way we think that an attendant merely performs a series of mechanical tasks by assisting people with disabilities by providing what he or she needs and desires, but also brings out the *tension* involved in care work.

Dependency is human nature; we all are dependent on one another for something. But in the case of people with disabilities, they are dependent on others for much longer periods due to a complex social environment that is not disability-friendly. Most of the time, we come to know that people with disabilities are oppressed and exploited in the name of help and care. They are placed in hospitals or asylums; thus, Michelle's father had decided to place her in an asylum. Even the care given to people with disabilities in the private sector isolates them from direct participation in community life. Care is framed in such a way that people with disabilities are entirely dependent on the attendant, and sometimes the attendant uses physical force to reaffirm his or her power and expresses his or her frustration. Balraj often gets frustrated when Michelle disobeys him and does not follow his guidance. His frustration is quite explicit when he pushes her into the water fountain, and Nandu, who is both the friend and carer of Pinky, scolds her repeatedly when she does not pay attention to sounds. Disability activists like Jenny Morris (1991) have contested the assumption that disabled people are dependent and burdensome. He makes a clear distinction between physical dependency and social dependency. Physical dependency means that an individual needs the help of someone to do a particular task—for example to get out of bed—while social dependency means that an individual has to ask someone for help because of the complexity of a social organization that is not disability-friendly. Disability activists argue that "independence is not about performing every possible task autonomously but rather having decision-making control over one's life. Independent living is more about individuals controlling their services than it is about individuals being completely self-sufficient" (Fritsch 2010: 3). Such activism changed the entire movement and people began to think of the need to change the social environment that would facilitate the independence of people with disabilities. People with disabilities need care attendants to be available to help with everyday activities such as bathing, eating, shopping, etc. They do not want to rely on volunteers or want to remain in institutions for their everyday activities. Disability activist like Bill Hughes prefers the term "personal assistance, help, support to care." Thus, the emotional aspect of care is bracketed, and assistance instead privileges the financial empowerment of disabled people both to participate in the market as bosses and to control their caring relationships. (Hughes et al. 2005: 268). Undoubtedly, personal assistance supports people with disabilities emotionally and physically too. Personal assistance has to be compatible in terms of culture, gender, and sexuality so that it enables people with disabilities to share their feelings and they do not feel alienated. The selection of personal attendants has to be made by people with disabilities so that they can make the relationship very effective. Pinky rejects the person with whom she used to practice and chooses Nandu. She feels comfortable with him and qualifies for the competition. Therefore, there must be the autonomy of people with disabilities in the hiring of personal attendants.

Such an approach assures that people with disabilities and their care attendants are not exploited. The relationship between people with disabilities and assistive devices, tools, animals, or persons presents a means to achieve individual independence. Thinking about the relations and extensions of the desiring body that exceed its containment is about displacing the sovereign subject, not simply pointing out the way in which we are all dependent or interdependent. Rather, we do so in order to conceptualize that which not only displaces and problematizes the language of dependence/independence but also demonstrates active assemblages of "becoming-in-the-world-with-others" as a way out of the self and the telos of autonomy (Price and Shildrick 2002: 72). The becoming-in-the-world-with-others approach is a new way of situating bodies with the question of intercorporeal ethics and imagines a different way of living together. It denounces the exploitation of capital.

Michelle lives in a separate room with her teacher with whom she spends most of her time. She rarely interacts with her parents. In the presence of her teacher, she feels the extension of her body; her teacher becomes her hands, eyes, and legs. She calls him whenever she needs something. In the absence of her teacher, she feels incomplete and imperfect. In the presence of her teacher, Michelle does not feel that she is disabled; in other words, she experiences her body as complete and whole. Michelle's subjectivity is in relation to her teacher at all times. She is very familiar with her teacher; it is as if she knows him in the same way that one knows his or her parts of the body. She searches for him every time he is not around. Pinky does the same. If she does not meet Nandu every day, she feels lost and fails to concentrate on her work. One may argue that because she loves him she wants to be with him all time. In fact, they both realize that they experience their fullest sense of self when they are together. The intercorporeal relationship does not take us in the direction of thinking about the rights of the people with disabilities in terms of their independence, but rather leads us to think about the relational assemblage that is created in the moments of intimate care. The shared moments between care attendants and people with disabilities force us to examine the way bodies are produced together and challenge the autonomy of the normative body.

According to Deleuze and Guattari, "a body is an intensive relation of parts, differentiated by the maximum and minimum thresholds of its power of being affected" (1987: 45). They use the concept of "becoming" to destabilize the idea of "being" and consider the entire life as a constant process of becoming.

It is not that a static and stable being enters into a new relationship that transforms the body, but rather bodies that symbolize intensive relation of forces or power continually produce affects in relation with others and form temporary assemblages. A body is then,

> an assemblage of forces or passions that solidify (in space) and consolidate (in time) within the singular configuration commonly known as an "individual." This intensive and dynamic entity is not, however, the emanation of an inner essence, nor is it merely the effect of biology. The Deleuzean body is rather a portion of forces that is stable enough—spatio-temporarily speaking—to sustain them and to undergo constant, though necessarily contained, fluxes of transformation. It is a friend of transformative effects whose availability for changes of intensity depends, first, on its ability to sustain and, second, to encounter the impact of other forces or affects.
>
> (Braidotti 2011: 159)

Therefore, the body's position of becoming cannot be known in advance; instead, it "becomes" with the "touch" of others. It is constantly produced in relational assemblage with others. Becoming concentrates more upon the creative and multiple assemblages rather than thinking about the individual subject. Kelly Fritsch argues that becoming is aimed at neither the emancipation of a collectivity nor an aggregate of subjects with a shared identity struggling to gain political and economic rights, as the disability rights movement might desire. Becoming aims to transform the static position of identity and transgress the fixity of it altogether. It is more important to understand the way it escapes the process of subjectification and reinscribes the subject. The concept of becoming pays attention to transcending the limits of subjects, it does not focus on how the subject has been constructed or is being constructed. It allows us to think about the point of the unsustainability of the subject in fixed form. It helps us to realize how the identity or embodiment is constantly displaced and confronted. It does not dismiss the politics of identity and subjectivity, but rather focuses on the fluid embodiment. It constantly undoes the contained sense of self that is founded upon the notion of independence and sovereign autonomy. Grosz argues that a body is a connection of heterogeneous surfaces, energies, and surfaces: "the body does not hide or reveal an otherwise unrepresented latency or depth but is a set of operational linkages and connections with other things, other bodies" (1994: 20). Assemblages do not follow any order, they are temporarily linkages of fragments, elements and flow of ideas whether they are animate or inanimate. They are composed of lines, speed, intensities, and movements. They are not found anywhere but are made. They are not constructed at a particular time, but rather are made constantly and connected. This is why the body is not a fixed individual; rather it is an assemblage of pleasures, organs, activities, passions, feelings, and behaviors. It is a grouping of various sorts of elements and different materials of all sorts. "The way in which bodies come together produce a non-totalised collection or assemblages, which in its active relations to other social practices, entities, and events, forms connections" (1994: 20). Therefore, bodily functions and the body's connections with others sometimes do and sometimes do not transmit the intensities. "Any assemblage owes its capacity and capability to become to the very vitality of materials that constitute it" (Bennett 2010: 23).

A personal carer who works as an assemblage is an embodied relation who challenges the normative construction of an autonomous being. Nandu, who is always there to help Pinky, feels that he is detached and goes to the fight and wins. During the dance practices, he just dictates to her and guides her to improve her performance. But he loses his identity perpetually and experiences a new form of subjectivity. He cannot stand as neutral and imagines himself as a blind man. He does not perceive himself as actively engaging in the dance practice but his physical energies are present and that make him engage in the practice routine. His body transforms from what was thought to be a container into a porous, multiplicity of outsides and insides. The sovereign subject experiences a loss of containment. The disability experience of Nandu expresses a leakage between their bodies, where they become-with-one-another in an assemblage.

Balraj, who carries his own subjectivity, helps Michelle to position her body, to make her wear a particular dress, and feeds her. Sometimes Michelle even exposes her private parts to him, and once she feels like kissing him and the act of doing so makes both of them feel vulnerable. Remaining with this vulnerability, Balraj is neither wholly subsumed nor able to maintain his distance. Rather, all are involved in a continual process of becoming together through the unmapped circulation of desire, so that although subjectivity is never completely abandoned, it remains a charge point of departure and return, leaking and flowing, closing and opening (Gibson 2006: 24). Balraj feels like he is being pulled back and pulled in. As Manning puts it, the event takes place neither in the subject nor the object, but in relation to itself (2009: 78). It is in this relation that the sense of self is constituted; selves build onto and through one another, bursting out of their skin containers in an intimate relationship with the environment (Manning 2009: 79). These all are the process of becoming that intermingle in this particular assemblage.

The assistance of care attendants accounts for the inability of people with disabilities, which is why the medical model treats disability as a disease. The inability of people with disabilities can be overcome with the help of an attendant. But the involvement of care attendants with their desires, intensities, vulnerabilities, leakiness, and connections can never be overlooked. The involvement of a care attendant frames a relational embodiment and queers the fixed identity of the autonomous subject, and such processes can never be explained by the language of independence. "The operation of desire as that which extends beyond the self to the other is a potential point of disturbance to the normativities of everyday life" (Fritsch 2008: 67). The coming together of bodies results in a loss of self-definition.

The theory of independency and autonomy increases the possibility to view disability as a lack and a deficiency. It also neutralizes the role of attendants and fixes them just as a tool that performs like an object. It also contributes to legitimizing the repressive systems that subscribe to the exclusion of people with disabilities. It exhibits the lack of disability in relation to normal people and compels people with disabilities to contribute to capitalist society. According to Hughes et al. (2005), "Transforming care into personal assistance means buying into the logocentric and patriarchal heritage of the enlightenment. It also means that the ethical imperative recognition of the Other is left out of the moral equation" (Hughes et al. 2005: 268). Therefore, various produced assemblages challenge the beings of the bodies and question the autonomy and independency that is implicitly asserted. Here, our focus is not on showing the relationship between one body and another, but rather it is on understanding intercorporeality as the fundamental structure of becoming-in-the-world-with-others. The process of becoming the body dismisses the notion of being and represents its inherent fluidity, lack of completion, and unsettled subjectivity. According to Weiss, "intercorporeality signals that the experience of being embodied is never a private affair, but is always already mediated by our continual interactions with other human and non-human bodies" (1999: 5). Shildrick adds, "Our sensing bodies are not only affected by others but actually 'effect the very constitution of embodied becoming" (2009: 25).

The disabled body does not only help in identifying the relational nature of embodiment but also challenges the sovereign self and radically shifts our sense of one another. It paradigmatically undoes the grounds upon which capitalist relations depend and changes our ethical responsibilities toward each other. Assemblages of becoming create new ways of being that do not reinforce inequitable relations. The concept of assemblage places emphasis on what we can create together rather than what we do for others.

> If the assemblage of a disabled person and her attendant is constantly closed-off by reasserting their statuses as a boss and a worker, what can be created at that moment is limited by this contractual relationship. However, in thinking through other possible ways of embodying this interaction through an intercorporeal ethics, caring is no longer simply about a set of mechanical tasks.
>
> (Hughes et al. 2005: 261)

New practices form new kinds of subjects and create different kinds of social relations that dismiss the same social inequities that have marginalized people with disabilities and others. Here we seek neither to glorify nor to dismiss the status of the marginal but to transform the very foundation of any political interaction. Engaging with the critical thinking of intercorporeality and becoming-in-the-world-with-the-others opens up new ways of understanding bodies that have the potential to emancipate both people with disabilities and others.

This chapter not only explores the stereotypical representation of women with disabilities but also formulates a new model for their liberation. It questions the state apparatuses that attempt to normalize anomalous embodiment. The discourse of modernity that prevails over self-dependency and individuality was questioned. It is a panoptic gaze of the patriarchal culture that domesticates women with disabilities. The analysis of cinematic texts is important to examine the way cinema perpetuates the prejudiced belief of mainstream society against people with disabilities and at the same time presents an alternative model through which to voice their experiences.

Chapter 7

New Directions for Future Work

Disability is one of the least explored fields and as such scholars need to examine the religio-political discourse that has constituted the systematic discriminatory structure of society that leaves no space for the body marked with differences. The consciousness of the people is governed prominently by religious ideologies. All cultures, including the Jewish culture, the Christian culture, and the Hindu culture, are regulated by their respective dominant religions and determine the societal norms. Norms identify the productive body for global modernity and certify it as a worthy living body. With respect to the disabled body, norms attempt to modify it in order to make it productive. The classical age discovered the body as an object and target of power. "It is easy enough to find signs of the attention then paid to the body—to the body that is manipulated, shaped, trained: which obeys, responds, becomes skillful, and increases its forces" (Rainbow 1984: 180). Through various ideological apparatuses, society aims to train the anomalous bodies to assimilate them into normative structures.

By using post-conventional and postmodernist theories, one can attempt to embark on the crucial ethical step of thinking differently in terms of people with disabilities. There is a need to refigure disability and move beyond normative frameworks that limit the possibilities for a radical reevaluation of the discourse of disability. This does not limit itself to the medical and social model of disability but explores the sociology of impairment. It questions the structure of ableism that reinforces the dominant cultural views of disability. It deals with the Christian religious practices that do not give disabled people the right to be a priest. It represents how religion as an important tool was used by society to discriminate against people with disabilities. There is a need to understand the religious practices that supervise the process of exclusion. Prejudiced beliefs—e.g., the disabled body is a punishment by God—are circulated by religious practices and are embedded in the consciousness of the people. This needs to be deconstructed to open up a space for people with disabilities. It critiques the model of charity that believes that people with disabilities are helpless and hapless, and that they require people's assistance and sympathy.

The institutionalization of hospitals and asylums represented the politics of the state to exclude bodies marked with differences. The hospital building was

DOI: 10.4324/9781032722054-7

organized as an instrument of medical action. It operated in the manner of a disciplinary institution and as a machinery of control that functions like a microscope of conduct. It was established in the standardization of industrial processes and products. During that time, disability was produced in a particular form. Due to their physical differences, disabled people were excluded from the labor market and consequently they were unemployed and poor. Foucault's work is concerned with the history of institutions and the shift that occurred in human life during industrialization. His works help to identify oppressive regimes that do not even open up the scope for emancipatory discourse. It goes without saying that these analyses do not explore the experiences of people with disabilities but allow individual identification with subject populations to inform and deepen the scholarly enterprise.

This book seeks to celebrate the differences of disabled people and secures differences' claim to ethical legitimacy. By investigating the problems of sociopolitical movements in the field of disability studies, it is found that the disability movement must use differences as a rhetorical and practical tool with a powerful ethical legacy to mature the labor of emancipation. The book fulfills its objective by debating in favor of inclusive differences and giving the emerging disabling practices their own voice to challenge any a priori form of fixing disability that attempts to fix it into a self-closed perspective. It moves away from the discussions concerned with differences in impairment and disability and promotes a methodological and conceptual shift from exclusive perspectives to inclusive differences. It focuses on the heterogeneity of practices that makes inclusive differences so eminently political. It challenges the hegemonic voices that do not give space for multiple voices. In Chapter 2, the hegemonic practices of the Indian government and its goal to promote commonality are questioned. It discusses the empowerment of practices that question common sociocultural and material orders that have taken the model of exclusion for granted.

Pain is a very important phenomenon in the discourse of disability to intervene in the knowledge produced about disability through pain. Pain is also used as a tool to structure the cultural politics of ableism. With the help of novels, the enigmatic relationship between pain and suffering is questioned. The narratives that believe that pain leads to suffering and disabled body experiences pain. The book examines the structural conditions that make the experience of chronic pain tragic. The discourse of athleticism, personal responsibility, individualism, and stoicism finds that pain causes suffering for people with disabilities. The connection between gender and sexuality that is intimately promoted by the discourse of athleticism cannot be overlooked. This echoes Alison Kafer's contention that "disability is experienced in and through relationships" (2003: 11) and adheres to the claim that pain also occurs in relationships. It concludes by arguing that suffering is both structural and profoundly situated.

The theories of Judith Butler and Gilles Deleuze have already had a far-reaching influence on contemporary critical work on the body, gender, sexuality, and identity. Their work suggests that there are different forms of embodiment and their associated behavior, particularly in relation to sexuality, helps a scholar to raise questions about what is legitimate and what is not. It expresses the intelligible nature of the disabled body that can never be subjugated. Analysis of the characters in the chosen novels reveals the impossibility of stabilizing a unified self who will become a subject in the symbolic. They are continually in the process of being produced and transformed. The work turns to minoritarian thinking and practices which are highly appropriate for the problematics of disability. It mobilizes an effective account of globalization that incorporates symbolic and imaginary aspects without losing touch with the disabled bodies. It suggests that globalization does not offer the opportunity for new locations, energies, and capacities but does open up a different form of fluid identity that encompasses the lives of disabled people.

The emerging discourse of animal studies can help us to analyze the constant association of people with disabilities with animals to naturalize their suppression. This new direction is necessary to study what Marcus says is the "strongest form of difference ... within our own cultural realm" (1986: 168). The study of animal-human interactions is very productive for further sociological exploration of these differences. We also need to refigure the animal and their interaction with nature and with human beings. According to Haraway,

> the actors are not all of us. If the world exists for us as nature, this designates a kind of relationship, an achievement among many actors, not all of them human ... nature is made, but not entirely by humans; it is a co-construction among humans and non-humans.
>
> (1992: 297)

This study also offers intersectionalities of positivism, post-structuralism, and phenomenological views of nature as well as of the human body. Intersections of these discourses disrupt the hierarchization of human versus non-human reductionist views of nature as well as of the human body.

The book also questions the rationalist approaches to human and non-human ethics and promotes concepts of friendship, care, community, and responsibility. It resists the dualism of reason and emotion and explores the continuity with and differences from other life forms. It discusses the representation of women with disabilities in movies and concludes that they have always been projected as being subservient to men. Their disabilities are portrayed as preventing them from having their rights and freedom. The normative patriarchal structure that constitutes them as the disabled subject goes unnoticed. Scholarship challenges the constraints in women's lives and obscures the categories of nationalism, womanhood, sexuality, race, and class. The chosen movies present a fundamental means through which these disabled women are subjected to hegemonic codes that reinforce social mandates related to heterosexuality and womanhood. However, through disabled women's narratives these discourses may be disrupted and the categories of womanhood, sexuality, and race can be undermined. Women with disabilities are also no exception when it comes to household chores. However, their efforts remain invisible. Their wages are low and they have the fewest opportunities for employment. The movies under study contest the perversions of cultural traditions and modernity.

An analysis of the media is important to understand its role in the construction of cultural identities. Women with disabilities are often victimized by the cultural narratives of stigma. Associating disabled women with tainted and discounted images produces a discrediting effect. The stigma attached to women with disabilities is more intense and effective than that to men with disabilities because they live in a patriarchal culture. Moreover, women as a category are already ostracized. Like gender, disability is biological; indeed, it is socially constructed from biological reality. The stigmatized identity of women with disabilities enforces the patriarchal culture's desire for control over the body.

Feminists have unmasked consumer capitalism's appropriation of women as sexual objects for male gratification. However, the media produces mythicized images of women that prioritize sexual pleasure for the able-bodied. Sexual images of women with disabilities are projected as privileging the able-bodied. Moreover, there is a missing discourse of pleasure for people with disabilities. Disability scholars and activists are still struggling to make access to the built environment equal for people with disabilities. They are fighting for disabled people's right to education, employment, etc. It is not suggested that accessibility to the built environment is not important for people with disabilities, but we also need to focus on the discourse of sexuality for people with disabilities. Full inclusion means access to pleasure. It is our collective responsibility to push further the agenda of educating ourselves and share the real truths about sexuality with the non-disabled community of the non-disabled too.

This book has tried to introduce the reader to the intellectual and political issues that emerge from the discourse of disability. It does not only produce emancipatory discourse for the people with disabilities but also debates in favor of all the marginalized bodies. A theory of disability for the liberation of all the marginalized bodies is needed because the theory of disability represents locations and forms of embodiment from which the dominant ideologies of society became visible and open to criticism. There is a need to circulate the idea that the disabled body is as real as an able body so that people with disabilities can occupy the space in public to which they are entitled.

Disability identity shares the same theoretical tenets with the categories of race, caste, gender, class, and sexuality. Disability does not only talk about the impaired body, it also engages with the exclusion of people based on their gender, class, caste, and race under the spectrum of patriarchal culture. A disabled woman is denied access to the social space because she has a female body. The caste system disabled the Dalits because they belong to a lower caste. All the people who are excluded by society are entitled to a disability identity. Their voices raised together against the normative culture will help to transform society and to build an inclusive society in which all the people can be accommodated irrespective of their differences. They may have different experiences but they all are the victims of normative culture.

The issues of employment with respect to people with disabilities must be explored. The Persons with Disabilities Act, 1995 provides 3% reservations in all government and public sector jobs, which I think is insufficient given the number of people with disabilities in India. Moreover, even this 3% is not implemented. Most universities do not have disabled teachers. It has become commonplace for universities to fail to fully implement the reservation policy for disabled candidates. Also, universities tend to homogenize different categories of disability by grouping different candidates with different kinds of disability under one category. This usually happens because they are not aware of the various categories within the category. I posit that such information should be circulated to the authorities to help them to understand that disability has its own diversity. The problems confronting a visually challenged person are different from those of a physically incapacitated person. Their diversity cannot be homogenized. This is not to suggest that they should not join forces to fight against the discriminatory system but rather there is a need to collate the experiences of various disability categories and address them scientifically to avoid overgeneralization of problems concerned with people with disabilities.

Disability scholars must debate the usage of various terms for people with disabilities. We often come across the words such as disabled, handicapped, differently abled, challenged on trains and buses, or in railway stations and other public places. Every term has an oppressive value. disability scholars understand that one employs a medical way of referring to disability in day-to-day life which will not bring about any change in the attitude of the people or in the meaning of disability. There have been major debates on the politics of language: how can one change people's attitudes by changing the words one uses to refer to disability? The word *bechara* (poor thing) is generally seen to attach to a disabled body. It accentuates the victim status of disabled people. As discussed earlier, each term is contextual and has its own cultural roots and meanings. The cultural meaning that is attached to an impaired body is the result of fate, and thus is beyond redemption. I would like to work on the politics of language and its stigmatized association with disabled people. Many disability scholars do not feel comfortable with the term "handicapped" and have challenged the way it is used to refer to people with disabilities, even in the official documents.

India is a vast country with many different languages and practices. We can never homogenize the experiences of people with disabilities living in different regions. Needless to say, disabled people have problems with society. They can associate with each other, and can share their experiences with regard to exclusion and discrimination. In-depth research work will be needed to collect their experiences and analyze along what lines they differ from each other and in what ways they are excluded. The relationship between state, society, and family in the context of disability has also yet to be adequately conceptualized.

This book does not deal with the issues surrounding cognitive disability which I consider are material for future research. Physical disability can be identified with bodily appearance, unlike mental disability, which is why physically impaired people can easily become victims of society. They are easily subjected to medical institutions. Their behavior always challenges the normal order. They are often confined to private spaces and their choices are rejected outright. They are an easy target for sexual and domestic violence. There is little existing literature that deals with the issues of people with mental disabilities. We need to examine the resources available to them and review the facilities for their education provided by the government. Our task will be to find out how easy it is for them to access such facilities and whether the government meets their educational needs. A survey should be conducted to examine the issues surrounding parenthood for people with intellectual disabilities. There is a need to address questions such as should people with intellectual disabilities bear children? Can parents with intellectual disabilities adequately care for their children? What are their sources of income and how do they manage in the home? How is the government working to meet their welfare needs? Is any help provided for them by the government?

Disability in India is still perceived as an individual problem even by policymakers, medical professionals, and teachers. This is largely because stigma and charity still continue to structure the way disability is viewed. By examining these issues, we will create awareness regarding disability and highlight the fact that disability is socially constructed. Our goal is to remove the stigma attached to disability that ostracizes people with disabilities. Research in these fields will increasingly project disabled people as *citizens*.

Bibliography

Abberley, Paul. "The Concept of Oppression and the Development of a Social Theory of Disability." *Disability, Handicap and Society*, vol. 2, 1977, pp. 5–19.

Addlakha, Renu. *Disability Studies in India: Global Discourses, Local Realties*. New Delhi: Routledge, 2013.

Alcoff, Linda. "Cultural Feminism Versus Poststructuralism: The Identity Crisis in Feminist Theory." *Signs: Journal of Women in Culture and Society*, vol. 13, no. 3, 2006, pp. 40–66.

Althusser, Louis. "Ideology and Ideological State Apparatuses (Notes Towards an Investigation)." *Lenin and Philosophy and Other Essays*. Edited by Ben Brewster. New York: Monthly Review Press, 1971, pp. 85–126.

Alur, Mithu. "The Lethargy of a Nation: Inclusive Education in India and DevelopingSystemic Strategies for Change." *Policy, Experience and Change: Cross Cultural Reflections on Inclusive Education*, edited by Len Barton and Felicity Armstrong. Dordrecht: Springer, 2007, pp. 91–106.

Anderson, Robert. "Stroke." *Living with Chronic Illness: The Experience of Patients and their Families*. Edited by Robert Anderson and Michael Bury. London: Unwin Hyman, 1969.

Anderson, Robert C. "Teaching (with) Disability: Pedagogies of Lived Experience." *Review of Education, Pedagogy, and Cultural Studies*, vol. 28, no. 3–4, 2006, pp. 367–379.

Aristotle. *Rhetoric*. Translated by W. Rhys Roberts. New York: Modern Library, 1984.

Armstrong, David. *Original Signs: Gesture, Sign, and the Sources of Language*. Washington, DC: Gallaudet UP, 2002.

Austin, John L. *How to Do Things with Words*. Cambridge, MA: Harvard UP, 1962.

Ballard, Keith. *Inclusive Education: International Voices on Disability and Justice*. New York: Routledge. 1999.

Barnes, Colin. *Disabling Imagery and the Media*. Halifax: Derby and Ryburn Publishing, 1992.

Barnes, Colin. "The Social Model of Disability: Myths and Misrepresentations." *Coalition, the magazine of the Greater Manchester Coalition of Disabled People*, August 1996, pp. 115–130.

Barnes, Colin, Mercer, Geoff, and Shakespeare, Tom. *Exploring Disability: A Sociological Introduction*. Cambridge: Polity Press, 1999.

Barnes, Colin, Oliver, Mike, and Barton, Len. *Disability Studies Today*. Polity Press: Cambridge, 2002.

Bartky, Sandra. *Femininity and Domination: Studies in the Phenomenology of Oppression*. London: Routledge, 1990.

Barton, Len. "The Struggle for Citizenship: The Case of Disabled People." *Disability, Handicap & Society*, vol. 8, no. 3, 1993, pp. 235–248.

Barton, Len. "Developing an Emancipatory Research Agenda: Possibilities and Dilemmas." *Articulating with Difficulty: Research Voices in Inclusive Education*. Edited by Peter Clough and Len Barton. London: Paul Chapman Publishing, 1998, pp. 59–69.

Barton, Len. "The Struggle for Citizenship: The Case of Disabled People." *Disability, Handicap and Society*, 1998, pp. 35–58.

Barton, Len. *Overcoming Disability Barriers*. New York: Routledge, 2006.

Baudrillard, Jean. *Symbolic Exchange and Death*. Cambridge: SAGE, 1976.

Bauman, Zygmunt. *Postmodernity and Its Discontents*. Cambridge: Polity Press, 1997.

Beauvoir, Simonede. *The Second Sex*. New York: Vintage, 2010.

Bennett, Jane. "The Agency of Assemblages."*Vibrant Matter: A Political Ecology of Things*. Durham, NC: Duke UP, 2010.

Bennett, Wayne, and Tilly, Christopher. *Body and Image: Explorations in Landscape Phenomenology*. San Francisco: Left Coast Press, 2008.

Benveniste, Emile. "Subjectivity in Language." *Problems in General Linguistics*. Edited by M. E. Meek. Coral Gables: FL: U of Miami P, 1971, pp. 223–230.

Bersani, Leo. *Is the Rectum a Grave? And Other Essays*. Chicago: Chicago UP, 2010.

Berube, Michael. *Life as We Know It: A Father, a Family, and an Exceptional Child*. New York: Vintage-Random House, 1998.

Bhatt, Usha. *The Physically Handicapped in India: A Growing National Problem*. Bombay: Popular Book Depot. 1963.

Bird, Lisa. *The Fundamental Facts: All the Latest Facts and Figures on Mental lllness*. London: Mental Health Foundation, 1999.

Braidotti, Rosi. *Nomadic Subjects Embodiment and Sexual Difference in Contemporary Feminist Theory*. 2nd ed. New York: Columbia UP, 2011.

Branson, Jan, and Miller, Don. "Beyond Integration Policy: The Deconstruction of Disability." *Integration: Myth or Reality?* Edited by Len Barton. London: Falmer Press, 1999.

Bredberg, Elizabeth. "Writing Disability History: Problems, Perspectives and Sources." *Disability & Society*, vol. 14, no. 2, 1999, pp. 189–201.

Browne, Susan*et al.With the Power of Each Breath: A Disabled Women's Anthology*. San Francisco, CA: Cleis Press, 1985.

Buckingham, Jane. "Writing Histories of Disability in India: Strategies of Inclusion." *Disability and Society*, vol. 26, no. 4, 2011, pp. 419–431.

Butler, Judith. "Performative Acts and Gender Constitution: An Essay in Phenomenology and Feminist Theory." *Theatre Journal*, vol. 40, no. 4, 1988, pp. 519–531.

Butler, Judith. *Gender Trouble: Feminism and the Subversions of Identity*. London: Routledge, 1990.

Butler, Judith. *Bodies that Matter: On the Discursive Limits of Sex*. London: Routledge, 1993.

Canguilhem, Georges. *The Normal and The Pathological*. New York: Zone Books, 1991.

Charlton James. *Nothing About Us Without Us: Disability, Oppression and Empowerment*. Berkeley: U of California P. 1998.

Chowdhary, Prem. "Socio-Economic Dimensions of Certain Customs and Attitudes: Women of Haryana in the Colonial Period." *Economic and Political Weekly*, vol. 22, no. 48, Nov. 28, 1987, pp. 2060–2066.

Connell, Raewyn. *Masculinities*, Berkeley, CA: U of California P, 1995.

Connell, Raewyn. "Masculinities and Globalization," *Men and Masculinities*, vol. 1, no. 1, 1998, pp. 3–23.

Cooter, R. *Surgery and Society in Peace and War: Orthopaedics and the Organization of Modern Medicine1880–1948*. Basingstoke: Macmillan, 1993.

Copjec, Joan. *Read My Desire: Lacan Against the Historicists*. Cambridge, MA: MIT P, 1994.

Copjec, Joan. *Read My Desire: Lacan Against the Historicists*. London: Routledge, 1998.

Corker, Mairian. "Sensing Disability," *Feminism and Disability*, vol. 16, no. 4, Autumn 2001, pp. 34–52.

Corker, Mairian, and Shakespeare, Tom. *Disability/Postmodernism: Embodying Disability Theory*. London: Continuum, 2002.

Crow, Liz. "Including All Our Lives; Renewing the Social Model of Disability." *Encounters with Strangers: Feminism and Disability*. Edited by Jenny Morris. London: Women's Press, 1996.

Darwin, Charles. *On the Origin of Species by Means of Natural Selection*. Oxford: Oxford UP, 1989.

Davis, Lennard. "Nude Venuses, Medusa's Body, and Phantom Limbs." *Enforcing Normalcy: Disability, Deafness and the Body*. Edited by DavidMitchell and Sharon Snyder. New York: Verso, 1995.

Davis, Lennard. "Nude Venuses, Medusa's Body, and Phantom Limbs." *The Body and Physical Difference*. Edited by DavidMitchell and Sharon Snyder. Ann Arbor: U of Michigan P, 1997.

Davis, Lennard. "Nude Venuses, Medusa's Body, and Phantom Limbs." *The Disability Studies Reader*. Edited by DavidMitchell and Sharon Snyder. New York: Routledge, 1997.

Davis, Lennard. "Introduction: Disability, Normality, and Power." *The Disability Studies Reader*. 4th ed. Edited by Lennard J. Davis. Routledge: New York, 2013.

Deleuze, Gilles, and Guattari, Felix. *A Thousand Plateaus: Capitalism and Schizophrenia*. Translated by Robert Hurley. Minneapolis: Minnesota UP, 1987.

Deleuze, Gilles, and Guattari, Felix. *Anti-Oedipus: Capitalism and Schizophrenia*. Translated by Robert Hurley. Minneapolis: Minnesota UP, 1987.

Derrida, Jacques. *Of Grammatology*. Baltimore, MD: Johns Hopkins UP, 1967.

Derrida, Jacques. *Limited Inc*. Berkeley, CA: SAGE, 1977.

Derrida, Jacques, and Bass, Alan. *Positions*. Chicago: Chicago UP, 1981.

Dorman, Johanna. *The Blemished Body: Deformity and Disability in the Qumran Scrolls*. Doctoral dissertation, U of Groningen, 2007.

Douglas, Mary. *Natural Symbols*. New York: Pantheon, 1970.

Douglas, Mary. *Purity and Danger: An Analysis of the Concepts of Pollution and Taboo*. London: Routledge, 2004.

Drinkwater, Chris. "Supported Living and the Production of Individuals." *Foucault and the Government of Disability*. Edited by Shelley Tremain. Michigan: U of Michigan P, 2015, pp. 229–244.

Erevelles, Nirmala. *Disability and Difference in Global Contexts: Enabling a Transformative Body Politic*. New York: Palgrave Macmillan, 2011.

Esping-Andersen, Gøsta. "After the Golden Age." *Welfare States in Transition: National Adaptations in Global Economies*. Edited by Gøsta Esping-Andersen. London: SAGE, 1996, pp. 1–31.

Esposito, Roberto. *Immunitas: The Protection and Negation of Life*. Cambridge: Polity Press, 2011.

Farrall, Lyndsay Andrew. *The Origin and Growth of the English Eugenics Movement 1865–1925*. New York: Garland, 1985.

Feasey, Rebecca. *Masculinity and Popular Television*. Edinburg: Edinburg UP, 2008.

Fine, Michelle, and Asch, Adrienne. *Women with Disabilities: Essays in Psychology, Culture, and Politics*. Philadelphia, PA: Temple UP, 1988.

Finger, Anne. *Past Due: A Story of Disability, Pregnancy and Birth*. London. Routledge, 1990.

Finkelstein, Victor. *Attitudes and Disabled People: Issues for Discussion*. New York: World Rehabilitation Fund, 1980.

Finkelstein, Victor. "Disability and the Helper I Helped Relationship: An Historical View." *Handicap in a Social World*. Edited by Ann Brechin, Penny Liddiard, and John Swain. London: Hodder and Stoughton, 1981, pp. 59–63.

Fisher, Seymour. *Body Consciousness: You Are What You Feel*. Englewood Cliffs, NJ: Prentice-Hall, 1973.

Fletcher, Agnes. *Overcoming Obstacles to the Integration of the Disabled People*. Disability Awareness in Action, 1995.

Foucault, Michel. *Madness and Civilization: A History of Insanity in the Age of Reason*. Translated by Richard Howard. New York: Random House, 1965.

Foucault, Michel. *The Birth of the Clinic: An Archaeology of Medical Perception*. Translated by Alan Sheridan. London: Tavistock, 1973.

Foucault, Michel. *Discipline and Punish: The Birth of the Prison*. Translated by A. Sheridan. London: Allen Lane, 1977.

Foucault, Michel. *History of Sexuality*. Vol. 1. Translated by Robert Hurley. London: Allen Lane, 1979.

Foucault, Michel. *Power/Knowledge. Selected Interviews and Other Writings1972–1977*. Edited by Colin Gordon. Brighton: Harvester Press, 1980.

Foucault, Michel. "The Subject and Power." *Michel Foucault: Beyond Structuralism and Hermeneutics*. Edited by Hubert L. Dreyfus and Paul Rabinow. Chicago: U of Chicago P, 1982.

Foucault, Michel. *Society Must Be Defended*. Translated by David Macey, Edited by Mauro Bertani and Alessandro Fortona. New York: Picador, 2003.

Foucault, Michel. *Abnormal*. Translated by Graham Burchell. New York: Picador, 2003.

Frazee, Catherine. "Body Politics." *Saturday Night*, 2 September 2000.

Friedman, John B. *The Monstrous Races in Medieval Art and Thought*. Cambridge, MA.: Harvard UP, 1981.

Friedman, Marilyn. *Women and Citizenship*. Oxford UP, 2005.

Fritsch, Kelly. "Intimate Assemblages: Disability, Intercorporeality, and the Labour of Attendant Care." *Critical Disability Discourses*, vol. 2, Sept. 2010.

Galvin, Rose. "A Genealogy of the Disabled Identity in Relation to Work and Sexuality." *Journal of Disability and Society*, vol. 21, no. 5, Aug. 2006.

Garland, Robert. *The Eye of the Beholder: Deformity and Disability in the Graceo-Roman World*. Bristol: Classic P, 2006.

Garland-Thomson, Rosemarie. *Extraordinary Bodies: Figuring Physical Disability in American Culture and Literature*. New York: Columbia UP, 1997.

Garland-Thomson, Rosemarie. "Integrating Disability, Transforming Feminist Theory." *NWSA Journal*, vol. 14, no. 3, Autumn 2002, pp. 1–32.

Garland-Thomson, Rosemarie, editor. *Freakery: Cultural Spectacles of the Extra-ordinary Body*. New York: Columbia UP, 2005.

Garland-Thomson, Rosemarie. *Staring: How We Look*. Oxford: Oxford UP, 2009.

Gibbs, Richard W. *The Poetics of Mind*. Cambridge: Cambridge UP, 1994.

Gibson, Barbara E. "Disability, Connectivity and Transgressing the Autonomous Body." *Journal of Medical Humanities*, vol. 27, 2006, pp. 187–196.

Girdlestone, Gathorne Robert. *The Care and Cure of Crippled Children*. New York: Arno Press, 1924.

Ghai, Anita. "Disabled Woman: An Excluded Agenda of Feminism". *Feminism and Disability*, vol. 17, no. 3, Summer 2002, pp. 49–66.

Giddens, Anthony. *Modernity and Self-Identity*. London: Routledge, 1991.

Giddens, Anthony. *Sociology*. 6th ed. Cambridge: Polity, 2006.

Giroux, Henry A. *Border Crossings: Cultural Workers and the Politics of Education*. New York: Routledge, 1992.

Glassner, B. *Bodies: The Tyranny of Perfection*. Los Angeles: Lowell House, 1992.

Gleeson, Brendan J. *Second Nature? The Socio-Spatial Production of Disability*, Doctoral Thesis, Department of Geography, U of Melbourne P. 1992.

Gleeson, Brendan J. *Second Nature? The Socio-Spatial Production of Disability*. London: Routledge, 1999.

Goffman, Erving. *Stigma: Notes on the Management of Spoiled Identity*. Harmonds-worth: Penguin, 1963.

Goffman, Erving. *Frame Analysis*. New York: Harper & Row, 1974.

Goffman, Erving, and Lemert, Charles C. *The Goffman Reader*. Cambridge, MA: Blackwell, 1997.

Greengross, Wendy. *Entitled to Love: Sexual and Emotional Needs of the Disabled*. London: Malaby Press, 1976.

Grosz, Liz. *Volatile Bodies: Towards a Corporeal Feminism*. Bloomington: Indiana UP, 1994.

Gwyn, Richard. "Captain of My Own Ship: Metaphor and the Discourse of Chronic Illness."*Researching and Applying Metaphor*. Edited by Lynne Cameron and Graham Low. Cambridge: Cambridge UP, 1999.

Hacking, Ian. *The Social Construction of What*. Cambridge, MA: Harvard UP, 1999.

Hahn, Harlan. "Public Support for Rehabilitation in Programs: The Analysis of US Disability Policy." *Disability, Handicap & Society*, vol. 1, no. 2, 2007, pp. 121–138.

Hahn, Nicolette. *The Righteous: Porkchop: Finding a Life and Good Food Beyond Factory Farms*. New York: William Morrow, 2009.

Hannabach, Cathy. "Anxious Embodiment, Disability and Sexuality: A Response to Margrit Shildrick," *Studies in Gender and Sexuality*, vol. 8, no. 3, 2007, pp. 253–261.

Haraway, Donna. *Primate Visions: Gender, Race and Nature in the World of Modern Science*. New York: Routledge, 1989.

Haraway, Donna. "The Promises of Monsters: A Regenerative Politics for Inappropriate/d Others," *Cultural Studies*. Edited by Lawrence Grossberg, Cary Nelson, and Paula Treichler. New York: Routledge, 1992, pp. 295–337.

Haraway, Donna. *Simians, Cyborgs, and Women: The Reinvention of Nature*. London: Free Association Books, 2003.

Harding, Sandra. *The Science Question in Feminism*. New York: Cornell UP, 1986.

Hawkins, Ronnie Zoe. "Ecofeminism and Nonhumans: Continuity, Difference, Dualism, and Domination." *Hypatia*, vol. 13, no. 1, 1998, pp. 158–197.

Hayles, N. Katherine. *How We Become Posthuman: Virtual Bodies in Cybernetics, Literature and Informatics*. Chicago: U of Chicago P, 1999.

Hegarty, Seamus, and Alur, Mithu. *Education and Children with Special Needs: From Segregation to Inclusion*. Berkeley, CA: SAGE, 2002.

Higgins, Paul. *Making Disability: Exploring the Social Transformation of Human Variation*. Springfield, IL: Charles C. Thomas Publisher. 1992.

Hirst, Michael, Thornton, Patricia, Dearey, Melissa, and Maynard-Campbell, Sue. *The Employment of Disabled People in the Public Sector: A Review of Data and Literature*. London: Disability Rights Commission, 2004.

Hirst, Paul Q., and Thompson, Graheme F. *Globalization in Question: The International Economy and the Possibilities of Governance*, 2nd edn. Cambridge: Polity Press, 1999.

Hockenberry, John. *Moving Violation: War Zones, Wheelchairs, and Declarations of Independence*. New York: Hachette Books, 1996.

Holden, Chris. "Globalization, Social Exclusion and Labour's New Work Ethic." *Critical Social Policy*, vol. 19, no. 4, 1999, pp. 523–529.

Hughes, Bill. "The Constitution of Impairment: Modernity and the Aesthetic of Oppression." *Disability & Society*, vol. 14, no. 2, 1999, pp. 155–172.

Hughes, Bill, and Paterson, Kevin. "The Social Model of Disability and the Disappearing Body: Towards a Sociology of Impairment," *Disability & Society*, vol. 12, no. 3, 1997, pp. 325–340.

Hughes, Bill, McKie, Linda, Hopkins, Debra, and Watson, Nick "Love's Labours Lost? Feminism, the Disabled People's Movement and an Ethic of Care." Sociology, vol. 39, no. 2, 2005, pp. 259–275.

Irigaray, Luce. *Speculum of Other Woman*. Translated by G. C. Gill. Ithaca, NY: Cornell UP, 1985.

Iwakuma, Miho. "The Body as Embodiment: An Investigation of the Body by Merleau Ponty." *Disability/Postmodernity: Embodying Disability Theory*. Edited by Mairian Corker, and Tom Shakespeare. London: Continuum, 2002, pp. 76–87.

Jha, Praveen. *A Right to Education in India*. New Delhi: Routledge, 2007.

Jha, Raj Kamal. *Fireproof*. New Delhi: Pan Macmillan, 2008.

Kafer, Alison. "Compulsory Bodies: Reflections on Heterosexuality and Able-bodiedness." *Journal of Women's History*, vol. 15, no. 3, Autumn 2003, pp. 77–89.

Kalyanpur, Maya. "Equality, Quality and Quantity: Challenges in Inclusive Education Policy and Service Provision in India." *International Journal of Inclusive Education*, vol. 12, no. 3, 2008.

Kanga, Firdaus. *Trying to Grow*. New Delhi: Penguin Group, 1990.

Karna, Gajendra N. *Disability Studies in India: Retrospects and Prospects*. New Delhi: Gyan Publishing House, 2001.

Kaushik, Bharti N. *Education of Disabled Students*. Jaipur: Rajasthan Hindi Granth Academy, 1977.

Keltner, Stacey. *Kristeva: Key Contemporary Thinkers*. Cambridge: Polity Press, 2011.

Kevles, Daniel J. *In the Name of Eugenics: Genetics and the Uses of Human Heredity*. New York: Alfred A. Knopf, 1985.

Kimmel, Michael. "Masculinity as Homophobia: Fear, Shame, and Silence in the Construction of Gender Identity," *Feminism and Masculinities*, Edited by Peter Murphy, Oxford: Oxford UP, 2004, pp. 182–199.

Kohama, Angela. *Inclusive Education in India: A Country in Transition*. Oregon: U of Oregon P, 2012.

Kristeva, Julia. *Power of Horrors: An Essays on Abjection.* New York: Columbia UP, 1982.

Kristeva, Julia. *Strangers to Ourselves.* New York: Columbia UP, 1991.

Kristeva, Julia. *Interviews by Julia Kristeva.* Edited by Ross Mitchell Guberman. New York: Columbia UP. 1996.

Kristiansen, Kristjana, Vehmas, Simo, and Shakespeare, Tom, editors. *Arguing About Disability: Philosophical Perspectives.* London: Routledge, 2009.

Kuppers, Petra. *Disability and Contemporary Performance: Bodies on Edge.* New York and London: Routledge, 2003.

Kuppers, Petra. *Disability Culture and Community Performance: Find a Strange and Twisted Shape.* Cambridge: Palgrave Macmillan, 2011.

Lacan, Jacques. "Aggressivity in Psychoanalysis." *Ecrits: A Selection.* Translated by A. Sheridan. New York: W. W. Norton, 1977.

Lacan, Jacques. *The Mirror Stage as Formative of the Function of the I in Ecrits: A Selection.* Translated by A. Sheridan. New York: W. W. Norton, 1977.

Lacan, Jacques. *The Four Fundamental Concepts of Psychoanalysis.* Translated by A. Sheridan. New York: W. W. Norton, 1981.

Lakoff, George, and Johnson, Mark. *Metaphors We Live By.* Chicago: U of Chicago P, 2003.

Langmore, Paul and Umansky, Lauri, editors. *The New Disability History: American Perspectives.* New York and London: New York UP, 2001.

Levin, David Michael. *The Opening of Vision. Nihilism and the Postmodern Situation.* New York and London: Routledge, 1997.

Linton, Simi. *Claiming Disability Knowledge and Identity.* New York: New York UP, 1998.

Longmore, Paul. *Why I Burned My Book and Other Essays on Disability.* Philadelphia: Temple UP, 2003.

Longmore, Paul K., and Umansky, Lauri. *The New Disability History: American Perspectives.* New York: New York UP, 2000.

Luhmann, Niklas. *Theory of Society: Cultural Memory in the Present.* Stanford, CA: Stanford UP, 2012.

MacKenzie, Donald A. *Statistics in Britain, 1865–1930.* Edinburgh: Edinburgh UP, 1981.

Manning, Rita. *Just Caring: Explorations in Feminist Ethics.* Bloomington: Indiana UP, 2009.

Marcus, George. "Contemporary Problems of Ethnography in the Modem World System." *Writing Culture: The Poetics and Politics of Ethnography.* Edited by James Clifford and George Marcus. Berkeley: U of California P, 1986, pp. 165–193.

Marks, Deborah. *Disability: Controversial Debates and Psychosocial Perspectives.* London and New York: Routledge, 1999.

Mayne, John. *A Treatise on Hindu Law and Usage.* Farmington Hills, MI: Gale, 2013.

Mayr, Ernst. *The Growth of Biological Thought: Diversity, Evolution, and Inheritance.* Cambridge, MA: Harvard UP, 1982.

Mayr, Ernst. *Toward a New Philosophy of Biology.* Cambridge, MA: Harvard UP, 1988.

McRuer, Robert. *Crip Theory: Cultural Signs of Queerness and Disability.* New York: New York UP, 2006.

Meekosha, Helen. "Body Battles: Bodies, Gender and Disability." *The Disability Reader: Social Sciences Perspectives.* Edited by Tom Shakespeare. Continuum: New York, 1998. Print.

Merleau-Ponty, Maurice. *Phenomenology of Perception.* Translated by C. Smith. London: Routledge and Kegan Paul, 1962.

Merleau-Ponty, Maurice. *The Visible and The Invisible*. Evanston, IL: Northwestern UP, 1968.

Metcalf, Barbara D. *A Concise History of Modern India*. Cambridge: Cambridge UP, 2006.

Mishra, Anil Dutta. *Mahatma Gandhi on Education*. New Delhi: Vikas Publishing House, 2011.

Mishra, Ramesh. *Globalization and the Welfare State*. Cheltenham: Edward Elgar, 1999.

Mitchell, David, and Snyder, Sharon. *The Body and Physical Difference: Discourses of Disability in the Humanities*. Ann Arbor: U of Michigan P, 1997.

Mitchell, David T., and Snyder, Sharon L. *Narrative Prosthesis Disability and the Dependencies of Discourse*. Ann Arbor: U of Michigan P, 2001.

Mitra, Sophie, and Sambamoorthi, Usha. "Disability Estimates in India: What the Census and NSS Tell Us." *Economic and Political Weekly*, vol. 41, no. 38, Sept. 23–292006, pp. 4022–4026.

Morris, Jenny. *Pride Against Prejudice*. London: Women's Press, 1991.

Murphy, Robert. *The Body Silent*. New York: W. W. Norton, 1987.

Nagar, Richa, Lawson, Victoria, McDowell, Linda, and Hanson, Susan. "Locating Globalization: Feminist (Re)reading of the Subjects and Spaces of Globalization." *Economic Geography*, vol. 78, no. 3, July 2002, pp. 257–284.

Narayan, Badri. "Demarginalisation and History: Dalit Re-invention of the Past." *South Asia Research*, vol. 28, no. 2, 2008, pp. 169–184.

Negrin, Llewellyn. *Appearance and Identity: Fashioning the Body in Postmodernity*. Cambridge: Palgrave Macmillan, 2008.

Nelson, Jack. editor. *The Disabled, the Media, and the Information Age*. Westport, CT: Greenwood Press, 1994.

Norden, Martin. *The Cinema of Isolation*. New Brunswick: Rutgers UP, 1995.

Nussbaum, Martha Craven. *Hiding from Humanity: Disgust, Shame, and the Law*. Princeton, NJ: Princeton UP, 2004.

Nussbaum, Martha. *Frontiers of Justice: Disability, Nationality, Species Membership*. Cambridge, MA: Belknap P of Harvard UP. 2007.

Oliver, Michael. *The Politics of Disablement: A Sociological Approach*. London: Palgrave Macmillan, 1990.

Oliver, Michael. "Disability and Participation in the Labour Market." *Poor Work*. Edited by Phillip Brown and Richard Scase. Milton Keynes: Open UP, 1991.

Oliver, Michael. *Understanding Disability: From Theory to Practice*. London: Palgrave Macmillan, 1996.

Oliver, Michael, and Barnes, Colin. *Social Policy and Disabled People: From Exclusion to Inclusion*. London: Longman, 1998.

Oliver, Michael, and Barnes, Colin. "Disability Studies, Disabled People and the Struggle for Inclusion." *British Journal of Sociology of Education*, vol. 31, no. 5, 2010, pp. 547–560.

Ott, Katherine. "The Sum of Its Parts," *Artificial parts, Practical Lives: Modern Histories of Prosthetics*. Edited by Katherine. Ott, David Serlin, and Steven Mihm. New York: New York UP, 2002.

Pal, Joyojeet. "The Portrayal of Disability in Indian Cinema: An Attempt at Categorization." *Phalanx*, 2012.

Patsavas, Alyson. "Recovering a Cripistemology of Pain: Leaky Bodies, Connective Tissue, and Feeling Discourse." *Journal of Literary and Cultural Disability*, vol. 8, no. 2, 2014, pp. 203–218.

Pawar, Urmila, and Moon, Meenakshi. *We Also Made History: Women in Ambedkarite Movement*. Translated by Wandana Sonalkar. New Delhi: Zubaan, 2008.

Pelka, Fred. *What Have We Done: An Oral History of the Disability Rights Movement*. Amherst: U of Massachusetts P, 2012.

Phadke, Shilpa. *Why Loiter?*London: Penguin Books, 2010.

Porter, Michael. *The Competitive Advantage of Nations*. London: Macmillan, 1990.

Porter, Theodore M. *The Rise of Statistical Thinking 1820–1900*. Princeton, NJ: Princeton UP, 1986.

Price, Janet, and Shildrick, Margrit. "Bodies Together: Touch, Ethics and Disability." *Disability/Postmodernism: Embodying Disability Theory*. Edited by Mairiam Corker and Tom Shakespeare. London: Continuum, 2002.

Priestley, Mark. *Disability Politics and Community Care*. London: Jessica Kingsley Publishers. 1999.

Priestley, Mark. *Disability and the Life Course: Global Perspectives*. Cambridge: Cambridge UP, 2001.

Priestley, Mark. *Disability and the Life Course: Global Perspectives*. Cambridge: Cambridge UP, 2011.

Rainbow, Paul. *The Foucault Reader*. New York: Pantheon Books, 1984.

Rorty, Richard. *Philosophy and Mirror of Nature*. New York: New York UP, 1980.

Rose, Martha L. *The Staff of Oedipus: Transforming Disability in Ancient Greece*. Michigan: Michigan UP, 2003.

Roulstone, Alan. *Enabling Technology: Disabled People, Work and New Technology*. Milton Keynes: Open UP, 1998.

Ruigrok, Winfied, and Van Tulder, Rob. *The Logic of International Restructuring*. London: Routledge, 1995.

Ryan, Joanna, and Thomas, Frank. *The Politics of Mental Handicap*. Harmondsworth, London: Penguin, 1980.

Samuels, Ellen. "Critical Divides: Judith Butler's Body Theory and the Question of Disability." *NWSA Journal*, vol. 14, no. 3, Autumn, 2002, pp. 58–76.

Sandhal, Carrie. *Bodies in Commotion Disability and Performance*. Ann Arbor: U of Michigan P, 2005.

Saussure, Ferdinandde. *Course in General Linguistics*. Translated by Wade Baskin. New York: McGraw-Hill, 1916.

Scambler, Graham. "Re-framing Stigma: Felt and Enacted Stigma and Challenges to the Sociology of Chronic and Disabling Conditions." *Social Theory and Health*, vol. 2, no. 1, 2004, pp. 29–46.

Scarry, Elaine. *The Body in Pain: The Making and Unmaking of the World*. New York: Oxford UP, 1985.

Schweik, Susan M. *The Ugly Laws: Disability in Public*. New York: New York UP, 1994.

Sen, Amrtya. *Inequality Reexamined*. Oxford: Clarendon P, 1992.

Shakespeare, Tom. "Cultural Representation of Disabled People: Dustbins for Disavowal." *Disability & Society*, vol. 9, no. 3, 1994,283–299.

Shakespeare, Tom, editor. *The Disability Reader: Social Science Perspectives*. London: Cassell Academic, 1998.

Shakespeare, Tom. *Disability Rights and Wrongs*. Routledge: London, 2006.

Shakespeare, Tom, and Watson, Nicholas. "The Social Model of Disability: An Outdated Ideology?" *Exploring Theories and Expanding Methodologies: Where Are We and Where Do We Need to Go? Research in Social Science and Disability*, vol. 2. Edited by Sharon Barnarrt and Barbara. M. Altman. Amsterdam: JAI, 2001.

Sharma, Umesh, and Deppeler, Joanne. "Integrated Education in India: Challenges and Prospects." *Disability Studies Quarterly*, vol. 25, no. 1, 2005.

Shildrick, Margrit. *Dangerous Discourses of Disability, Subjectivity, and Sexuality*. London: Palgrave Macmillan, 2009.

Shildrick, Margrit, and Mykitiuk, Roxanne, editors. *Ethics of the Body: Post-conventional Challenges*. Cambridge, MA: MIT Press, 2005.

Shotter, John. *Cultural Politics of Everyday Life: Social Constructionism, Rhetoric and Knowing of the Third Kind*. Toronto, ON: U of Toronto P, 1993.

Siebers, Tobin. *The Subject and Other Subjects: On Ethical, Aesthetic, and Political Identity*. Ann Arbor: U of Michigan P, 1998.

Siebers, Tobin. *Disability Theory*. Ann Arbor: U of Michigan P, 2008.

Siebers, Tobin. "Tender Organs, Narcissism, and Identity Politics." *Disability Studies: Enabling the Humanities*. Edited by Brenda Jo Brueggemann, Sharon L. Snyder, and Rosemarie Garland-Thomson. New York: PMLA, 2010.

Sinha, Indira. *Animal's People*. London: Simon & Schuster, 2007.

Snyder, Sharon L., and Mitchell, David T. *Cultural Locations of Disability*. Chicago: U of Chicago P, 2006.

Sontag, Susan. *Illness as Metaphor*. New York: Farrar, Straus and Giroux, 1978.

Stienstra, Deborah. "*The Intersection of Disability and Race/Ethnicity/Heritage Languages/ Religion*." Presented at the Intersections of Diversity Seminar, Ottawa, 8 March 2002. http://canada.metropolis.net/events/Diversity/litreview_Index_e.htm.2002.23rd.

Stienstra, Deborah. "DisAbling Globalization: Rethinking Global Political Economy with a Disability Lens." *Global Society*, vol. 16, no. 2, July 2002, pp. 109–121.

Stiker, Henry Jacques. *A History of Disability*. Ann Arbor: U of Michigan P, 1999.

Taylor, Sunaura. "The Right Not to Work: Power and Disability." *Monthly Review*, vol. 55, no. 10, 2004.

Taylor, Sunaura. "Vegans, Freaks, and Animals: Toward a New Table Fellowship." *American Quarterly*, Special Issue: *Species/Race/Sex*, vol. 65, no. 3, September 2013, pp. 55–64.

Tepper, Mitchell. "Sexuality and Disability: The Missing Discourse of Pleasure." *Journal of Sexuality and Disability*, vol. 19, no. 4, 2000.

Thomas, Carol. *Female Forms: Experiencing and Understanding Disability*. Philadelphia: Open UP, 1999.

Thomas, Linda. *Language, Society and Power: An Introduction*. London: Routledge, 1999.

Thomas, M., and Thomas, M. J. "Status of Women with Disabilities in South Asia." Asia *Pacific Disability Rehabilitation Journal. Selected Readings in Community-Based Rehabilitation, Series 2: Disability and Rehabilitation Issues in South Asia*, vol. 9, no. 2, 1998, pp. 60–64.

Tudor, Deborah. "Twenty First Century Neoliberal Man." *Neoliberalism and Global Cinema*. Edited by Jyotsna Kapur and Keith Wagner. Routledge, 2011.

Turner, David M., and Stagg, Kevin. *Social Histories of Disability and Deformity*. London: Routledge, 2006.

UNESCO. *The Salmanaca Statement and Framework for Action on Special Needs Education*. Paris: UNESCO, 1994.

United Nations. *Convention on the Rights of Persons with Disabilities and Optional Protocol*. New York: United Nations, 2007.

Waddington, Lisa B. "Reassessing the Employment of People with Disabilities in Europe: from Quotas to Anti-Discrimination Laws." *Comparative Labor Law Journal*, vol. 18, no. 1, 1996, pp. 62–101.

Watson, Nick. "Well, I Know This Is Going to Sound Very Strange to You, but I Don't See Myself as a Disabled Person: Identity and Disability." *Journal of Disability and Society*, vol. 17, no. 5, 2002.

Weber, Max. *Sociological Theory*. New York: McGraw Hill, 1996.

Weiss, Gail. *Body Images: Embodiment as Intercorporeality*. London: Routledge, 1999.

Weiss, Meira. "Territorial Isolation and Physical Deformity: Israeli Parents' Reaction to Disabled Children." *Disability & Society*, vol. 12, no. 2, 1997, pp. 259–272.

Wendell, Susan. *The Rejected Bodies: Feminist Philosophical Reflections on Disability*. New York: Routledge, 1996.

Wolfensberger, Wolf. "Human Service Policies: The Rhetoric Versus the Reality," *Disability and Dependence*. Edited by Len Barton. Lewes: Falmer, 1989, pp. 23–42.

Wolfensberger, Wolf. *The Principle of Normalization in Human Services*. North York, ON: G Allan Roeher Inst Kinsman, 1993.

Wright, David, and Digby, Anne. *From Idiocy to Mental Deficiency: Historical Perspectives on People with Learning Disabilities*. New York: Routledge, 1996.

Young, Iris Marion. *Inclusion and Democracy*. Oxford: Oxford UP, 2000.

Young, Iris Marion. *Justice and the Politics of Difference*. Princeton, NJ: Princeton UP, 2011.

Žižek, Salvoj. *Violence: Six Sideways Reflections*. London: Picador, 2008.

Zola, Irving Kenneth. "Medicine as an Institution of Social Control." *Sociological Review*, vol. 20, 1972, pp. 487–504.

Zola, Irving Kenneth. "Self, Identity, and the Naming Question: Reflections on the Language of Disability." *Social Science and Medicine*, vol. 36, no. 2, 1993, pp. 167–173.

Websites

ADL. *A Brief History of the Disability Rights Movement*. https://www.adl.org/resources/backgrounder/brief-history-disability-rights-movement. Accessed 14 November 2023.

Commission of the European Communities. *Communication from the Commission to the Council, the European Parliament, the European Economic and Social Committee and the Committee of the Regions*. https://eur-lex.europa.eu/LexUriServ/LexUriServ.do?uri=COM:2003:0567:FIN:EN:PDF. Accessed 23 December 2015.

Department of Economic and Social Affairs, United Nations. *Convention on the Rights of Persons with Disabilities*. https://social.desa.un.org/issues/disability/crpd/convention-on-the-rights-of-persons-with-disabilities-crpd. Accessed 14 November 2023.

Department of Economic and Social Affairs Disability, United Nations. Implementation of the World Programme of Action Concerning Disabled Persons. https://www.un.org/development/desa/disabilities/implementation-of-the-world-programme-of-action-concerning-disabled-persons-a49435-part-2.html. Accessed 27 December 2015.

Department of Economic and Social Affairs Disability, United Nations. *United Nations Decade of Disabled Persons 1983–1992*. https://www.un.org/development/desa/disabilities/united-nations-decade-of-disabled-persons-1983-1992.html. Accessed 27 December 2015.

Department for Education. *National Statistics: Special Education Needs in England*. https://explore-education-statistics.service.gov.uk/find-statistics/special-educational-needs-in-england. Accessed 14 November 2023.

Felluga, Dino. "General Introduction to Psychoanalysis." *Introductory Guide to Critical Theory*. https://www.cla.purdue.edu/academic/english/theory/psychoanalysis/psychintroframes.html. Accessed14 November 2023.

Government of India. *Right to Education Act*. 2005. http://www.india.gov.in/spotlight/spotlight_archive. Accessed 27 December 2011.

Historic England. *Disability in the 19th Century*. https://historicengland.org.uk/research/inclusive-heritage/disability-history/1832-1914/. Accessed 10 November 2015.

Historic England. *Disability in the Early 20th Century 1914-1945*. https://historicengland.org.uk/research/inclusive-heritage/disability-history/1914-1945/. Accessed 10 November 2015.

Indian Institute of Technology Kanpur. *Macaulay's Minute on Education*. http://home.iitk.ac.in/~hcverma/Article/Macaulay-Minutes.pdf. Accessed 14 November 2023.

Legislative Department. *The Constitution of India*. https://legislative.gov.in/constitution-of-india/. Accessed 14 November 2023.

Ministry of Home Affairs, Government of India. *A Treatise on Indian Census Since 1981*. https://censusindia.gov.in/census.website/. Accessed 14 November 2023.

Ministry of Human Resource Development, Government of India. *Sarva Shiksha Abhiyan: A Programme for the Universalization of Inclusive Education.* https://samagra.education.gov.in/inclusive.html. Accessed 14 November 2023.

Ministry of Human Resource Development, Government of India. *Inclusive Education of the Disabled at the Secondary Stage (IEDSS).* https://www.education.gov.in/iedss. Accessed 14 November 2023.

Ministry of Social Justice and Empowerment, Government of India. *The Rights of Persons with Disabilities Bill,* 2012. https://cdn.nic.in/SJ/PDFFiles/DisabilityBill2012.pdf. Accessed 15 November 2023.

Ministry of Statistics and Programme Implementation, Government of India. December 2003. https://www.mospi.gov.in/national-sample-survey-officensso. Accessed 14 November 2023.

Ministry of Statistics and Programme Implementation, Government of India. *National Sample Survey report no. 583.* https://pib.gov.in/PressReleasePage.aspx?PRID=1593253. Accessed 5 November 2023.

Office of National Statistics. *National Statistics: Special Educational Needs in England.* London: ONS, 2005. http://dfes.gov.uk/rsgateway/DB/SFR/s000584/SFR24 2005.pdf. Accessed 10 November 2013.

Qualification and Curriculum Authority. *Annual Report and Accounts 2005–06.* https://assets.publishing.service.gov.uk/media/5a7ba716e5274a7202e188d2/1195.pdf. Accessed 24 December 2015.

UNESCO. Inclusive Education*: The Way of the Future, Forty-eighth Session of the International Conference on Education.* Reference document: ED/BIE/CONFINTED 48/3. Geneva: UNESCO, 2009. http://www.ibe.unesco.org/fileadmin/user_upload/Policy_Dialogue/48th_ICE/CONFINTED_48-3_English.pdf. Accessed 14 November 2023.

UNESCO. *The Salamanca Statement and Framework for Action on Special Needs Education.* http://www.unesco.org/education/pdf/SALAMA_E.PDF. Accessed 2 November 2011.

UNICEF. *Our History.* https://www.unicef.org/india/our-history. Accessed 14 November 2023.

United Nations Enable. *Fact Sheet on Persons with Disabilities.* http://www.un.org/disabilities/documents/toolaction/pwdfs.pdf. Accessed 30 March 2013.

United Nations Enable. *The Standard Rules on the Equalization of Opportunities for Persons with Disabilities.*https://www.un.org/esa/socdev/enable/dissre00.htm. Accessed 15 November 2023.

World Bank. *People with Disabilities in India: From Commitments to Outcomes.* July 2009. https://documents1.worldbank.org/curated/en/577801468259486686/pdf/502090WP0Peopl1Box0342042B01PUBLIC1.pdf. Accessed 14 November 2023.

World Health Organization. *Rethinking Care from Disabled People's Perspectives.* https://www.independentliving.org/docs6/barnes200106.pdf. Accessed 14 November 2023

World Health Organization. *Disability and Health Overview.* https://www.who.int/health-topics/disability#tab=tab. Accessed 23 December 2015.

Further Reading

Abbinnett, Ross. *Culture and Identity: Critical Theories*. Cambridge: SAGE, 2003.

Aguilera, Raymond. "Disability and Delight: Staring Back at the Devotee Community." *Sexuality and Disability*, vol. 1, no. 4, 2000, pp. 255–261.

Ahmad, Aijaz. *In Theory: Classes, Nations, Literatures*. London: Verso, 1992.

Ahmed, Sara. *Differences That Matter Feminist Theory and Postmodernism*. Cambridge: Cambridge UP, 1998.

Albrecht, Gary L., Seelman, Katherine D., and Bury, Michael. *Handbook of Disability Studies*. 1st ed. London: SAGE, 2001.

Ashcroft, Bill, and Griffiths, Gareth. *Key Concepts in Post-Colonial Studies*. London: Routledge, 1998.

Atkins, Kim. *Self and Subjectivity*. Malden, MA: Blackwell, 2005.

Bal, Mieke. *Narrative Theory: Critical Concepts in Literary and Cultural Studies*. London: Routledge, 2004.

Banerjee, Sikats. "Armed Masculinity, Hindu Nationalism and Female Political Participation in India." *International Feminist Journal of Politics*, vol. 8, no. 1, 2006, pp. 62–83.

Barker, Chris, and Galasinski, Dariusz. *Cultural Studies and Discourse Analysis*. Berkeley, CA: SAGE, 2001.

Barnartt, Sharon, and Scotch, Richard K. *Disability Protests: Contentious Politics, 1970–1999*. Washington, DC: Gallaudet UP, 2001.

Beresford, Peter. "Poverty and Disabled People: Challenging Dominant Debates and Policies." *Disability & Society*, vol. 11, no. 4, 1996, pp. 553–567.

Black, Rhonda. S., and Pretes, Lori. "Victims and Victors: Representation of Physical Disability on the Silver Screen." *Research and Practice for Persons with Severe Disabilities*, vol. 32, no. 1, 2007, 66–83.

Bogdan, Robert. *Freak Show*. Chicago: U of Chicago P, 1988.

Brain, Robert. *The Decorated Body*. New York: Harper & Row, 1979.

Cadwallader, Jessica. "Suffering Difference: Normalisation and Power." *Social Semiotics*, vol. 17, no. 3, 2007, pp. 375–394.

Campbell, Fiona Kumari. *Contours of Ableism: The Production of Disability and Abledness*. New York: Palgrave Macmillan, 2009.

Cann, Paul. *Unequal Ageing: The Untold Story of Exclusion in Old Age*. Bristol: Policy, 2009.

Catts , Hugh W., and Kamhi, Alan G. *The Connections Between Language and Reading Disabilities*. London: Lawrence Erlbaum Associates, 2005.

Certeau, Michelde, and Giard, Luce. *The Practice of Everyday Life*. Ed., New Rev. and Augm. Minneapolis: U of Minnesota P, 1998.

Charlton, James. *Nothing About Us Without Us: Disability Oppression and Empowerment*. Berkeley, CA: U of California P, 2000

Chivers, Sally. *The Silvering Screen: Old Age and Disability in Cinema*. Toronto: U of Toronto P, 2011.

Chivers, Sally, and Markotic, Nicole. *The Problem Body: Projecting Disability on Film*. Ohio: Ohio State UP, 2010.

Chomsky, Noam, and Foucault, Michel. *The Chomsky-Foucault Debate: On Human Nature*. New York: The New Press, 2006.

Chowdhary, Paul D. *A Handbook of Social Welfare*. Delhi: Atma and Ram Sons, 1981.

Clements, Luke, and Read, Janet. *Disabled People and the Right to Life: The Protection and Violation of Disabled People's Most Basic Human Rights*. London: Routledge, 2008.

Coleridge, P. *Disability, Liberation and Development*. Oxford: Oxfam, 1993.

Craton, Lillian. *The Victorian Freak Show: The Significance of Disability and Physical Differences in 19th-Century Fiction*. Amherst, NY: Cambria Press, 2009.

Dreyfus, Hubert L., and Rabinow, Paul. *Michel Foucault: Beyond Structuralism and Hermeneutics*. 2nd ed. Chicago: U of Chicago P, 1983.

Dolmage, Jay. *Disability Rhetoric*. New York: Syracuse UP, 2013.

Due, Reidar. *Deleuze*. Cambridge: Polity, 2007.

Ellis, Katie, and Kent, Mike. *Disability and New Media*. New York: Routledge, 2011.

Enns, Anthony W., and Smit, Christopher R. *Screening Disability: Essays on Cinema and Disability*. Lanham, MD: UP of America. 2001.

Fiedler, Leslie. *Freaks: Myths and Images of the Secret Self*. New York: Simon and Schuster, 1976.

Francis, Robert. *Murphy: The Body Silent*. New York: Norton, 2001.

Fraser, Nancy. *Stretching the Radical Imagination: Beyond the Unholy Alliance of Identity Politics and Neoliberalism*. New York: Verso, 2010.

Frauley, Jon. *Criminology, Deviance, and the Silver Screen: The Fictional Reality and the Criminological Imagination*. New York: Palgrave Macmillan, 2010.

French, Sally. "Disability, Impairment or Something In-between?" *Disabling Barriers—Enabling Environments*. Edited by John Swain, Vic Finkelstein, Sally French and Michael Oliver. London: SAGE in association with the Open U, 1993, pp. 37–57.

Freud, Sigmund. *Totem and Taboo*. New York: Vintage, 1946.

Freud, Sigmund. *Three Essays on the Theory of Sexuality*. Translated by J. Strachey. London: Basic Books, 1962.

Freund, Peter. *The Civilized Body*. Philadelphia: Temple UP, 1982.

Fries, Kenny. *The History of My Shoes and the Evolution of Darwin's Theory*. New York: VSA Arts, 2006.

Frosh, Stephen. *Sexual Difference: Masculinity and Psychoanalysis*. London: Routledge, 1994.

Gerschick, Thomas J. "Toward a Theory of Disability and Gender: Feminisms at a Millennium." *Journal of Women in Culture and Society*, vol. 25, no. 4, 2000, pp. 1263–1268.

Gilead, Sarah. "Liminality, Anti-Liminality, and the Victorian Novel." *Nineteenth-Century Fiction*, vol. 53, no. 1, Spring 1986, pp. 183–197.

Goodley, Dan. *Disability Studies: An Interdisciplinary Introduction*. Los Angeles, CA: SAGE, 2011.

Goodley, Dan, Hughes, Bill, and Davis, Lennard. *Disability and Social Theory: New Developments and Directions.* New York: Palgrave Macmillan, 2012.

Hall, Stuart. *Cultural Identity and Diaspora.* London: Lawrence and Wishart, 1990.

Hall, Stuart. *Representations: Cultural Representations and Signifying Practices.* Los Angeles, CA: SAGE, 1997.

Harvey, David. *The Condition of Postmodernity: An Enquiry into the Origins of Cultural Change.* Oxford: Blackwell, 1990.

Helen, Meekosha. "Decolonizing Disability: Thinking and Acting Globally." *Disability & Society*, vol. 26, no. 6, 2011, pp. 667–682.

Hevey, David. *The Creatures Time Forgot: Photography and Disability Imagery.* London: Routledge, 1992.

Jones, Rose. "Impairment, Disability and Handicap: Old Fashioned Concepts?" Journal of Medical Ethics, vol. 27, no. 6, Dec. 2001, pp. 377–379.

Judovitz, Dalia. *The Culture of the Body Genealogies of Modernity.* Ann Arbor: U of Michigan P, 2001.

Klein, Anne C. "Presence with a Difference: Buddhists and Feminists on Subjectivity." *Hypatia*, vol. 9, 1994, pp. 112–130.

Knoll, Kristina R. "Feminist Disability Studies Pedagogy." *Feminist Teacher*, vol. 19, no. 2, 2009, pp. 122–133.

Koch, Tom. "Disability and Difference: Balancing Social and Physical Constructions." *Journal of Medical Ethics*, vol. 27, no. 6, Dec. 2001, pp. 370–376.

Kumar, Krishna. *Political Agenda of Education.* New Delhi: SAGE, 1991.

Leary, Timothy. *Foucault: The Art of Ethics.* London: Continuum, 2002.

LeBesco, Kathleen. *Revolting Bodies?: The Struggle to Redefine Fat Identity.* Amherst: U of Massachusetts P, 2004.

Lecourt, Dominique. *Marxism and Epistemology: Bachelard, Canguilhem and Foucault.* London: NLB, 1975.

Lefebvre, Henri. *Critique of Everyday Life.* London: Verso, 2005.

Lemke, Thomas. "'The Birth of Bio-politics': Michel Foucault's Lecture at the Collège de France on Neo-liberal Governmentality." *Economy and Society*, vol. 30, no. 2, 2001, pp. 190–207.

Lemke, Thomas. *Biopolitics: An Advanced Introduction.* New York: New York UP, 2011.

Lemert. *Human Deviance, Social Problems, and Social Control.* Englewood Cliffs, NJ: Prentice-Hall, 1967.

Lipkin, Joan, and Fox, Ann M. "Res(Crip)ting Feminist Theatre through Disability Theatre: Selections from the Disability Project Source." *NWSA Journal*, vol. 14, no. 3, Autumn 2002, pp. 77–98

Locke, Terry. *Critical Discourse Analysis.* London: Continuum, 2004.

Loomba, Ania. *Colonialism-Postcolonialism.* London: Routledge, 1998.

Lowenstein, Adam. *Shocking Representation: Historical, Trauma, National Cinema, and the Modern Horror Film.* New York: Columbia UP, 2005.

Mahlstedt, Andrew. "Animal's Eyes: Spectacular Invisibility and the Terms of Recognition in Indira Sinha's Animal's People." *Interdisciplinary Literature*, vol. 46, no. 3, September 2013.

Mann, William C., editor. *Smart Technology for Aging, Disability and Independence.* New York: John Wiley and Sons, 2005.

Matthews, Nicole. "Contesting Representations of Disabled Children in Picture-Books: Visibility, the Body and The Social Model of Disability." *Children's Geographies*, vol. 7, no. 1, 2009, pp. 37–49.

Marrati, Paola. *Gilles Deleuze: Cinema and Philosophy*. Baltimore, MD: Johns Hopkins UP, 2003.

Marx, Karl. *Capital*. Translated by Ben Fowkes. London: Penguin Books, 1990.

Masemene, M. *Constitutionalism and Access Legislation, Paper Presented to the CIB Expert Seminar on Building Non-Handicapping Environments*. Harare: Harare, 1992.

Massey, Doreen B. *Space, Place, and Gender*. Minneapolis: U of Minnesota P, 1994.

Menon, Nivedita. *Sexualities*. New Delhi: Women Unlimited, 2007.

Millar, Robert McColl. *Language, Nation, and Power: An Introduction*. Basingstoke: Palgrave Macmillan, 2005.

Millett-Gallant, A. *The Disabled Body in Contemporary Art*. New York: Palgrave Macmillan, 2010.

Mohapatra, Atanu. "Portrayal of Disability in Hindi Cinema: A Study of Emerging Trends of Differently-Abled." *Asian Journal of Multidimensional Research*, vol. 1, no. 7, December2012.

Moser, Ingunn. "Disability and the Promises of Technology: Technology, Subjectivity and Embodiment within an Order of the Normal." *Information, Communication & Society*, vol. 9, no. 3, 2006, pp. 373–395.

Osteen, Mark. *Autism and Representation*. New York: Routledge, 2007.

Paterson, Kevin, and Hughes, Bill. "Disability Studies and Phenomenology: The Carnal Politics of Everyday Life." *Disability and Society*, vol. 14, no. 5, 1990, pp. 597–610.

Race, David G. *Intellectual Disability Social Approaches*. Maidenhead: McGraw-Hill/ Open UP, 2007.

Rapley, Mark. *The Social Construction of Intellectual Disability*. Cambridge: Cambridge UP, 2004.

Reddy, Raghava. "From Impairment to Disability and Beyond: Critical Explorations in Disability Studies." *Sociological Bulletin*, vol. 60, no. 2, 2011, pp. 287–306.

Reich, Robert B. *The Work of Nations*. London: Simon and Schuster, 1991.

Riddell, Sheila, and Watson, Nick. *Disability, Culture, Identity*. Harlow: Pearson Education, 2003.

Riley, Charles A. *Disability and the Media: Prescriptions for Change*. Hanover, NH: UP of New England, 2005.

Rutherford, Jonathan, editor. *Identity: Community, Culture and Difference*. London: Lawrence and Wishart, 1990.

Schriempf, Alexa. "(Re)fusing the Amputated Body: An Interactionist Bridge for Feminism and Disability." *Hypatia*, vol. 16, no. 4, Autumn, 2001, pp. 53–79.

Scull, Andrew. *Madness in Civilization: A Cultural History of Insanity*. Princeton, NJ: Princeton UP, 1982.

Scully, Jackie L. *Disability Bioethics: Moral Bodies, Moral Difference*. Lanham, MD: Rowman & Littlefield, 2008.

Sethi, Rumina. *The Politics of Postcolonialism Empire, Nation and Resistance*. London: Pluto, 2011.

Shapiro, Joseph. *No Pity: People with Disabilities Forging a New Civil Rights Movement*. New York: Times Books/Random House, 1993.

Shilling, Chris. *The Body in Culture, Technology and Society*. London: SAGE, 2005.

Smith, Angela. *Hideous Progeny: Disability, Eugenics, and Classic Horror Cinema*. New York: Columbia UP, 2012.

Smith, Bonnie G., and Hutchinson, Beth, editors. *Gendering Disability*. New Jersey: Rutgers UP, 2004.

Swain, John, and French, Sally. "Towards an Affirmative Model of Disability." *Disability & Society*, vol. 15, no. 4, 2000, pp. 569–582.

Tinkcom, Matthew, and Villarejo, Amy. *Keyframes: Popular Cinema and Cultural Studies*. New York: Taylor & Francis, 2001.

Tromp, Marlene, editor. *Victorian Freaks: The Social Contexts of Freakery in Britain*. Columbia: Ohio State UP, 2008.

Wagner, Roi. "Silence as Resistance Before the Subject, or Could the Subaltern Remain Silent?" *Journal of Theory, Culture and Society*, vol. 1, no. 26.

Weber, Samuel. *Return to Freud: Jacques Lacan's Dislocation of Psychoanalysis*. Cambridge: Cambridge UP, 1991.

Wilkerson, Abby. "Disability, Sex Radicalism, and Political Agency." *NWSA Journal*, vol. 14, no. 3, Autumn 2002, pp. 33–57.

Wills, David. *Dorsality: Thinking Back through Technology and Politics*. Minneapolis: U of Minnesota P, 2008.

Wilson, Timothy D. *Strangers to Ourselves: Discovering the Adaptive Unconscious*. Cambridge, MA: Belknap P of Harvard UP, 2002.

Wolfe, Cary. *What Is Posthumanism?* Minneapolis: U of Minnesota P, 2010.

Young, Robert. *Colonial Desire: Hybridity in Theory, Culture, and Race*. London: Routledge, 1995.

Young, Robert. *Postcolonialism: An Historical Introduction*. Oxford: Blackwell, 2001.

For Product Safety Concerns and Information please contact our EU
representative GPSR@taylorandfrancis.com
Taylor & Francis Verlag GmbH, Kaufingerstraße 24, 80331 München, Germany

* 9 7 8 1 0 3 2 7 2 2 0 6 1 *